Wealth:
An Owner's Manual

*A Sensible, Steady, Sure Course
to Becoming and Staying Rich*

Michael Stolper

with
Everett Mattlin

Best wishes.

HarperBusiness
A Division of HarperCollinsPublishers

A hardcover edition of this book was published in 1992 by HarperBusiness, a division of HarperCollins Publishers.

HarperCollins books may be purchased for educational, business, or sales promotional use. For information please write: Special Markets Department, HarperCollins Publishers, Inc., 10 East 53rd Street, New York, NY 10022.

First paperback edition published 1993.

The Library of Congress has catalogued the hardcover edition as follows:

Stolper, Michael, 1945–
    Wealth : an owner's manual / Michael Stolper, Everett Mattlin.
        p.   cm.
    Includes index.
    ISBN 0-88730-540-7
    1. Finance, Personal.   2. Wealth.   3. Quality of life.
    4. Investments.   I. Mattlin, Everett B.   II. Title.
    HG179.S8437   1992
    332.024—dc20   91-42316

ISBN 0-88730-645-4 (pbk.)

    95 96 97 RRD 10 9 8 7 6 5 4 3 2

Acknowledgments

This book is the result of numerous two and three day sessions closeted in hotels in Maryland, New York, and La Jolla with Everett Mattlin, my co-author, and a writer by profession. I was instructed to get the best writer possible. I succeeded.

This book encompasses twenty years of professional and personal experience. Having never expected to be in a position to acknowledge anything, I intend to take full advantage of this opportunity. First, to my father who taught me that integrity and capital are the elements of freedom; my mother, who demonstrated that humor and compassion can get you through anything; and to my sons, Scott, Andrew, and Jordan, who bring me constant joy.

I have been blessed professionally with kind and reasonable clients; relationships with a number of America's legendary investors, many of whom are my friends; and co-workers who are like family: Carole Rhoades, whose unqualified friendship has sustained me for fifteen years; Margaret McKean, the one person I know who is both intellectually and morally qualified to be President; and Barbara Malone, whose skill and equanimity are an inspiration to all. Finally, the people who have taught me what great investors have in common and protected me from imposters: Tom Bailey, founder of Janus Fund; Roger Engemann of Pasadena Growth Fund; Rick Aster of The Meridian Fund, and the many others whose talents have brought increased prosperity to my clients. A final note of thanks to Len Kessler, whose efforts made the difference.

Contents

INTRODUCTION

BECOMING WEALTHY AND STAYING THAT WAY

How do you define *rich?*

It's mostly in the eyes of the definer, isn't it? For the rock-bottom poor, the envied ideal is the family with a modest duplex and a seven-year-old Chevy. For the family with a four-bedroom suburban ranch house and two late-model cars, the ideal is the really rich *People* people who don't have to worry about what bills the mailman is delivering today. As John Jacob Astor III is supposed to have said, "A man who has a million dollars is as well off as if he were rich."

I have my own definition of rich. It's a pragmatic definition: you have become rich when you have accumulated enough money to be able to maintain your accustomed lifestyle without having to work anymore. Your money is now doing the work for you, throwing off enough passive income to support you in comfort without your lifting a finger or a brain cell. If you want to continue to work, fine, but it's by choice, not necessity.

And I think most people would define rich that way. The fantasy for most of us is to live the way we're living, or preferably better, without having to sweat for it.

That's certainly the retirement goal of most of us, whether we hope to retire at 45 or 65. The mortgage will be paid off, the college tuitions behind us. There'll be money coming in

1

from a pension and social security, and from our own savings. There'll be enough to be comfortable, to travel, to live without financial worry.

How much savings is that going to take? How high a pile do we need to build during our working years to have the supplemental income we need to live as lazily as we'd like? Well, a million should do it for most. That would throw off, after taxes, about $50,000 a year. On top of a decent pension, with the house free and clear, you could enjoy a very comfortable life-style.

The word *millionaire* still has a nice ring to it. It still conjures up an image of someone who is "independently wealthy," and who can enjoy an enviable life-style without working to sustain it. And ten years ago, a total net worth of a million might have done the trick, but today, after inflation's toll, particularly in the 1970s, you probably need a million, or near it, *in addition* to the value of your home, if you are going to live in effortless comfort.

Nevertheless, in common parlance, *millionaire* still stands as a synonym for *rich*. By that definition, the number of the rich in this land may surprise you. Kevin Phillips, in his recent bestselling *The Politics of Rich and Poor*, estimates there were 1.5 million millionaires in this country in 1988, a number he says he drew from "multiple sources." I wouldn't be surprised, with the appreciation in assets since then, if there aren't twice that number today.

Of course, there are, in addition to the merely rich, those who used to be called "the filthy rich," and are now, since the Reagan era, euphemistically referred to as "high net worth individuals." At least 1000 people in this country are believed to be worth $100 million, and at last count *Forbes* found 274 *billionaires* in the world, 96 of them Americans, when family fortunes are included. Something like 70,000 people in this country have annual *gross incomes* of $1 million or more.

But most of us don't feel the need for that kind of money. We don't yearn for multiple mansions, yachts with gold-plated bathroom fixtures, custom-body cars, or live-in servants. Living comfortably, pretty much the way we've been living, without labor, would do just fine.

A million in income-producing funds will make it happen. And getting there is not as formidable as it might seem. If there are already a few million people who have done it, you, too, can join the club. If you haven't already. In fact, it is almost inevitable if you have a good job or professional practice, set aside some money routinely, invest sensibly, and don't have rotten luck, such as a serious illness. Throw in a little *good* luck and you can get to that status well before you are 65.

Consider: In 1990, more than 4 million households enjoyed an income of $100,000 or more. Suppose your average income over 30 years, from the age of 30 to 60, is $100,000 a year. Put aside just 6 percent of that a year and you would have $180,000 at the end of the 30 years. But don't forget the power of compounded investment returns. If your savings earn a modest 10 percent a year, which is what stocks have historically provided, and you take care of taxes from your income, at age 60 you will have not $150,000, but that $1,000,000 you need to move to easy street.

The Instant Rich

Most people who are wealthy today acquired their money in just that old-fashioned, Calvinistically approved way—a lifetime of working and putting aside. The only paths to instant riches used to be an inheritance, the sale of one's business (maybe to another company, maybe in a stock offering), a big divorce settlement, or some bolt out of the blue, like winning the state lottery.

But within the past ten years or so we've seen the creation of a whole new class of instant millionaires—the byproduct of the restructuring of corporate America. All those mergers, acquisitions, leveraged buyouts, and recapitalizations you've read about have left a host of people with a million, or several million. They were highly placed executives in companies that were bought or that merged with other companies, and their jobs were taken over by their counterparts at the acquiring or dominant survivors; they were given early retirement with a lump-sum package that, after nearly 30 years of service, with accumulated stock options thrown in, came to a couple million dollars.

These people went from what I call the "working wealthy,"— highly compensated for their knowledge and skills but with no substantial amount of money to worry about—to being out of work but with a great deal of money sitting in their bank accounts. Most of them have no idea what to do with it. That's when I am called in. My business is to help the rich cope with their riches.

One of my clients, for example, was in the upper management of a publishing company that was sold. He was told the acquiring company had someone who would take over his function, that he was, in that nasty word, "redundant." But with the company stock he'd acquired over the years, what he had in a savings plan, and the generous retirement package they gave him, he walked out, at the age of 57, with nearly $10 million. That kind of money just sitting there made him very, very nervous. He was almost in a panic when he called my office.

It can be even simpler than that. In 1988 RJR Nabisco was taken over in a $25 billion leveraged buyout, and in such transactions shareholders are paid off at handsome premiums to the prices the stocks were selling at before the raiders pounced. I have one client who owned a great many shares of RJR Nabisco. Her grandfather had bought a few hundred shares of R.J. Reynolds Tobacco Company stock decades ago and left them to her. The company had merged with Nabisco Brands, the stock had split many times, and she just kept stashing the new certificates in a safe deposit box. From time to time she thought about selling her shares but she couldn't bring herself to do it. She would have had to pay a heavy capital gains tax, and the stock always seemed to work its way higher. And what else would she do with the money anyway? Then, suddenly, doing nothing was removed as a choice. Stock that may have had a cost basis of a couple of dollars a share was taken away from her at $109 a share. She'd been converted to cash, or, as financial types say, her asset had been liquified.

The volume of such transactions has been enormous. In the past ten years or so tens of billions of dollars have been paid out to shareholders. After the late 1980s collapse of the junk bond market, which financed many of these deals, the buyout and merger mania has died down. But companies are still being bought and sold, and many people come out of these transactions very, very wealthy.

Wall Street Babel

Somebody who comes into sudden wealth from these "corporate events," or who has accumulated a sizable nest egg over many years, is obviously going to have different financial needs and concerns than someone still building toward that day. The rich have to invest their money to keep it. Those working their way toward wealth have to invest to get there.

But whether you are rich or on your way there, you have to wrestle with many of the same questions. If you have accumulated any money, be it $10,000 or $10 million, you are an investor, whether you like it or not. Keeping your money in a money market account at the bank is just as much an investment decision as buying stocks and bonds.

In recent years all of us—those trying to build assets and those most interested in protecting them—have been barraged with an overwhelming array of investment alternatives, many of them difficult to understand. Successful businesspeople can be as confused as schoolteachers. And when it comes to investment, the bullets you dodge are as important as the bull's-eyes you score.

If you consult your friends or your lawyer or your accountant about what to do with your money, you usually end up with different and conflicting pieces of advice. And if you choose to handle matters on your own, you quickly realize how hard it is to make decisions. The stock market scares you. You can't forget 19 October 1987, when market values plummeted 20 percent in one day. "Volatility" seems to be a euphemism for the phenomenon that stocks go down about four times as fast as they go up.

Bonds were traditionally conservative, safe investments, but then came the double-digit inflation of the 1970s. If you sold your bonds, you got back less than you paid for them, and if you held them to maturity, you got back dollars whose buying power was decimated. In any case, how do you go about investing in a market of Treasuries, government agencies, corporates, municipals, foreign bonds, mortgage-backed securities, zero coupons, junk bonds, convertibles, and the odd hybrids Wall Street has concocted?

Real estate always seemed like a sure investment, until the last few years, when values flattened, then collapsed. There were some warning signs. Real estate salesmen became celebrities, carpenters became patrons of the arts, and, most important, almost everyone who owned a home made more money by accident than they ever did through purposeful labor. Some very smart people in the business predict that a recovery may not come about for another ten years or more. In any case, how would you go about investing in real estate? If you buy, say, a small strip shopping center, by yourself or with a few partners, who will decide when the parking lot needs blacktopping and fight with delinquent tenants? You could give money to some firm that invests in real estate, but then most of the real estate limited partnerships of the 1980s have proved, according to *Barron's*, a "disaster."

All the other investment possibilities—precious metals, oil and gas, collectibles, commodities, currencies, options and futures and options on futures, mortgage-backed securities, index funds, sector mutual funds, variable return insurance policies, single-premium annuities, and the plethora of other financial inventions—simply leave you bewildered. You cannot understand them all, and you fear that the people pitching them to you might conveniently forget to tell you about the risks they entail.

And even if you decide which types of investment are right for you, what do you do then? Invest on your own, with the help of a broker? Totally on your own, using a discount broker? Through mutual funds? Your bank's trust department? An investment counseling firm? How do you pick a manager? And know if he's doing a good job for you?

No wonder so many people huddle into money market funds. They feel foolish because they know the funds and certificates of deposit are not where they are going to earn the highest returns over time, but they are apprehensive about doing anything else.

Your Money Guide

This book will simplify investment matters and lay out a straightforward path you can follow. If you have substantial assets, you will find out how to determine your spending needs, develop income-generating portfolios to cover them, and invest the balance for further growth. If you are still in the process of getting rich, this book will help you devise a savings and investment program to reach your goals. Budgeting, saving, and investing, as well as a host of side issues that distract and can potentially disrupt a financial plan, will all be dealt with.

And who am I, you ask, to be giving all this advice? What are my qualifications?

First of all, I have a master's degree in finance. Then I was a stockbroker for seven years. I had to learn early on about all the major investment markets. I also learned what brokers do for a living. They are salespeople, not financial advisors, no matter what fancy names their firms now give them. But 20 years ago I decided the best way I could serve my clients was to look for outside professional managers of their money. Those managers may be mutual funds (and I am a director of three mutual fund management companies, responsible for investing about $6 billion of shareholder money). Or those managers may be investment counselors. I know that all of these investment professionals have no motive except to perform. They buy and sell when they think it is time to buy and sell, not when they need commissions to pay for a new kitchen.

For two decades, then, I have tracked the money management industry, traveling not just the United States but the world to find out which managers—be they at mutual funds or investment counseling firms—out of thousands are truly competent, what expectations are realistic, how to monitor them to know if they are continuing to do what they were hired for.

I've learned how to spot the gifted managers and what clues signal that their will to strive has peaked. I've learned how to study performance numbers to uncover distortions or manipulations. I think I know how to identify talent because I've seen years of results from the people I've hired.

Equally important, I have spent the same 20 years meeting with some 2000 clients. I have learned how people of wealth think, what worries them, what kinds of investment mistakes they tend to make, and what sorts of investments make sense for them. I have seen them struggle in deciding how much they should spend and how much they should spare for their estates. I've heard their anxieties about the responsibilities that wealth brings.

They also talk to me about matters that are not strictly financial, though they often stem from their financial position, particularly if their wealth has come suddenly. They've found, for example, that strains develop in relationships with old friends who haven't had the same measure of success. The expectations of their children change and can create family strife. They are pursued by numerous people who want to be their advisers or expect them to become benefactors. Of course, wealth is a blessing, but it can be a mixed blessing. If you are wealthy, it should be comforting to know that the problems you face are not unique and to find out how others have learned to deal with the stresses.

In listening to these people of wealth tell me their stories, I have found out how most of them got rich in the first place. I've learned that even if you are not an entrepreneur or a fortunate participant in some headline-making corporate event, you can gradually, confidently, enter the ranks of the upper 2 percent of financial achievers.

I have, in short, years of research conducted in the field and hands-on experience with the owners and investors of money. This book will share that knowledge with you. I will show you how the rich got that way and suggest some strategies that make the getting easier. And with those who are already rich I will share the advice I give my clients about how to allocate and invest money to ensure that the good life it brings will continue.

Working toward financial independence and holding on to it can, in fact, be easy, but it is not simple. There is a big difference between *simple* and *easy*. Complex matters become easy only when you have come to understand them, and I have devoted years to discerning the right paths to wealth and wealth preservation. This book will help you to define the best course to follow at whatever stage of life and wealth you are in, to design a financial blueprint that will make you feel that you are in control, and to avoid the most common mistakes. We will sort through the confusion of investment options and learn how to acquire wealth and then preserve and augment it.

Much of my advice is simple common sense. It may even seem somewhat unexciting to those of you who have wealth or hope for it. Good. That's what I want—to help the readers of this book avoid the excitement of detours and disasters. If you are looking for a get-rich-quick manual, this is not your book. Instead, it presents a sensible, steady, and sure course to becoming and staying rich.

Many books have been written—a number of them, in my opinion, irresponsible—about how to acquire wealth, but few address themselves to those already wealthy. The wealthy are my clientele. I know how they worry about losing what they have gained in life and how often, in confusion about how to handle their money, they do foolish things with it. The anxiety and urgency they feel—because so many options are open to the affluent—are wholly unnecessary. If your ship has come in, there is no need to send it back into stormy seas. All those opinions you get, all those deals and investment "opportunities" you see, and all the confusion they generate—I just say, "Calm down. Let's take our time. We'll review all the possibilities and make a plan that will put everything in order. Remember, you are wealthy now. Relax and enjoy your new sense of security and status. You didn't know it before—how could you?—but that is what money is for."

1

LIFE AFTER WEALTH

1. With Money Come Responsibilities

Most people who have come into money or who have retired
after a long career have had some assets that they have been
investing over the years, whether on their own or with the
help of professionals. But they've never had responsibility for
the kind of money they now have on their hands.

They sell a business or receive an inheritance and are handed
a big check. Or they retire and are given, in a lump sum, the
proceeds of their company's savings, defined contribution and
profit-sharing plans, and/or stock option plans. Or they were
self-employed and can now withdraw their Keogh and IRA
money.

True, they made investment choices about their own company's pension plan, their employer's defined contribution
plan, or their own Keogh and IRA accounts. But now that
they have retired from the work force, they have gathered together more money than they ever had to worry about before,
and they have many more options about what to do with it.
Including spending it.

They know what this newly gathered money can do for
them. They expect comfort, travel, the leisure to pursue the
interests they never seemed to find the time for, status, and,
most important, security, both financial and psychological.

And they are right. That is what they dreamed of and that
is what they now have.

But along with the elation there is also a good deal of anxiety. The celebration is often muted. They know things have changed, and it takes a while before they realize how, and how much, things have changed. People now responsible for considerable assets realize they are in a position where, along with the possibilities, they now have a lot they can lose. A 10 percent drop in the stock market feels quite different when you have $500,000 invested than it did when you had $50,000 invested. There is a near-universal tendency for people to express losses in dollar terms and gains in percentage terms.

Generally these people now possess enough money to live as well as they have been living, and maybe better. So they sense that if they do something with the money that proves too risky, they could lose enough capital to have a nasty effect on the life-style they can now enjoy without working.

They know, too, that if they do take risks and increase their wealth, it will have no real effect on the way they are living because the life-style they have is comfortable and familiar. Some big gains would be nice for their inheritors, but if life-style is pretty much set, to risk the loss of capital to a degree that would threaten this life-style would be the height of folly because there's so little upside.

Life won't get appreciably better, but it could get appreciably worse. They have more to lose than to gain. No wonder the money makes them nervous.

Think about your own situation. If you were handed enough money that you never had to work again and could still live as well as you're living now, what incentive would you have to take risks with the money? If you heard about a piece of real estate for sale that looked ridiculously cheap, a seemingly lay-up opportunity to make big bucks, you would have to remind yourself that if you put your $1 million on the line and things, for whatever reason, didn't work out, your million could turn into one-half million. All of a sudden you would have lost $40,000 in pretax income, which is the difference between staying at the Ritz Carlton and at Motel 6.

Where Are the Gurus?

Feeling apprehensive and disoriented as the result of the "liquification of their assets," and inadequate to decide what action to take, the newly affluent look for guidance. If they sold their business or if the company they worked for was sold, they may talk to the investment banking firm that handled the transaction; it usually has a brokerage or investment advisory subsidiary. They may ask their attorney or accountant to steer them to competent advisors. They will probably talk to their local banker, though they are wary of that source of help. The "personal banking" units that have been set up in recent years to woo the wealthy treat you with courtesy and patience, but bank trust departments do not exactly have a reputation for investment prowess.

Those looking for financial guidance for their recently gathered assets probably have had a stockbroker over the years, often a relative or friend, who's bought them occasional stocks or some municipal bonds. But they doubt they can rely on him or her to help with the major money they now have. Their broker has never done a particularly good job of making money for them in the past, and they know brokers make a living by buying and selling: no transactions, no commissions. They want a long-term plan, not a trading account. If brokers were paid on a performance basis, it might be a different matter.

If these newly minted affluents have friends who are wealthy, they naturally ask them how they run *their* financial affairs. There is a presumption in our society that because someone is rich, he or she knows a lot, though many wealthy businesspeople are quite naive about investments. Still, I would encourage people to make it a habit to talk to other people in similar circumstances and compare notes. Find out what they have been going through and have decided to do about their money. It will give you some perspective.

These may be former business associates, lawyers, or just friends and acquaintances, but they should be people you respect. There are plenty of people who are well-off but absolutely clueless about the world other than the part of it that enriched them. Set up non-agenda social lunches with those you *do* respect, and chat about what you are doing and what they are doing. First, it keeps you engaged with the world of commerce. Second, if the dialogue is candid—and it is likely to be if you, too, open up—it gives you a sense of how others are handling their business affairs, which helps you assess how you are managing your own.

All people who have money are torn between the feeling that they should be doing more with it than they are and the fear of getting hurt financially by doing too much and making rash commitments. It is comforting to talk to others and to know they have the same problems. I don't think people should be financially insular. Our sources of advice shouldn't be limited to the people we are paying for that advice, because investment advisors—yes, including myself—have accumulated biases, as does anyone who renders advice in a narrow field, and it's good to know other people who think differently.

The need for such communion with others struggling with similar decisions has even led to support groups in some communities. Most commonly, people who have inherited or expect to inherit considerable wealth get together to share the problems their affluence has brought them. At the very least, conversations with others in a similar situation scratch an itch, because we are all curious about what other people do with their money.

It is no wonder that the financial planning industry has grown so rapidly in the last decade or two because these planners would seem to be the natural source of unbiased expertise, especially those who charge a fee and do not earn their compensation by putting clients in limited partnerships or selling them annuities.

But I've found that most of the wealthy people I counsel distrust financial planners because they suspect these people have a reach that exceeds their grasp. They wonder if one person, whose qualifications may be a crash course in personal finance, can really advise judiciously about insurance, estate planning, stocks and bonds, real estate, and the more arcane areas of investment. That kind of omniscience doesn't jibe with one's experience as a businessperson or professional. I think people are right to be skeptical in most cases. I'll have more comments on financial planners in a later chapter.

Sources of advice about managing money:

- · Your stockbroker—has he made more money for himself than he's made for you?

- · Your banker—comforting, but usually produces pedestrian results

- · Your attorney and accountant—may be able to steer you to competent investment professionals

- · Other wealthy persons—good to compare notes with but may be no more knowledgeable than you

- · A financial planner—be wary of presumptions of omniscience

---

2. The Reality Check

It's at the point when the newly enriched have considered their sources of advice and come away confused that I often get called into the picture. People are referred to me by one of my clients or by a stockbroker, lawyer, or accountant. Or they read about me in *The Wall Street Journal* or some other periodical and give me a call. Usually they come to my office in San Diego; sometimes I am traveling and can go to their offices.

Perplexed and anxious about how to deal with the money they now shepherd, they want my advice on all sorts of decisions. Should they take a piece of this money and indulge in some of the things they've always fantasized about? Should they build their dream house, or instead pay off what's left of the mortgage on the house they're in? Would a second home be a good idea, from the standpoint of investment and taxes as well as of life-style? Should they make large gifts to their children? The kids understandably feel entitled to share in their parents' good fortune, but the parents worry about what sum they can gift without stripping away their children's motivation to succeed in life. Should wills be changed? Should trusts be set up?

And, of course, people want to know how their wealth should be invested; that is usually their biggest immediate worry. Should they put the money into municipal bonds? Do they belong in the stock market? How about the "deals" they now hear about? On the one hand, they are terribly afraid of doing something stupid that would jeopardize their new sense of affluence and security. On the other hand, many—particularly the entrepreneurial spirits—think they should be doing something "smart" with the money that will make it grow and prove they are savvy about seizing the opportunities their capital provides.

Along with their anxieties, they are still pinching themselves about their good fortune. The fact that they are in my office talking about it sort of validates that it really has happened. One of the ways that I help them is to give them some sense of what their new affluence means.

For example, a man who had sold his business for $4 million came to see me. He was disoriented and disturbed by his new situation. He was 60 years old and had been spending about $100,000 a year. His concerns spilled out: he wouldn't be working anymore, he'd have no earned income, inflation would eat at his assets. Could he still spend as he had been spending, could he spend more? So I said, "Stop for a minute. Just consider. You are used to spending $100,000 a year, right? You now have $4 million. So think—if you never earned a penny in interest, it would take you 40 years to run out of money, at which time you would be 100 years old. That should give you some comfort."

This exercise of dividing the amount of capital you have by your level of consumption is a quick litmus test of your own affluence. It's so obvious, but people never think in those terms. I could see the man visibly relax in his chair.

Different Strokes

People being people, inclinations about what to do with new wealth vary widely. Some want to live it up; most have no great desire to change their life-style. A few see their new money as an opportunity to fund some enterprise or investment scheme that will make them even richer. Most, however, are prone to cling to what they now have, afraid that Fortune won't smile on them more than once. Some are sophisticated about investment markets; many have kept every cent they ever owned in the bank. Some are happy they can now leave their children inheritances that will ensure a measure of security and comfort they themselves never received from their parents. Others are convinced children who are given too much never learn self-reliance and end up miserable.

So when people do pull up a chair in my office, or I in theirs, I want first to find out what they are like, what motivates them, what they expect from their new wealth. I start by asking them to tell me a little something about themselves, and then I listen. Almost always they tell me a great deal. There are so few people to whom they can talk about their money. Most people would rather talk about their sex lives than their money. But they *have* to talk about money with me, so a kind of intimacy is created.

Most people love to talk about their businesses. When someone tells me, "My key employees all walked out of the place with at least a million bucks," I know that they don't view people as commodities, and that can be important when we have to deal with each other and with investment advisers.

They talk about their families. He'll say, "John, my oldest son—he's 32—has had a chronic drug problem." And his wife will say, "Yes, but it's getting better." And he'll pat her on the knee and say, "Yes, dear, and it was getting better last year, too." This is a problem we are going to have to deal with in our planning.

I ask questions, too, of course. I always ask about children, about what obligations, such as education, remain. We talk a lot about the children—what they want to do for the kids now and after they are gone, and if there are any particular problems, such as a child (like the drug-addicted son) who needs special consideration because of physical or psychological problems. We will go into this topic at length in a later chapter.

I ask if their parents are still living, if any sort of inheritance can be expected in the future—an unpleasant topic to raise, but certainly relevant to financial plans. Often I hear, "Neither of our parents has anything." Aside from the possibility that financial obligations toward those parents may be involved, that statement tells me a little more about where these people are coming from. There may be something of a depression mentality we will have to deal with.

When people talk about themselves and their past, they send messages. They tell how their psyches have been shaped, what neuroses will have to be dealt with. The wife's involvement in decision making about financial matters is important, too, particularly if she's the dominant player.

I ask them about more personal things—their hobbies, for instance. If they have none, I know they're going to have a more troublesome transition period and that investments stand a good chance of ending up as their hobby. And if they do have hobbies, I like to know what they are. It fills out the picture, and what I am doing, really, is twisting the dials. It is important to get to know the people I am advising on financial matters, because then I can understand how much risk they will be comfortable with, what kind of time horizons they think in terms of, and whether or not they are likely to do something foolish with their money.

I try to deal with people as though I am a counselor concerned not just with their money but with them as people as well. The economic solutions to people's problems are generally quite clear. The difficult part is integrating those solutions with their temperamental needs as individuals. I have found that the total process works best when you consider different solutions, all of which could be effective, and modify the solutions based on the strength of your reactions to them. You opt for what makes you most comfortable.

The three most pressing questions for the newly wealthy:

- Should I now buy some of those things I've dreamed about?
- Where should I invest the money?
- What should I do, financially, about our children?

3. Wish Lists

Early on I ask people about their "wish lists." The money that was tied up in a business, a retirement plan, or a family trust is now in their own power. In the first flush of affluence, is there any money they want to skim off the top to fulfill long-held desires?

People are usually very ambivalent about what to do now that they are actually able to do it. "Okay," they tell themselves, "it's time. I have worked hard and long, and now I want some of those goodies I've dreamed about." But they aren't sure it's right to be so indulgent, at least too quickly.

Maybe it is a boat they want to buy. Or a sports car. Or a home in the Florida Keys. For some, it's an airplane; usually that's the wish of someone who learned to fly in the service. Sometimes it's a long-standing passion to own fine antiques or paintings.

I encountered one couple, both highly compensated physicians, who had a vision that was almost sacred to them: they would become collectors of major works of art. They saw themselves attending Sotheby auctions and having their picture in *Vanity Fair*. But you need a great deal of money for that sort of thing, of course, and this couple had nowhere near enough. They thought I had a pipeline to investment geniuses who could quickly turn their million into $20 million so they could proceed with their ambitions for celebrity. I told them I didn't think anybody could meet their investment goals and we parted company. On a more exemplary note, I know another man who is moderately wealthy who used a good part of his inherited wealth to set up a foundation to take care of abused children. Once they have money, people become excited about achieving all sorts of long-desired goals.

Spending Inhibitions

However, most people who have finally come into considerable money are not sure if they should immediately proceed with those goals or fulfill their wishes. These are new kinds of decisions, and most people are uncomfortable with them.

They ask themselves: "Can I really afford it? Shouldn't I maybe wait a bit? Or invest the money and dedicate some of the *income* to my wishes instead of going out and spending a big piece of capital? I just don't feel right about taking $200,000 to buy a boat. Not only will that $200,000 no longer throw off any income, maintaining the boat is going to cost a lot of money. It would certainly be very indulgent of me—and selfish, because if I invested that money, it could grow and I'd have more to leave the kids." And on and on. My clients look to me for permission they feel they can't give themselves. It is agony for them to spend big money because they are not used to it. They've been accumulators of capital. They can't bring themselves to spend what they worked so hard to put together—especially on something that's hardly an essential.

So many of us have been imbued with the notion that it is practically a sin to spend principal. This notion isn't universal but it is very, very common, and it seems to cross generational and ethnic lines. I've seen someone who has turned $1 million into $2 million in the stock market in less than four years get stomach pains over drawing out $40,000 to buy a new car. And it doesn't matter if the person has $20 million rather than $2 million. So people often compromise; they make themselves feel better by buying a $25,000 car. But it is still tough for them to "dip into principal."

Spending on themselves instead of building a bigger inheritance is a very troubling issue for many, and it triggers the question that we will explore in depth in a later chapter—how much to leave the kids. Of course, that's a lifetime activity for many of us, worrying about what should be ours and what should be reserved for our children. Should I take a vacation or put the money aside for their college education? Should I buy that BMW or make a gift to the kids this year? People go back and forth between wanting to make their children rich and feeling that they are entitled to the niceties of life. "I'm 60 years old, my kids are in their 30s. They'll have 40 years ahead of them after I'm in a box." So they'll buy the boat and comfort themselves with the thought that the kids can share in it.

Not everybody goes through this inner turmoil. Some people are very clear about the whole matter: "The kids have got enough and I'm not going to worry about it." And there's no correlation between the size of the assets and the degree of worry. Some people are clear, but others torture themselves.

A Boat Can Sink You

Sometimes, of course, people really *don't* have enough money to buy whatever it is they crave without incurring unpleasant consequences. I just say, "Fine and well, buy the boat if that's what you want so much, but this is really going to cut down your income and put a crimp in the rest of your life-style. Just be sure of priorities." People get into deep trouble when they spend so much that they are at the edge financially. Then the markets go through a rough period—stocks and bonds fall— and suddenly their sense of affluence changes. They had $2 million, so they bought their boat, and then—wham!—stocks are down 15 percent and the million they kept in stocks isn't worth a million anymore, and they get frightened.

We've all gone through that. Stocks are going up and we feel rich and extravagant; then stocks go down and we feel like we can't afford to go out to dinner, much less take the cruise we'd planned. And once you are retired, you feel helpless, impotent. You can't do anything about it anymore, the way you could when you were able to put together another deal or work longer hours at your profession. You have lost the ability to alter, in any direct fashion, your economic well-being.

So you go and buy your boat when you're feeling plush and three months later the market drops 15 percent. You don't want to sell your brand-new, glorious boat, but you've just lost $150,000 in the market and you panic because you can see another (30 percent?) drop. The sense of threat becomes unbearable. You can't take the stress, and—it's only human to try to reduce or eliminate stress—you don't sell the boat but you sell the stocks. If you get yourself in a position where you are stretched, you are all too likely to do something that freezes your financial dilemma. You are going to blow out your investments and make it so you can never catch a rebound— because you seldom have the courage to reenter the arena, at least until you are sure "this isn't just a trap," by which time stock prices are already 20 percent higher.

To keep that from happening, you must structure your balance sheet so that the stresses can never become so acute that drastic, self-defeating measures become necessary.

Before you even go into stocks, you should have enough money in inviolable income-producing securities to know that your income needs are taken care of.

Then you can say to yourself, "Sure, my stocks are down 15 percent, but my income from the million I left in Treasuries is safe. I can keep the boat and not worry." And time is your ally, not your adversary. You don't need that 15 percent. The stocks will come back, and if it's later rather than sooner, the money will go to your kids.

But if there isn't enough money to ensure the necessary income stream, then my most definite advice is to forget the boat. First things first.

I have found that most people do splurge a bit with their newly realized wealth but they seldom go overboard. When people come into a lot of money at the age of 40 or 45, they tend to go "toy" shopping, splurge on all sorts of stuff. I've seen an instance or two of a fairly young guy who was drawing $100,000 in salary out of his high-tech company that was sold for $20 million, and he went wild. But usually by the time you reach your 50s you don't care much anymore about acquiring more material things. You might buy a condo in the Caribbean that the whole family can use, but you are not likely to build a $2 million house for just yourself and your spouse. There's a point in life when the currency of acquisition has been devalued. You are beyond the desire to be envied for your yacht or Ferrari or mansion. (At least this is true outside the city of New York, which seems to have its own special rules.) Past a certain age, people find their joys in other people, not in possessions.

Most people's lives between 55 and death will be relatively unchanged in terms of creature comforts. The expressions of new wealth that I've seen are rather modest. We always buy the car we should instead of the car we want; now these folks can finally buy the car they want, and that's more likely to be a Jaguar than a Lamborghini. They'll take that dreamed-of cruise

and indulge in a deluxe cabin on the Queen Elizabeth II—
things they associate with luxury that seemed out of their reach
before. But cruises are $10,000 items, not $100,000 items. And
they have more to do with experiences than with possessions.

The litmus test for satisfying a wish list:

Do I have enough money to buy a certain item or experience without jeopardizing the income stream that
supports my life-style?

---

4. Status Quo Life-styles

After the wish list is taken care of, it is time to think about
everyday living. Again, I don't find that people who are now
in possession of a sizable amount of money make any grand
changes in their lives. They want to go on living pretty much
as they did before.

One reason they don't spend is their desire to hang on to
what they have. It separates them from their less affluent past.
Even with $500,000 or a million or several millions in the bank,
people don't start spending lavishly, because it makes them
feel good to look at their net worth statement and see a large
and comforting number. They relish this sense of security and
pride more than they desire high living. Some individuals also
take pride in an understated life-style. Sam Walton, whose Wal-
Mart stores have made him a billionaire, is pleased to have the
world know that he drives a pickup truck.

Age, again, is certainly the pivotal factor in how people behave once the chips are cashed in. Those who become wealthy
when they are still under 40 are far more likely not only to go
on an initial buying spree but also to live it up thereafter. But
unless you receive an inheritance early in life or are a whiz kid
who starts up a computer company at 21 that you sell at 31,
money—real money—doesn't arrive until middle age, which is
another one of life's cruel ironies. If your parents were about 25
when you were born and the last surviving parent dies at 80,

that makes you 55 when you come into your inheritance. Most entrepreneurs who build a business don't think seriously of selling out and cashing in until they are in their mid-50s, when they start to feel they are slowing down and worry that they won't be as aggressive as they were. Those high-up enough in a corporation to be offered early retirement that leaves them with millions are likely to have reached 50. And, of course, those who follow the normal retirement pattern are well past 50.

The money comes, then, at a time of life when most people no longer have the desire to do anything very grand with it. Their life-styles are familiar and comfortable, and they don't really want to change them all that much.

The size of a fortune also makes a difference, of course. If you have just come into $5 million, you are far more likely to switch to custom-made suits and designer dresses than if you have $500,000. But I've had clients suddenly in possession of $5 million, even far more, who find they prefer to live on about the same, rather modest scale as in the past.

The other factor that defines how much a life-style changes is the way the money arrives. A family that has saved for 35 years, watching its nestegg grow bit by bit, is not likely to change the habits of a lifetime and start spending madly when the chips are cashed in at retirement. However, if the money comes unexpectedly—you get a generous and unsolicited offer for your business, or the company you work for is acquired and you are eased out with several million in total compensation—there is far more temptation to move into a higher sphere of luxury. But even in those cases the outlay may be muted. Studies of people who have won lotteries show that most, except for the very young, don't change their life-styles dramatically.

Extravagance Is a Relative Term

When the people who come to me for help in their investment planning start to talk about their spending, I try not to be judgmental. They are looking to me for absolution, if they suspect they have been living too high on the hog, and for a ticket of entitlement to continue along the same lavish path. I can grant both. If they say, "We don't live extravagantly," I'll just say, "It doesn't sound like it," even if the number's $1,000,000 a year. And the truth is, there is no standard. People ask me, thinking with some guilt of what they spend, "What is normal?" I tell them, honestly, that "normal" in this instance is entirely a function of how people with the same resources choose to live. The only thing that matters is that the income be adequate to support the outflow.

It seems to be very easy to spend whatever there is to spend. Consumption rises with the level of income. But a million a year? Well, there are multiple houses with servants in all of them. There is a staff that goes beyond the domestics—a resident accountant, for example. There may be a driver for a regal car, and it is not uncommon to find an airplane as well. A couple of country club memberships. Frequent and elaborate trips. Round-trip tickets to London on the Concorde are $8000 each, and two rooms at the Savoy—Johnny needs his own room, of course—run $800 a day. Some shopping at Harrod's, naturally. Back home, there are the black-tie functions—you can go to one a week—where the tickets cost $1000 each, the dress costs $3500, the shoes cost $500, and the purse costs $800. And then, too, the kids spend a lot, even after the years of private schools. "We helped Susie out when she bought her $300,000 house"—things like that. You wonder how people do it? That's how they do it. As I say, it's easy.

A lot of people live as though they are entitled to whatever they want in life. God will provide for them. And God usually does. Would you believe that they still feel deprived? They have $30 million, but someone else has $50 million; they have a plane but someone else has a Lear jet, and more and bigger houses, too. You don't think you would be that way if you had that kind of money? "Gee, if I had $10 million, I wouldn't know what to do with all that money." Wanna bet?

It's all a matter of what you are used to. Since most of us are used to a lot less extravagance, we feel rich if we can just maintain our accustomed life-style, perhaps upgraded slightly, when we have ceased our labors. And if we have assiduously saved and invested a percentage of our earnings, whatever that level of earnings may have been, we will most certainly reach that point.

5. Developing an Action Plan

The first step in making a financial plan that will fit your new circumstances is figuring out what you have been spending.

It always surprises me that most people don't know how much they spend. So I tell my clients just to take an evening and go through last year's checkbook. That'll tell you what your level of consumption is. Sure, there will always be something special during the year: You had to put a new roof on the house or pay for your daughter's wedding. But that's all right. There will usually be something like that *every* year—a new car, help for the kids, or a big donation to a college for a thirty-fifth reunion.

Then you have to think about what may have changed, what you would like to change, what you might be spending in the years to come. And you have to be realistic about it. A couple will say they have been spending $100,000 a year. Then we calculate that if they now put all of their investable assets in Treasuries, they will have an income of $200,000 a year. "Oh, no," they say, thoroughly appalled, "we don't need that much income!" Okay, they don't need all of it. But think some more about that $100,000 figure. Your time is your own now, for example; you can travel whenever you wish. And you want to enjoy some of the rewards of all those years you worked and scrimped to reach this point in your life, so you feel you deserve to fly first class, at least now and then, and to stay in staterooms and first-class hotels, and to eat at the best restaurants. You will probably give more elaborate Christmas gifts. You may get more involved in charities now and want to make larger donations. You may want to give money to your children. Even if you don't build a mansion or buy a yacht or upgrade your life-style all that much, you are still likely to spend at least somewhat more than you used to. Few things are as addictive as limousines and first-class seats.

You will also discover another curious phenomenon: Some of your standard expenses will rise. Those who can now justifiably be called wealthy acquire would-be partners in their success. If a year ago you had a business but today you have $10 million, you will find that many of your routine costs go up in some proportion to your new fortune. Your legal costs may rise significantly, for example, even though the services you require are roughly the same. Your tax preparation and other accounting work may also go up considerably, though, again, no more work is called for. In fact, even if all your income now comes from dividends and interest, which means that tax returns are certainly no more complicated than in the past, you find that the service provider feels entitled to share in your good fortune. You are a million-dollar package now, not a mere wage earner. The justification? You'll get none. Just a higher bill.

Universal? No. Common? Yes.

My advice is to try to head off this assumption that each should pay according to his means. Tell these folk beforehand that you will not look upon that kind of discrimination kindly. Say to your accountant, "My affairs have become remarkably uncomplicated since the business was sold. Presumably, that will be reflected in my accounting costs." That should send a message to Garcia.

But most people don't do this. They become a good deal more cavalier about money when they have a lot of it. They raise their eyebrows and pay the bill. America is one of the few places on the globe where pickpockets have offices and initials after their names. Don't you be taken.

It is almost certain, then, that your expenses will increase, but in most instances I've seen, the amount of additional outlay over what was spent in previous years is modest. I'd put it in the vicinity of 10 percent to 20 percent. Your expenses won't leap from $100,000 to $200,000, but there is a good possibility they will climb to $115,000.

But not much more than that. Once your house is paid for and your kids are educated, you don't need a whole lot of money. You might eat out four nights a week because the kids are gone, but that's about as much as you can stand. You get sick of that, too. Maybe you spend $400 or $500 a month on food. Then there's the maintenance and insurance on your house, the utilities, and other such expenses, that maybe add up to another $1000 a month. You do tend to travel more and to travel in style, but you can do that, too, only to a limited extent. Go to London for a week (without Johnny), for instance, and you spend $400 a day on a hotel room and $200 on food, so maybe the whole trip costs about $1000 a day. If you do two such trips a year, you'll spend about $15,000. And you'll go to New York for a couple of three-day weekends a year, for some good food and theater; that'll be another $3000 a year.

That adds up to $18,000, or $1500 a month, for travel. Throw in the other expenses, and I would say that if you have $5000 to $7000 a month to spend—about $80,000 a year—you can cover your home costs and still live very, very well.

If you are skeptical about that figure, remember that you are through furnishing your house. You're tired of recovering the furniture. You stop collecting "things." With the kids gone, out on their own—the empty nest syndrome—many people downscale their living quarters. They sell the house with the pool and move into an apartment, and maybe buy a condo in Scottsdale. And very few people are going to travel as much at 75 as they did at 55 or 65. Even if your health is good, it takes more out of you. As you get older, you are more likely to spend money on activities that involve your children and grandchildren. You take your son and daughter-in-law and their two kids to Jamaica for a week. Some would call this "investing in photo opportunities."

So let's assume that $80,000 a year would do rather nicely. To throw off $80,000 a year from 8 percent bonds, after taxes, relying on your own assets, would take about $1.5 million. But if you retire from a company with a good pension plan, you might be getting $40,000 or $50,000 from that source. Social security kicks in with another $12,000. So you might need only another $25,000 income from your own capital to bring you up to that level. So instead of $1.5 million, $500,000 should do it. If you want to give handsome donations, make gifts to your kids, and buy and maintain a condo in Hawaii, you would need more. Then, $1 million in investable funds, as we said in the first chapter, would take care of everything.

Of course, if you retire *before* you are eligible for a pension and social security, it is a different story. Those quitting work at 50 or 55 have to make up that difference somehow, and some use up a part of their own capital to bridge the years until the retirement plans kick in.

6. Keeping Score

As you draw up plans fresh into your retirement, you are only making assumptions. You will have to keep checking on those assumptions to see if your spending patterns are about as you expected. That's the only way to know how the pattern of spending has changed in your new situation. Most people, as I've said, are pleasantly surprised. They find they live not much above their customary level. The cash in their checkbook even builds up, and they are able to add to their investment portfolio.

Some people will discover, however, that they have been hitting the checkbook a bit too hard. This is especially true in the first year or two for those whose money has come suddenly. Not used to affluence, they don't know how much they are entitled to spend, but feeling flush, they tend to spend a lot. If they have $1 million and have put it into 8 percent bonds, they spend the $80,000 in income, and if they have $2 million, they spend $160,000. I've noticed that this tendency to consume 8 percent of investable capital is a very common phenomenon. The trouble is that people who do this have forgotten that taxes have to be paid on that income.

Many of these people will then try to improve their returns by going into riskier investments. They buy junk bonds, for example, so that they can spend at the same level and pay their taxes without eating up capital. But most people quickly see how dangerous that is. What would happen to their capital and their income if the investments go sour? So they sober up and cut back on the spending. Or, if it is possible, they shift assets into *safe* higher-income-producing securities. They sell some stocks and put the proceeds into Treasuries.

You can keep track of expenditures and investments on your home computer. Convenient, easy-to-master software is now available. *Managing Your Money* and *Quicken* are both good programs. But a lot of people don't know that you can hire a bookkeeper for $25 an hour, which will end up costing you about $100 a month, to do the job for you. You could ask your accountant to handle it, but that will cost a multiple of the tab you get from a bookkeeper who works out of his or her home. Many of my clients have someone who does their income statements quarterly.

Knowing how things are progressing is critical to your peace of mind, to the sense that you have control of your life. You won't be crying out at the end of the year, "My God, we have $100,000 a year in income and there's nothing left! What's going on here?" If you know where the money's going, you can make changes, instead of just suffering anxiety attacks. The balance sheet, which lets you know whether you are winning or losing in your investments, can be done annually, because most of the changes in your net worth are going to reflect your investment program, and a quarterly accounting would mean little. But you should track expenditures every three months.

If you own any investment property or other nonmarketable assets, value them conservatively on your net worth statement. I'd value a piece of commercial real estate, for example, at cost. If you paid $200,000 for it and you think it is now worth $400,000, and you revalue it to that figure on your net worth statement and you then get struck by lightning, the appraiser of your estate may come out and write down $400,000, or maybe $430,000 for good measure. You may estimate its value at $400,000 today, but as we've all found out in recent years, real estate *can* go down in value as well as up, so to state values to reflect a property's estimated current worth—perhaps to make yourself feel good about what an astute investor you've been—is not realistic in any case. If you value conservatively instead, there's also a chance that you will reduce your estate tax liability. Why put down a value that your widow or widower will have to argue was really on the high side? Assets that are marketable are different. You can't carry Exxon at $6 a share.

When you do add up your net worth and contemplate what you will be leaving your heirs, don't forget those taxes. Taxes are an ugly reality that we tend to shove to the back of our minds. Let's say you have a portfolio worth $2 million and a million of it represents capital gains. If you sell, you'll be paying a capital gains tax of 40 percent by the time the state and city grab their share, and, if you drop dead, it's probably going to be even worse than that. If you sell, pay the taxes, and then drop dead, even less is left to your heirs. So in your accounting, reserve for that tax liability, because that's what is *really* going to be left behind. You don't know when the tax will be paid or precisely how much it's going to be, but it's an account payable you can't escape. Obvious? Yes, of course. But it never ceases to amaze me how many people don't consider this basic fact of life and death.

Your annual tally:

- Mark changes in your net worth, reflecting appreciation or depreciation in value of securities, real estate, or other investments.
- Ascertain any changes in your level of spending.
- Adjust accordingly:
  If income is greater than expenses, add to investments.

  If expenses are greater than income, either curtail spending or shift equity investments into income-producing investments.

---

7. Asset Allocation—The Simplified Version

Some items on your net worth statement, of course, represent investments in your life-style—your home, cars, furniture, art, jewelry, and other personal possessions. Those assets, along with any remaining interests in a business or professional practice, are tied up. The free, investable assets—cash, stocks, bonds, money market funds, partnerships, investment real estate—are those that can throw off the income that will support your life-style without labor.

To feel secure and good about your new wealth, the first thing—the main thing—to consider is income.

Quality of life is a derivative of income, not of capital. Sure, income is what buys the four-star restaurants and the five-star hotel rooms, but I am talking about the basics—high and steady income that keeps the money flowing into your checking account so that you meet your expenses and still look with satisfaction at your balance at the end of the month. That's far different from what your net worth may be. Net worth has real meaning only if you choose to borrow money or get divorced. Otherwise, net worth is almost an abstraction in terms of how it affects your wallet and your daily needs.

That is my "system" for investing wealth. Remarkably simple, isn't it? Figure out how much you and your spouse need to maintain your life-style. Then isolate enough of your capital to invest in Treasury bills and notes to throw off that amount of income.

If there are funds remaining, then start to think about "risk" investments. My preference for risk investments comes down to one: common stocks.

Treasuries for income, stocks for risk. Period. That is my pared-down version of the process you have probably read and heard about in the last couple of years: asset allocation. What is usually meant by asset allocation, be it for an institution like a pension fund or for an individual, is a division of investable funds to reflect two factors: the investor's needs and preferences, of course, but also the relationship among investment alternatives. That is, if stocks have been returning more of late than you would expect looking at historical data, you lower your allocation to stocks in favor of another market that hasn't been doing as well as in the past. The theory is that normal relationships will reassert themselves. I agree with that perspective, and we will see how it can be applied when making investments in the risk category. But income needs come first, and the allocation to investments that supply that income is sacred, whatever opportunities there may be because of disparities in asset class valuations.

Asset allocation also means, ipso facto, that money is spread around, that you don't keep it all in one asset basket. If you have enough of it, as the pension funds do, you can parcel it out to an amazing degree—domestic bonds, international bonds, domestic stocks, international stocks, corporate bonds, Treasury notes and bonds, mortgage-backed securities, real estate, private placements, commodities, cash equivalents (probably money market funds for you, but items like commercial paper for institutions), venture capital, precious metals, options and futures, oil and gas, farmland, timberland, and so on. A highly diversified portfolio certainly lowers risk and volatility, because one market will be going up while another is going down. And you can shift your assets from one market to another as you see relative values change. That's the way the big institutional investors handle their portfolios these days. The phenomenon is one more result of the world's having been computerized. All the accumulated data on relationships among various investment classes have convinced people that they can forecast an appropriate exposure to each.

Institutional investors have started shifting allocations on a shorter and shorter time table, and I have deep reservations about that. One has to make a good many assumptions—such as an expected rate of inflation—that are fed into a computer model to get meaningful output, and such forecasts tend to be inaccurate for a host of reasons, unraveling the whole system. Relationships of an investment class to its historical norm or to other investments can be out of whack for years, and new factors—of late, the importance of overseas stock and bond markets, for example—upset traditional relationships. I agree that returns from markets do tend to revert to their historical norms, but only over long stretches of time. I also agree that you can reduce the volatility of a total portfolio through diversification. But I do not believe that you can cleverly reallocate the portfolio month by month, or even quarter by quarter, to a host of markets both to reduce volatility and increase returns. Even if it did work, people would tinker with the system to conform to their emotional swings.

If I don't think the institutions, with all their own and Wall Street's computer power and Ph.D.s in mathematics, can do it right, I need hardly state that you, the individual investor, cannot do it right either. Yet people keep trying all the time, following some newsletter that advises them to switch from stocks to cash to bonds, usually by a phone call to a mutual fund family. Short-term market timing works sometimes and costs you money most times.

People First, Performance Second

In any case, most asset allocation models are designed to optimize investment returns. My priority is different: the comfort of the investor. My sole agenda is to keep the man or woman of wealth safe, secure, prosperous, and relatively worry-free. You have to consider the emotions that people experience during significant transitions in their lives. At the age of 55 or 65, people want to reduce rather than add to the number of items on their balance sheet. They don't want or need investments spread all over the financial spectrum. They want a limited number of relationships with managers of assets and a reduced level of bookkeeping and accounting. And they want liquidity, because they figure they are going to drop dead every day that they haven't.

That's why I stick to just Treasuries and stocks. Take real estate, a major investment alternative that throws off income as well as offers the possibility of growth of capital. But how do you invest in it? Most people aren't keen about owning properties directly, because they don't want to deal with all the complications of property management and tenant craziness. They could pay someone to manage the properties, of course, but they would still get phone calls about whether they want to patch or replace a leaking roof, or whether to throw out a tenant three months delinquent in his rent. Properties are headaches.

From a practical point of view, then, you could invest in real estate securities—real estate investment trusts and development companies. But then you just own more stocks—stocks that go up and down with the market and have to be analyzed like any other security. That is not what is usually meant by allocating assets to real estate. You could, instead, put money in limited partnerships that invest in real estate, but aside from the miserable records of most of these partnerships of late, if you want your money, you can't get at it. When you get to a certain point in life, you want everything liquid, simple, and tidy.

Another point: When you allocate your money to stocks and bonds, international securities, real estate, venture capital, oil and gas, some collectible (such as art or coins), and whatever else you come up with, imbued with the notion that you will reallocate as risks and rewards seem to change, you are immediately and perpetually plagued by doubts. Watching what is happening in those markets, you daily ask yourself, "Should I cut back on the stocks and shift more into bonds? Should I have more in international investments in response to this morning's headlines? Do I have enough in gold? Is real estate ready for a comeback? Should I do this or should I do that?" It's one thing for academics to contemplate allocation formulae on their computer screens, but it's another matter to have to deal with a portfolio on a day-to-day basis. If you have continuing ownership in a whole range of investment options, you have nonstop decision making to gnaw at you. And there are no road maps to certain success.

Suppose you think you have identified an offbeat investment opportunity. You have decided that junk bonds have become ridiculously cheap. You won't commit much of your money, because you realize this is a risky move; after all, you could prove wrong. If you go ahead and buy the bonds, you could indeed make some money. But what so often happens is that you have an inconsequential amount of money in an investment that proves highly consequential on the aggravation scale. If 3 percent of your money is in junk bonds and junk bonds take a dive, you tend to focus 100 percent of your attention on that 3 percent of your portfolio. The investment means next to nothing in terms of your net worth, but you worry constantly about what's happening to it.

When I talk about this with people, they are relieved. It gives them permission not to try to be investment gurus in taking care of their assets. They can just go and live their lives. They don't have to optimize their investments; instead, they can optimize their experiences. Your investments should be structured so that they don't require a lot of time and energy and so that they don't build anxieties. Of course, if you own stocks, you want to feel you are performing well; you don't want to have to apologize for your investments to anybody, including yourself. But being at the top of the performance heap isn't necessary. You just want to have investments that you understand and that you can monitor in a responsible way. Your biggest fear—not having money—can be put at rest. You can be comfortable. That's why people hire me, really. I am in the comfort business.

The only two investments you really need:
- Treasury notes for income
- Common stocks for income and capital growth

---

8. Sanctuary in Treasuries

My simple view of asset allocation, then, is that there are only two asset categories you should worry about. One deals with what I call *sanctuary,* the other with *risk.* Sanctuary money you'll keep in Treasury bills and notes. Risk is the investment category in which serious amounts of principal can be made or lost. Risk money you put into stocks.

It must be apparent by now that the amount of money you allocate to the sanctuary category is that which is enough to generate disposable income that meets your cost-of-living needs. If you are retired—you have cashed in your chips and want to live off your wealth—I would set that figure at approximately 125 percent of your needs in the year just before you retired. The reason it's 125 percent instead of 100 percent, or even 120 percent, is twofold. First, as we've discussed earlier, when events occur that make you affluent, you do end up spending more money—10 percent to 20 percent more— even if you think you won't. You travel more, your gifts and donations are more generous, you live it up a bit. But there's a second, just as important, reason: You should end each month with excess funds in your checking account. That way you will feel like a net generator of capital rather than a liquidator of your life's principal. And that is a very good feeling indeed.

As noted earlier, most of us are squeamish about spending capital, so having sufficient income to cover even major expenditures is an enormous relief. It's bad enough if you have to sell 500 shares of some stock to buy a car, but it's maddening to sell the shares and then see them jump in price. You castigate yourself for being stupid as well as indulgent. People beat themselves up over this sort of thing: "Look at the opportunity cost of that damn car," they scream at themselves. The stomach pains can get very severe. When you organize your affairs so that you can buy that car out of excess cash that's piled up in your checking account, your stomach rests easy.

Is tying up money in securities that provide income but don't add to your net worth the most efficient use of capital? Absolutely not. Is it an effective way to avoid ulcers? Absolutely yes. I've seen the relief in people's eyes when they realize they are not going to have to drive themselves crazy every time they have to spend big money.

Of course, there are those who don't worry about such things as maintaining capital and financial security, even as they get on in years. I think of one man who takes chances that I believe are crazy. He retired with about one-half million dollars in investable funds and he's kept the whole bundle in stocks. As it happens, he's had great investment results, averaging nearly 20 percent a year in returns. After taxes, he's probably got a net return of about 14 percent—about $70,000 a year. He has just himself to worry about, so he lives very well on his $70,000. He's got a big house in a resort area and a pair of Mercedes, and he travels everywhere. But to my way of looking at things, this man has a death wish. In his place, I'd be terrified that I'd outdistance my capital. I ask him, "What will you do if you take a big hit in the market and your account goes down to $400,000 and you still try to live the way you do now?" But he doesn't care. He's been living very comfortably for 15 years, he's still got his one-half million dollars, and he'll just go on taking his chances. Few of us, however, are built that way psychologically.

A slight subterfuge assures my clients of a bit more of an income cushion. Suppose your investable assets add up to $2 million. You have found that you've been spending about $80,000 a year, which means you need about $130,000 in gross income before taxes take their bite. Suppose, further, that you have $50,000 coming in from a pension plan and social security, or perhaps you are still generating that much income from consulting or other part-time work. I would advise you to put $1.5 million into intermediate Treasury bills. That would throw off pretax income of an additional $120,000 or so a year. So now you have $170,000 in gross income, or about $100,000 in after-tax income. You have the $80,000 you used to spend to maintain your life-style, plus another 25 percent to cover whatever additional money you are likely to spend now. The other one-half million in investable funds can go into stocks, to provide growth. And that will throw off 2 percent to 3 percent in dividend income that will give you another $10,000 or so a year, after taxes, to spend. So you can buy a new car every couple of years, take a Mediterranean cruise or its equivalent every year, and still have money in your checking account at the end of the month. I don't mention this little dividend ploy to people, though sometimes they pick up on it. But it's a nice bit of extra. They'll get a rush of affluence because they have all that income coming in, and that makes the world a far more hospitable place.

How much should you invest in income-producing Treasuries?

1. Enough of your capital to generate the income that can maintain the life-style you had before retirement

2. *Plus* enough to generate 25 percent additional income to cover life-style enhancements, take care of major expenses such as new cars, and provide a margin of comfort

9. What About Inflation?

Once they reflect on all the money they are putting into fixed income securities, people, very understandably, start to worry about inflation. Their income will be fixed, but the things they buy go up in price every year. Even if inflation is 4 percent or 5 percent, or only 3 percent, it's a problem, because people are living longer, and, over decades, inflation could substantially lower the buying power of those fixed dollars. They would fall behind in their standard of living.

Yes, inflation is a problem. But let's look at the realities. First of all, as pointed out earlier, if you had to dip into capital every year, you could probably live to 100 without using it up. But aside from that, if you take a closer look at your personal lifestyle, you will see that inflation is not going to hit you that hard.

Go back to your cost-of-living list. Each item is not going to inflate by 5 percent just because the inflation rate is 5 percent that year. Food expenditures will definitely inflate, but these probably represent about 5 percent of your disposable income. The single most important factor in your living costs is housing. If your home is paid for—and I always encourage paying off mortgages—there's no problem there at all. If you still have a mortgage, it's probably at a fixed rate, so that won't be going up by 5 percent. Rises in medical costs eventually get covered by Medicare. And then there are the children. If you still have one or more children in college, that expense keeps going up— it probably runs somewhere between $1000 and $3000 a month for each child, depending on where he or she goes to school. But when that is over, you'll find you have another $30,000 a year in disposable income. I would say the chances are more than good that your cost of living is not going to go up at the national rate.

What's more, if you still have money in stocks, and maybe some in real estate holdings, they are likely to go up in value at a rate equal to or higher than the rate of inflation. If you are wealthy enough to have more money in stocks than in bonds— say, you have a million in bonds because that throws off enough income to take care of living expenses and $2 million in investable funds left over to put into stocks—you and your heirs should stay well ahead of inflation. But if you don't own stocks or real estate, inflation's impact on your life will still be very minor. At the worst, you'll end up spending some of your principal, in which case the impact of inflation would be felt by your beneficiaries, not by you.

If you are still worried about inflation, put 5 percent or 10 percent of your net worth in gold. I usually suggest a mutual fund that specializes in gold investments. If you are really hung-up on this matter, you should just go out and buy gold coins, Maple Leafs or Eagles. If you are serious, do it now, because if we do start to reinflate, you are too likely to panic and put 40 percent of your money into gold at the wrong time. With 5 percent or 10 percent already committed, you'll feel protected as prices rise. In some ways, gold is a way to hedge your own emotionality and to avoid doing something disproportionate if we do reinflate. I call it "pre-scratching the itch."

Actually, I think that keeping some money in gold as inflation insurance isn't a bad idea, but most people in this country aren't interested. Whether they view it as anti-American or are just unfamiliar with the idea of gold as an inflation hedge, few choose to own it. Because it has never been important in this country, as it is in many parts of the world, it doesn't provide any meaningful psychological security. I certainly don't push it with my clients as part of their investment program.

The truth is, the only real inflation hedge is the ability to make more capital. And if you are no longer working, you are

---

Inflation is not a major concern because

1. Your own cost of living at retirement age is not likely to increase at the national inflation rate.

2. Some of your investments will probably rise in value faster than the inflation rate.

3. You can dip into capital to maintain your life-style without exhausting that capital during your lifetime.

unlikely to take the necessary risk to make that capital through investments. You can't deal with inflation by trying to get more income out of your present stockpile of capital. So don't worry about it.

10. How Much Ready Cash Do You Need?

People worry about cash: How much do they need to keep in money market funds or in a money market account at the bank? "For emergencies," they say. "In case something happens, you know."

Again, what are the realities? Suppose there is an emergency and you need immediate cash. You have a Master Card or VISA card. So if you have to buy an airplane ticket at very short notice because an aunt has passed away in Omaha, there's no problem. We're all so used to being told to keep six month's income, or whatever the sum, in ready cash for emergencies, but it really isn't necessary now that we have credit cards, often with ready-cash advance privileges, whose balances can be paid off over several months.

That's the economic reality, but the psychological reality is that most people like to have some ready cash for whatever it is they worry about. In their minds, anything below a certain level makes the world a frightening place. For some people, that level is $3000; for others, it may be $50,000 or $150,000. Whatever my clients tell me, I say, "Fine, that sounds like a good number." If the husband says $3000 and the wife says $5000, I'll say, "Well, maybe $5000 is a better number." The point is that the amount assuages any anxiety about meeting perceived needs.

That number, however, is a creation in each person's mind. The truth is that you need almost no cash. Most people today use credit cards for anything that costs a lot, and even if they like to pay off the card charges in 30 days, they'll probably have enough income coming in to handle the tab. But to tell people this is like telling someone who feels bad that he or she doesn't feel bad. If someone feels bad, I just acknowledge it.

Decide how much cash you need to keep in the bank to feel secure, put that amount aside, and rest easy.

For that is what you are trying to accomplish—to feel good about your finances. That's why, to reiterate, the asset allocation policy I recommend deals only with bonds and stocks. This way, people have only two things that need concern them. My system is not designed to optimize economics. It is designed to create the highest level of comfort commensurate with the least amount of risk. I believe in overweighting temperamental considerations at the expense of financial considerations. Money should contribute to people's happiness, not upset them.

If you own Treasuries, for example, and you read in the paper that bonds have gone down in value, you might say to yourself, "Forget it. My $1 million yesterday is worth $940,000 today, so what? It's irrelevant. My income from the bonds is going to be paid like clockwork." What's more, I tell people not to buy 30-year bonds but 5-year bonds and 7-year bonds, so you'll get your $1 million back before long. And if you also own stocks, and the market is blasted, you are insulated from any risk that you will have to change the way you live. You may have to wait for the stocks to come back in value, but in the meantime you've got that $80,000 a year coming in from the bonds, so you are not going to be hurt where it really counts.

Your comfort level is another reason to stick with Treasury bills and notes. They are the safest of investments, and this is, after all, the sanctuary sector of your assets. You have $2 million of investable funds and you need $100,000 a year in gross income to live on? Fine. Put $1.2 million into Treasuries paying 8 percent and your needs are taken care of. The rest can then go into some investment that should, over time, earn more than 8 percent. And that's stocks. It's as simple as that.

How much cash do you need to keep on hand?

For economic reasons: None

For psychological reasons: Whatever makes you comfortable

11. A Conservative Bond Strategy

However, this is important: don't buy just any Treasuries that pay 8 percent. Typically, I do not recommend going out further than seven years—that is, buy notes maturing in seven years, possibly ten years, but nothing longer than that. Twenty-year bonds pay higher interest, but if you own seven-year notes and interest rates go up and the value of the bonds go down, you have to wait only seven years to get your principal back and reinvest it. So you can sweat it out. But if you have to wait 15 years, or 20 years, especially when you are in your 50s or 60s, those years will seem like forever. You can get more income by lengthening the maturities or buying lower quality bonds—corporates instead of Treasuries—but you have to keep reminding yourself that this is the sanctuary part of your capital, and you are not trying to be opportunistic with it, not trying to increase your capital with it. That job is only for whatever money is left over after the sanctuary is taken care of.

I strongly discourage my clients from going out more than ten years in maturities, and, as I said, I prefer a maximum of seven years. The longer the maturities, the greater the fluctuation in values as interest rates rise and fall, and you don't need that worry. You want to be safe and confident and comfortable. Middle-aged people, having witnessed the ravages of inflation for a big part of their lives, are frightened when they put money out for longer periods of time.

Entrepreneurs, regardless of age, who have sold their businesses are also wary of long-term paper. They aren't very happy about buying bonds in the first place. As businessmen, they have been borrowers most of their lives. But lending—which is, of course, what you are doing when you buy a bond—seems unnatural to them. As a matter of fact, they often think lenders are fools. They've borrowed from the banks and taken risks in their businesses that they thought the bankers never really understood. Most of them have gone through periods when they were leveraged to the hilt, and sometimes business soured to the point where they wondered if they would be able to keep the doors open. On occasion they felt they were lying to the banks, borrowing ostensibly for inventory when they needed the money to make their payroll. If they are now going to be lenders themselves, they at least feel more comfortable lending to the U.S. government and knowing the loans are for short periods of time.

I know one man whose memories of being close to the precipice on a number of occasions have made him ultraconservative with his investments. The first thing he did when he sold his business was to build a home that cost about $2.5 million, and he paid cash for it. Then he calculated that the house was going to cost him about $25,000 a year in taxes and another $40,000 or so in general maintenance. He put a million dollars into Treasuries so that all the costs of operating the house were prefunded, and he bought 20-year bonds so that he wouldn't have to worry about those expenses for the foreseeable future. The money that was left over he put into ten-year Treasuries; nothing went into stocks. He said it was more important to him that his income never go down than that his capital go up. "A couple of times it was just a toss of the dice whether I ended up bankrupt or I ended up rich," he said. "I got lucky and I'm rich, but I don't ever want to worry about that sort of thing again." Now he knows he'll never have to give up his $2.5 million house.

Spread the Risk

I also strongly recommend what those in the bond business call *laddering*. That means that, if you are buying bonds that mature as far out as ten years, you divide your sanctuary money into fifths and put one-fifth each into notes that mature in two years, into those that mature in four years, into six-year notes, into eight-year notes, and into 10-year bonds. This truly protects you against interest-rate fluctuations and therefore assures you that the income you need will be there.

Consider what can happen if you don't ladder and all of your notes mature at the same time. Suppose you decide that interest rates are going to drop, so you want to lock in the high current rate. You put all of your million into 10-year bonds paying 10 percent. If interest rates do drop to $7\frac{1}{2}$ percent, great, you're a hero. But if instead they go higher, to 12 percent, you have sacrificed some $200,000 in income that you could have had over the 10-year life of the bonds if you were getting your money back every couple of years for reinvestment at the higher rate.

Or suppose you decide that interest rates are heading higher than 10 percent, so you keep all your money in short-term Treasury notes. But instead, rates fall to $7\frac{1}{2}$ percent. You don't lose principal: when your notes mature in two years, you get your $1 million back. But when you roll your money over into current Treasuries, your income will drop by 20 percent. And since most of us operate our lives out of income, not out of capital, you just took a very big hit. Having your income reduced by 20 percent is considerably more painful than missing an opportunity to make a capital gain.

So don't get too cute with the fixed portion of your assets, the part that pays the income you will need. By laddering, only a portion of your money is at risk to interest-rate changes, and you are protected against any major loss of income. You are settling for the average return over a given length of time. That's not particularly clever, I realize, but it protects you against doing something stupid.

That's important for another reason: Any stupidity tends to compound itself. The psychology of investors in the real world is that when they make a mistake, say in forecasting interest rates, they usually try to vindicate their action and prove their genius by making another call, which more likely than not turns out equally disastrous. I have a master's degree in finance and I've been in this business 20 years, but I can't forecast interest rates. And I don't know anybody else who can either, including some of our most eminent economists. Oh yes, a lot of people sometimes forecast rates correctly, but sometimes they don't, and none of them forecasts with enough precision enough of the time that I would bet money on their prognostications. It would be foolhardy for you to think you can do any better.

If you follow my notion of sanctuary, which is to use Treasuries and ladder them, you don't need professional management for your notes. The only way a manager could add value to a Treasury portfolio would be by making big bets on the direction of interest rates—and enough's been said on that topic already—or by trading the hell out of the account, swapping issues to pick up eighths and sixteenths of a percentage point in additional income. In the latter case, you move millions around to make hundreds—if you're lucky.

You don't need that, and you certainly don't need to pay somebody just to buy and hold the securities and collect the interest. The fees for fixed income management are commonly $\frac{1}{2}$ percent. If you are earning 8 percent in interest, you'd give up 6 percent of your gross income to have someone collect the money and balance the books, which seems high, even if you are rich. So don't look for a fixed income manager. Buy your Treasuries yourself. You can buy them directly from the Federal Reserve, but it is easier, and inexpensive, to have your bank do it for you.

Your income-producing portfolio:

· 20 percent in Treasury notes that mature in two years
· 20 percent in Treasury notes that mature in four years
· 20 percent in Treasury notes that mature in six years
· 20 percent in Treasury notes that mature in eight years
· 20 percent in Treasury bonds that mature in ten years

---

12. Considering the Alternatives

There are other income-producing investments, of course, besides Treasuries—single premium annuities, for example. The insurance company pays an interest rate competitive with intermediate bonds, but the annuity income is not taxed until the money is paid out. That favorable tax treatment is controversial and may disappear, since Congress may say "no more" and not grandfather such investments from back taxes. But aside from that, I worry about the financial solvency of the insurance issuers, because, as we have learned, we are in a world where insurance companies are in trouble from the junk bonds and nonperforming real estate in their portfolios. You could put part of your sanctuary allocation in annuities, as a Treasury note substitute, to gain the tax advantage, but because of the insurance company risk at this time, I wouldn't put more than 20 percent of my money in them.

I would not recommend municipal bonds. Often your return isn't much different than what you get from Treasuries, after taxes are paid, and you never know whether you have a problem with these bonds until you get notice of default. There's no oversight; nobody pays attention to them, certainly not the brokers who sold them to you, since brokers seldom understand the credits they are peddling. States, counties, and cities get downgraded from time to time. It happens quickly and you find out about it after the fact. You can't even find the price of the bonds in the paper. What's more, if you put your own portfolio of bonds together, you tend to pay too much when you buy them and you get robbed when you sell them. If one of my clients insists on municipals, I prefer the unit trusts sold by Nuveen, Van Kampen Merritt, and some other managers, even if there is a load fee. At least there's diversification of issues, you know what the returns are going to be as long as the bonds don't get called, and somebody is watching if a credit problem arises.

I see no point in buying government agency paper either— the notes issued by the Federal Home Loan Bank, or the Federal Farm Credit Corporation, and such. The incremental return over Treasuries is minimal, especially after you pay state taxes on the agencies, so why bother? Mortgage-backed securities, particularly those issued by the Government National Mortgage Association, have been very popular, mostly because they usually pay more than Treasuries. But then there's a different problem: When you receive your payments, part represents interest and part is repayment of principal, and the trouble is that people get their check and throw it into their checking account, and it all gets spent. You run a great risk of spending principal and not even realizing it. Again, I have to integrate how human beings behave with the economic issues.

People hate it when I discourage these alternatives. You know the way people shop around to find the certificates of deposit that pay $\frac{1}{4}$ percent more than another bank's. Most people take great pride in getting an edge. But I argue that credit markets are ruthlessly efficient, and if you are getting a percentage of greater return, there has to be more risk. So if you want to stray from Treasuries, I say to you, "Fine. If you want to do it, do it. I wouldn't."

Indeed, those are words I say frequently. I like a tidy world. I like to know that over here is my sanctuary, my anchor to windward, and over there is my risk. It is when you blend the two—when you try to increase the return on the sanctuary or increase the income on the risk—that you bastardize the process and get yourself in trouble. For most people "income" also means "safety," for they want to know that the assets they put in income-producing securities are not going to be destroyed. If it is going to be sanctuary, then it's damn well going to be sanctuary, and as long as there is a U.S. government issuing paper, I have nothing to worry about. The securities I want to worry about are those that can make 15 percent returns, not $\frac{1}{2}$ percent more than Treasuries. If I have enough money in Treasuries to generate the income I need, so that I know that even if my other assets go up in smoke, my life-style won't be affected, then I have increased my tolerance for risk in whatever I choose to do with the rest of my money.

13. The Risk Component

With the sanctuary element taken care of, we can get to the risk category. Risk is anything that offers the chance to make or lose serious money. That would include stocks, of course, but also junk bonds, long-maturity bonds (since a 55-year-old person may not be around to see a 30-year bond mature), real estate, venture capital, collectibles, and the other alternatives we've already mentioned.

What risk category is chosen, after the income-producing part is taken care of, is a function of a person's age, financial situation, and preferences. As we've seen, I advise common stocks. Most people who own investment real estate hang on to it, but they don't add to it. Those who don't already own it don't want to start owning it, because they do not want to assume the complications of investments that are management-intensive. Venture capital and the rest of the options are too risky for most investors. So that leaves stocks, which may not be ideal investments, but they involve fewer inconveniences at a time in life when convenience and liquidity are more important than other considerations.

Another chapter will explore how you should approach the stock market—whether on your own or through mutual funds or investment counselors, whether you need more than one manager or style, and whether you should have some non–U.S. companies in your portfolio. But for many people, there simply isn't enough money for stocks. They need to keep what assets they have in Treasuries, so they'll have the income they require to support their desired living standard. All I can say to such people is, "Look, you have a choice here. You don't have to do what I suggest, but the quality of your life is derivative of your income, and my advice is to put your money in Treasuries, live well, and stop trying to grow your capital by investing in the stock market. That will only increase your anxieties, and your money is supposed to relieve you of anxieties. If you become compulsive about optimizing every cent, the money will ruin your life. Go for the income and enjoy life. You can afford to do that now. You're not going to live forever. Develop the income and invest in memories."

Some people just can't stand that. They are so used to being able to say to themselves every December 31, "I am worth more today than I was on January 1," that they cannot bear the thought of having all their money in investments that cannot grow in value. The stock market soars and they feel God's giving away money and they don't have a basket, and it drives them wild.

For every one of my clients, I find it useful to lay out a high-risk strategy and a zero-risk strategy and see what responses I get. I try to focus on the client's comfort zone. I have to find a rational economic solution that is coupled with a temperamental solution, and if I hit it right, then I get a lot of head-nodding: "Yeah, that makes sense."

For some, that means no stocks at all, even if there is more than enough money to provide the needed income. If you feel comfortable with 100 percent in bonds, because the possibility of losing money is unthinkable, and you want a world that is safe, secure, and predictable, then forgo the appreciation potential of common stocks. People who need that sense of certainty happily sign the contract, and the older we get, the more likely we are to be in that category.

For others, however, involvement in the stock market to even a modest degree, so that they stay players in the game, seems as necessary for their psychic health as their daily one-half hour on a Nordic Track is for their physical well-being.

If you are one of those persons, put some of your money in the stock market so that when it goes up, you don't feel left out. If it is going to kill you not to be a participant, then do it. But know the offset—the possibility that you will have to adopt a more modest life-style if the market doesn't cooperate.

2

HOW THE AFFLUENT
GOT THAT WAY

1. Youth Is a Time for Spending

Gail Sheehy's best-selling book of several years ago, *Passages*
(E.P. Dutton, 1976) dealt with discernible patterns in the psychological states of people as they advance through the stages
of life. There are financial passages, too, that we all tend to go
through. The periods of our lives have a lot to do with how
we relate to money—how much is coming in, how much is
going out, and how we invest whatever we have saved, inherited, or realized from some fortuitous event. These periods
have a lot to tell us, too, about how wealth is amassed over a
lifetime.

Not much should be expected in the way of wealth gath-
ering in our early adult years. Sheehy calls them the "Trying
Twenties," an exhilarating time, when we "Shape a Dream,
that vision of ourselves which will generate energy, aliveness
and hope." Your expectations are boundless. Never mind that
there's such a disparity between what you know and what you
believe yourself capable of accomplishing. You haven't been
ground down yet by realities, or by your own limitations. All
is hope.

At this time of life, too, your energy levels are at their
highest, buoyed by expectation, not yet weighted down by

disappointments. If you are an office worker, every time you walk by the chief executive officer's room, you can say to yourself that you'll be sitting in there one day. After all, this is the United States: there are scores of role models who started with nothing and ended up rich. You don't consider that even if you do have the right stuff, it is going to take a long time before your goals can be achieved.

There's no cynicism at that age. I mean real cynicism, not intellectual posing. Cynicism is the emotional equivalent of scar tissue, and that's acquired through negative experiences. There's been no opportunity yet for failure and discouragement. You haven't had enough illusions shattered to be cynical.

Financially, the 20s are a time when you are checking off your list of deferred gratifications. Your own apartment—*own* is the all-important word here—is probably at the top of the list. But the list is a long one, and very specific. "I've always wanted a sports car." "I've always wanted to go to Europe." "I've always wanted to ski in Colorado." "I've always wanted a Nakamichi sound system."

Savings? Forget it. If you can't wear it, drive it, watch it, listen to it, or eat it, it has no place in your life. Your assets are invested in consumer electronics. It's probably the period of purest hedonism in anyone's financial evolution.

I remember what I was like in my 20s. I was so convinced that I would be a millionaire by the time I was 30 years old, I never gave a second thought to spending every cent I made. When I got to be 30 and wasn't even close, there was certainly a moment of reflection that suggested maybe, just maybe, I'd better deal with some future worries. Still, I was going to be rich all right; it was just going to take a bit longer.

We are not considering here, I might add, the anomalies of recent times, when a 27-year-old bond trader can make $300,000 a year. He usually ends up saving money simply because his income gets ahead of his list. But not always. Don't underestimate the ability of the young to spend. I've seen cases where very young people have come into a great deal of money suddenly. Often it is because grandparents have gifted them with some asset (with an accountant's

blessing: "Get it out of your estate") that throws off considerable income, and they manage to spend it all. At that age
they seem to have the capacity to consume any amount of
income.

And probably they should. I've come to consider it an enlightened attitude. At what other period of your life do you
have so much free time, so few ties, and so little responsibility? There are plenty of years ahead to be a grown-up and
to start building your fortune. Parents usually disapprove of
all this spending, though it doesn't do much good. Parents
tend to frown on children embracing a hedonistic lifestyle—
one that they may well aspire to themselves—because they
feel the youngsters haven't paid their dues, haven't worked
hard enough to afford that kind of high living. But the parents
bust their chops until they're 65 and then are too tired out to
do much with the money. So I'm all for the young consuming
to the level of their income.

Parents have another worry—that their children, who seem
to be spending every penny they make, aren't going to settle
down and make something of their lives. And that does happen, of course especially when assets the kids have been gifted
turn into hard cash. It's back to the RJR Nabisco example in
the introductory chapter. Grandma and Grandpa thought they
were giving their grandchild stock that would throw off $25,000
in dividend income, and suddenly it ends up being $3 million
in capital. Now the young person's psychology changes. He
or she feels rich, which is realistic, and being rich when you
are that young can inhibit ambition. Generally speaking, the
younger people come into considerable money, the less the
likelihood that they are going to do something financially wonderful with their lives. They may not turn into layabouts, but
it is less likely that they will make any huge effort to achieve
in a business or profession.

But those are the exceptions. The kids who work for their
bucks and then spend to the hilt will come up against the realities soon enough. So let them accumulate goods and good
times in those starting-out years. This is a time of life when
getting rich is a matter of dreams and not of disciplined programs.

2. The Family-Building Years: The Future Becomes a Factor

The footloose period tends to end with marriage, from the late 20s into the early 30s. Before a family's started, with both husband and wife bringing in good money, the consumerism probably continues, but it is directed toward more substantial acquisitions—primarily a larger apartment or first home, furnished with things that aren't made out of crates. The real change in lifestyle and financial objectives comes with the contemplation or arrival of children. That is the watershed. Adulthood, with all of its awesome responsibilities, descends. You are a parent; therefore, logic insists that you must become an adult at last.

All of a sudden, there are all these massive, terrifying obligations, these necessities that must be faced and, you suspect, funded. You can no longer merely spend the paycheck. The hedonism must end. You want to stop renting for sure, and own your own place. You'll need a bigger car, maybe a station wagon. You want more life insurance now than your company's benefits program provides. And you start thinking immediately—it seems to happen three days after the baby's home from the hospital—about education. Didn't you just read somewhere that in today's dollars tiny Elizabeth's college years are going to cost you in the neighborhood of $100,000?

So the savings ethic is born. The fundamental decision is made, and laid down as a law of the household, that consumption can no longer exceed income—that, as a matter of fact, it has to be less than income. You may indeed have to curb consumption, though, happily, there is often a modest mismatch in one's 30s, because you now have about ten years of experience under your belt, and if you are reasonably good at what you do, income is rising more rapidly than consumption. The surprise is on the up-side. You are paying off your modest house and still managing to set aside some money every month.

And that's it. You have just read it—the key to acquired wealth. If you are not born rich or had wealth thrust upon you by fortuitous circumstances, the sure way to make it on your own is to save and let your savings compound. That is the "secret" I have learned from the thousands of wealthy people I have counseled.

Not very exciting, is it? Or appealing. But I am afraid that there is only one, very elementary answer to the question, "How do I get rich?" That answer is: deferred gratification. People who are now affluent have had the ability over the years to look at a menu of options for their money and make that one unpleasant choice—deferral, doing without, putting aside instead—with considerable frequency.

Most of my clients have been blessed with relatively high incomes through the later years of their careers, but not necessarily astronomical incomes—six-figure but not seven-figure. The ones who have become what I would call middling rich, with a few million dollars but nowhere near enough to place them among the *Forbes* 400 rich, built up their incomes over the years, but they kept their lifestyles comfortable, not opulent. In blunter terms, they stopped short of spending every penny they had.

Thirty Years of Compounding

This discipline started in the "thirtysomething" years, the settling-in phase. Consider: we are talking about a 30-year span, from 35 to 65. Thirty years of continuous put-asides and accumulated investment earnings made millionaires of these people by the time retirement came. As we saw in the introductory chapter, putting a modest percentage of your income into a mutual fund every month and leaving it there to compound for those 30 years will assure you of your million. Some are lucky enough to earn a higher return, so that the million comes before they are 65. It may be boring but it works.

The savings are invested conservatively—sometimes in bluechip stocks or rental properties, but usually in respected mutual funds, which is certainly the easiest way. The people who have realized their financial goals rarely go into oil wells, venture schemes, or more exotic investments. As we've seen, they don't even have to save a great deal or earn a very high return on their savings. There's no need. Time and compound interest take care of the rest (see Table 2.1).

Table 2.1 The Power of Compounding

$300 Monthly, Invested at Age...	At Age 65 Will Be Worth...
20	$3,144,750
30	$1,138,991
40	$398,050
50	$124,341

Assumes a 10% return from common stocks. Taxes are paid from another source.

I realize that paying off a mortgage every month is an important form of saving and asset building. Few young families view it that way, however. Rather, they see the house as what they get *now*, a current reward for not spending every penny they make on cars, vacations, and Polo wardrobes. But it is a very solid investment, even forgetting probable appreciation over the years. You can't consume it; it stays there. Few are crazy enough, however young, to do something wildly impulsive, like blowing the house to pay for three years of wandering through Europe.

But the people with the vision or the determination to accumulate money do more than pay down the mortgage. They manage to find some money to set aside on top of that payment. I call these people's spend-a-little-less and save-a-little-more approach to life "measured consumption." Money is systematically earmarked for additional savings, most certainly for IRAs, Keoghs, contributory company retirement plans like 401(k)s, and any other tax-advantaged opportunities they are offered.

And you have to start when you are young, in your 30s, both to build the habit and to take advantage of the compounding. Consider those college costs. They may be on our minds almost from the moment the doctor confirms pregnancy, but it's so easy to put off the funding, telling ourselves the money will somehow be there when we need it, that we will certainly be making more money 18 years down the road than we do now. But this attitude touches on my whole philosophy about personal and family finances.

My basic premise, as you now know, is that quality of life, financially, is defined by income. More importantly, it is defined by *passive* income—income that you don't have to work for. How much passive income you can generate determines the choices of what you can do with your life. To the extent that you have prefunded your obligations, even when it meant reducing your style of living early on in your married life, the sooner you are free to go your own way and thumb your nose at the world.

Most of us face three major financial obligations during our lifetimes that need funding:

1. Paying off the mortgage on our house
2. Taking care of our children's education
3. Making sure we will have sufficient retirement income

The sooner you can cross those items off your list, the earlier in life you have achieved release from the chains of the proletariat. You may not have to go to work at all, depending on how well you want to live. About the only necessities that are left, after the Big Three are paid for, are food and the utility bills. Of course, you can then pursue some other kind of work that you've always thought about that pays far less or pays nothing but benefits society. Or you can work sporadically. Or work as usual, but only because that suits your fancy. But at least, if you get these obligations that enslave you to the system out of the way, you have all the choices.

The "secret" to becoming wealthy:

Save money regularly and invest it conservatively in common stocks. Compounding takes care of the rest.

---

3. Paying for College When the Kids Are Toddlers

I can suggest a way to get your children's educations taken care of right off the bat. It's inexpensive, if you start early enough. I'm a big advocate of handling this obligation through zero coupon bonds. These are bonds, issued by the U.S. Treasury, that are sold at a discount from face value, much the way that U.S. Savings Bonds are. At maturity you get all your interest as well as return of principal. Since you forgo current interest income, you can buy these safest of bonds at a relatively affordable price. For your first child you could buy one bond maturing in 18 years, another in 19, and others in 20 and 21 years. Four $25,000 bonds, paying 8 percent, should do the trick. Laying out only $22,400 over the four years after the child's birth will provide the $100,000 you need to cover college costs (Table 2.2).

I even go so far as to advise borrowing the money to buy the zeroes, if you have to, and paying back the loan over, say, the next four years. It may hurt to come up with that amount of money every month. And I realize zeroes are not the most efficient use of capital, since you could earn higher rates of return, if history is any precedent, by putting the money regularly into a stock mutual fund. But it's simple, direct, and free of uncertainty. After just a few years of paying off what you borrowed to buy the bonds, you will have one whopping obligation out of the way.

As the family grows, it may not be possible to put aside enough money every month to prefund this obligation of educating all the kids, but do as much as you can. What you are

Table 2.2 Taking Care of College Costs: Four $25,000 Bonds

8% Zero-Coupon Bonds Maturing in	Cost
18 Years	$6,256
19 Years	$5,793
20 Years	$5,364
21 Years	$4,966
Total	$22,379

Value at maturity = $100,000

At a child's birth, buy four zero-coupon U.S. Treasury bonds (the coupon is assumed to be 8%), one to mature in each of the child's college years. The total cost of the bonds will be $22,377, but their value when the child is in college will be $100,000.

trying to accomplish is an acceleration of the process of reaching that point where the lines cross. You are saying that you would rather achieve some level of economic independence at 45 than at 60. It's very difficult at the age of 30 or 35 to think that way, but as I look at things, it's clearly a superior strategy. The sooner you reach that state of financial karma, the simpler your life is going to be.

> Start paying for college educations as soon as the kids are born: Buy zero-coupon Treasury bonds that mature when they are 18, 19, 20, and 21.

4. The Disappearing Mortgage

I have another strategy I'd like to offer, which is both a savings and an investment ploy. It has been written about a good deal, but few have taken notice. It is, simply, to accelerate paying off the mortgage on your home.

If you are just buying a house, consider taking out a 15-year mortgage instead of a 30-year mortgage. It won't cost you as much more in monthly payments as you probably think. If you have a 10 percent mortgage of $175,000, your monthly payments for a 30-year mortgage would be $1536. If you shorten that to a 15-year mortgage, your monthly payments would be $1,880—less than $350 additional a month.

But whatever the terms of your current mortgage may be, you can try to prepay part of it every month, beyond your contractual commitment. Even a few hundred dollars extra every month will dramatically shorten the terms of payment (Table 2.3). It is another way of choosing to invest rather than consume, and in this case your investment is earning whatever your mortgage rate is.

Suppose that rate is 10 percent. Your decision in that case is, "Am I better off paying off my mortgage, say at the rate of $300 more a month, so that I am assured of earning a 10 percent pretax return, or am I better off taking that $300 and putting it in a stock market mutual fund and trying to earn 12 percent to 15 percent?" It's a tough decision. You are guaranteed the

Table 2.3 Retiring Your Mortgage Early

	Interest Rate	Payment	Total Payout	Years Making Payments
Conventional 30-year mortgage	10%	$1,536 per month	$552,960	30
30-year mortgage, but homeowner pays an additional $300 a month	10%	$1,836 per month	$352,512	16

By paying $300 additional per month on a 30-year $175,000 mortgage, you retire your mortgage approximately 14 years earlier and save more than $200,000.

10 percent return if you pay off that mortgage, whereas the 12 percent to 15 percent is iffy.

In my opinion, paying off a mortgage is not a bad deal, and the higher your mortgage rate, the better the deal. Many home owners have 11 percent mortgages. Yet if someone asks me, "Where can I get a guaranteed 11 percent return," and I answer, "Pay off the mortgage on your house," they look at me like I am crazy. They counter, "But if I pay off my mortgage, I won't have a tax deduction." But one day you'll have more income. When the mortgage is paid up, you'll have, say, more than $1000 a month to spend, even after allowing for the value of the tax deduction.

That's why people defer satisfactions—to get rich and enjoy future satisfactions. Paying off the house may not be the most efficient economic utilization of capital, but my answer is, "Who cares?" We're talking about quality of life, and quality of life is a function of having enough passive income to pay the bills.

To get rid of a mortgage obligation faster:

- When you buy, take out a 15-year instead of a 30-year mortgage.
- If you already have a 30-year mortgage, make additional payments monthly.

---

5. The Savings Discipline

Doing without something desirable to put aside money to fund the kids' education and build assets, whether through an investment program or accelerated mortgage payments, is not easy. There are many people who are almost incapable of living that way. You could always argue that there is no point in saving for the future when you could get cancer and die at 40. These are decisions people have to make for themselves. All I know is, that most of the people who have become wealthy have been savers rather than spenders.

These people seem to have an innate thrift ethic. I don't mean that it is obsessive, or that they are misers. They won't stay at fleabags when they travel or buy their clothes in thrift shops. But they won't book suites or go to custom tailors either. That sort of thing represents an extravagance that is quite uncomfortable for them. They feel instinctively that the very expensive things in life are out of their realm of entitlement. And they live that way when they are 35 and 55 and 75. It is just the way they are.

Usually, it is not an obsession with wealth that drives them, but just the desire to have a cushion of comfort. Something within them keeps them from spending every last dollar, and they build up cash as a consequence.

Indeed, if you ask these people why they live modestly and save instead of spending, with the exception of a few genuinely goal-oriented planners, they probably couldn't articulate an answer. Aside from educating their children, their goals are vague. They might mention retirement, but retirement doesn't become a meaningful reality until they are well into their 50s, by which time they've been systematic savers for decades. They just have an inner sense that if they spend all the money they are making, they are spending too much.

I can't entirely explain the psychology of these people, but it doesn't take a psychiatrist to conclude that money is, for them, a defense against insecurity. The nature of the insecurity, however, varies. Some people are chronically afraid of unemployment. Others are chronically afraid of illness and incapacity. Still others are chronically afraid of the economy's collapsing.

Money is a shield against whatever specific neuroses relate to financial insecurity.

There's a generational phenomenon at work, too. If your parents had vivid recollections of the Depression, then, consciously or unconsciously, you received messages your entire childhood that the world isn't a place you can trust financially. If you have memories of your family's circumstances changing from one level to a lower level—and there were few people who were unaffected by the Depression—you bear some psychic scarring. You just know, and feel, that the world's not necessarily always going to be hospitable, and it's incumbent upon you to defend yourself against the worst. When you try to say, "The hell with it, it's time to splurge a little," you find that there are ghosts that prevent you, or that won't let you enjoy it even if you do cut loose a little. Those ghosts are the voices of parents, who laid down the commandment of living modestly and saving regularly. Your parents may be dead for 30 years, but you still hear the lecture.

For people of my generation, or younger, whose parents did not experience the Depression, the entire life experience has been one of rising affluence. Certainly, since World War II there's been a half century of increasing prosperity. Many people lack the thrift ethic because they have no sense of a need for it.

Still, there are savers in this generation, too. Maybe it does take a psychologist to explain why some people are chronic savers, just as others are chronic spenders. Some people, for example, don't feel they deserve their incomes. These are often people who enjoy what they do, so it doesn't really seem like work for them. When highly compensated for that "work," their paychecks seem unjustified. Therefore, they can't bring themselves to consume it all, because they just know that one day somebody is going to find out they don't deserve all this money and take it away from them. Such people suffer from a different kind of insecurity.

When inveterate savers do spend money, they spend it only after careful consideration. They think in terms of alternatives. "If we don't go to Italy for our vacation this year, but spend it at Disney World instead, we'll save $4000. What could we do with that $4000?" Sometimes they'll just up and go to Italy.

They may decide the trip will enrich the children and serve as a familial bonding experience that can't be measured financially. But there is always that awareness that you can't have it all. You don't take the big vacation and buy new furniture for the family room all in the same year. There is a keen sense of responsibility about every outlay of major dollars.

Save the Cash and Let the Credit Go

Such people almost certainly won't borrow money to pay for the trip or the sofa and chairs. I've observed that people like this seldom buy on credit. They rarely have debt outside of a mortgage. It is unthinkable to take out a loan to buy a new car, for example. They replace a car every four or five years, and they pay cash. Consciously or unconsciously, they recognize a car as a wasting asset, and the money is there for a replacement or the family waits until it is. It's a very smart thing to do; financing cars costs a pile of money over a lifetime.

These people pay their VISA bill at the end of the month. You won't see them run up a $2000 bill at Nordstrom's that they pay off in $200 installments over a year. If they haven't the cash to buy what they want, they make do with what they have. The only exception may be their children's education. They'll borrow to pay tuitions if they have to, but otherwise they live not only within, but below, their means.

They are enlightened about the money they do spend. They are thrifty, in the best sense of that word. They buy term instead of whole life insurance. They are not averse to waiting to make major retail purchases—suits, gowns, furniture—until the sales are on. Yes, they'll take their quarter-off coupons to the supermarket. They are careful, almost tight, with their money.

I've learned to do it. I economize when I can. When I buy a car, I do it through auto brokers rather than dealers, and I save a considerable sum. I shop at warehouse clubs, and the discounts add up to extraordinary savings. I don't find that such a simple, consumer-driven option involves any inconvenience. And I bother with what others might consider penny-ante stuff. When AT&T came out with its credit card, with no annual fee, I stopped using my VISA card, which costs $50 a year. If I live another 30 years and AT&T honors its commitment never to charge a fee, I'll save $1500. (I pay off my balance every month, so I don't have to worry about differences in finance charges.) I just believe that if I am going to save $1500, guaranteed, I'd be a fool to pass up the opportunity. I'd have to hate money to do otherwise.

It wasn't so long ago, as we all know, that a family's decision to spend or not to spend was made by the husbands. It was their prerogative as the sole breadwinners in the family. The fact that there are two wage earners in so many families today allows people to live better, but it conspires against savings disciplines. Who is to make the spending decisions? Today there may even be parity in the contribution to the family purse, or the wife may be the higher earner. Working women are certainly not willing—nor should they be—to subordinate their wishes to the life-styles of the men in their lives. We've all seen the old sitcoms in which the husband bellows, "What do you mean, you spent $200 on a pair of shoes!" Nowadays the wife can yell back, "I'll spend *my* hard-earned money any way I please!"

This can obviously lead to problems, even acrimony, in deciding a family's spending patterns. The husband may be a big consumer and the wife a determined saver, or vice versa. But the clock can't be turned back. If there is a disagreement about what constitutes a reasonable expenditure of money, and what should be relegated to savings, working couples will just have to hammer out a compromise as best they can.

A dollar saved is more (considering taxes) than a dollar earned:

- Pay off charge card charges monthly.
- Save up, instead of borrowing, for new cars.
- Take advantage of sales and discount stores.
- Buy term instead of whole life insurance.
- Avoid all non-mortgage debt.

6. A Warning to Dyed-in-the-Wool Spenders

Saving just isn't important to many people. For them, money is simply the currency of life. It is what buys you experiences and possessions that are enriching. They give little thought to their financial future because the present is what they care about. Even though they may have very big incomes, they will rarely accumulate capital.

There's a laundry list of things money can provide. Some people want it for security, as we've seen, others for status, or power. (The ones who equate money with power are the speculators, the big risk takers. They want to turn small money into big money overnight, and they are willing to take extraordinary risks to make it happen. When people get very, very rich, it is usually a power agenda, not an insecurity agenda, that has driven them.) For a lot of people, though, status or power or security are inferior utilizations of money. They want it for the pleasures it can buy now. They spend and spend gladly.

They may end up rich, but it will be fortuitous. Their house has escalated in value beyond their wildest expectations. Or a small investment has produced extraordinary returns. But even windfalls are likely to consumed. With these people, it's easy come, easy go.

A great many people have no desire to enter the race for wealth. It's the old question asked in a 1971 book title: "Do you sincerely want to be rich?" And for many people, probably most people, the answer is, "No. I sincerely want to be comfortable, but rich doesn't have a lot to do with my life. Sure, it would be nice, but. . . ." Okay, you have a choice. You have to decide who you are. But decide, don't merely drift. Sit down with your spouse over Sunday morning coffee and say, " Do we really care about money?" The answer may be "No" and that you want to consume what you earn, enjoy life to the full, and not worry about the morrow. It's your decision.

But that talk is important. You have to come to grips with who you are and who you are not. And prepare yourself for the consequences, for you are taking some big risks. Life is not always harmonious. If you are one of those persons who spends to the hilt—and maybe beyond—at some point in your life, you had better take stock and consider the future.

There comes a time, too, when you have to recognize that your income has largely peaked, that your career is not likely to take you incrementally higher, so that you cannot depend on future raises to bail you out of present excesses or raise your standard of living. If you are 48 and still a fourth vice president, it isn't likely that you are going to enjoy the compensation of a chief executive officer down the line. If you ignore the facts and live on the delusion that your income will rise in quantum leaps from birth to death, and you are always living on the edge in the belief that you will be provided for more extravagantly by your next career advancement, or stock option bonanza, or whatever you put your hopes on, then you'll never save anything, and trouble almost certainly lies ahead. Some of your goals aren't going to be achieved, and you will have to adjust your life-style accordingly.

Look at what has been happening in corporate America the past few years. Largely because of the threat the Japanese have imposed on us, companies have been restructuring and tightening, and we've seen systematic purgings of middle management. It kind of drives home the message that the world doesn't always have to be supportive. The fact that you go to work every day and do your job, and even do it well, doesn't mean that your job is absolutely secure. It doesn't mean that you're going to be assured cost-of-living-plus increases every year. It doesn't mean that all your medical costs are going to be taken care of. In a globalized economy, this competitive pressure is something that is not going to go away. A different script is being written, and people know it. Their insecurity has risen. Savings rates have been going up.

7. The Conversion of the Nonsavers

It isn't easy to start putting money aside if you've never been a saver and if you haven't that inner compulsion to tithe yourself in homage to insecurity. But given sufficient motivation—fear of eventual poverty or the vision of eventual wealth—the saving habit can be cultivated. And the earlier you begin, the surer your success.

Any commitment that forces saving—the mortgage that has to be paid, as opposed to rent, or the loan you took out from the bank to buy zero coupon bonds—is obviously a valuable discipline. The least painful way to save, I have found, is to participate in any scheme that involves a payroll deduction. Money that never reaches your checking account is money that you aren't tempted to spend.

Most obviously, you absolutely should participate in any savings or defined contribution retirement plan your employer has set up. Anyone who doesn't participate, particularly in a plan in which the employer matches, in whatever part, the employee's contribution, has to be brain-dead. Many employers contribute 50 cents for every dollar the employee relinquishes, up to a certain dollar limit. Where else can you get an immediate 50 percent return on your money? I would borrow money from the bank to participate to the limit if I had to. Yet many, many employees never sign up for these plans. They can find every kind of excuse to justify needing every penny they earn. That word *need* has to be redefined if saving is ever to become a reality.

What kind of investment choice should you make when you consider the options of your employer's savings and retirement plans? Most people take the "safe" option of a guaranteed investment contract that pays a fixed return. It is like a bond, except that the interest paid is readjusted annually and your investment can never go down in value. But people entering these plans when they are young have the luxury of time, and the overwhelming evidence is that common stocks are the safest—as well as the highest-return—investment, because they stay ahead of inflation. Up to the age of even 50, I'd put all my money in stocks. Since you are probably not going to retire until you are 60 or 65, your stock investments have at least ten years to recover from any downturn in the market. That is the economic reality. Temperamental considerations, for those who are nervous about putting all of their money into stocks, may dictate that a percentage of their plan contributions go into fixed income investments, but I would urge you to think about the economic facts of life and go with as high a stock allocation as you can bring yourself to accept.

But don't stop with your employer's defined contribution plan. Do as much as you can to skim money off the top of your salary. For example, some mutual funds allow you to buy shares through a monthly investment plan that automatically debits your bank account. The Janus Group and Twentieth Century Investors allow a zero initial investment and automatic monthly pay-ins of as little as $50. Again, the money comes out before you have a chance to spend it.

Years ago, recognizing my own frailties and ability to consume, I found another way to discipline myself to put money aside that may be of use to you. Like everyone else, I had an inexhaustible list of things that I "desperately" needed, and I knew if my earnings went into my checking account, they would very likely be used to cross something off the list. So even in my 20s I would go to the bank and borrow money— say, $10,000—and I would put that money into a mutual fund. Then I would pay the bank off, out of my earnings, at the rate of $500 a month, or at whatever schedule I could afford at the time. I had a $500-a-month obligation that I had to honor. When the loan was paid off, I had an asset, and with a little luck the $10,000 was worth say, $15,000.

Over the years, as my income rose, I would simply up the scale. I've even borrowed as much as $100,000. Of course, I could have just written monthly checks to my savings account or a mutual fund, but I knew I rarely would. Every month I would find a reason not to do it: "I'm just so tired. I need to go away for the weekend or I'll go crazy." We all know the rationalizations one can invent. But I couldn't duck the obligation to repay my loan.

Sometimes I have bought the mutual fund shares, from a no-load fund, then deposited them in an account at the discount broker Charles Schwab, which would lend me 50 percent of the value of the shares—like a margin account at any broker's. (I didn't buy the original shares through Schwab, because the firm would have charged me a fee for the transaction; I went directly to a no-load fund.) The rate on what I'd borrowed was attractive—the broker's call rate or some modest amount above that—and I viewed this interest cost as the price of discipline. I would then take the borrowed margin money and buy more fund shares. And I would, every month, endeavor to pay off as much of that Schwab debt as I could, on top of the bank loan. Yes, the value of the shares I had bought could have gone down, but because my time horizon was long enough—more than five years—I could be pretty sure of appreciation. Even if that appreciation didn't entirely cover the interest costs, it didn't matter to me very much, because my prime motive was to force myself to save rather than consume. I didn't have to worry about a margin call, because the bank would keep rolling over my loan as long as I was making my interest payments. Sure, it hurt. I was left with very little discretionary income. But that was the idea—to keep consumption to a minimum. One of my rewards—probably what I wanted on a psychological level—was a sense of virtuous deprivation. If something came up and the payments became too onerous, I would liquidate some of the shares. My capital grew nicely. It is a tactic that can be practiced on any scale you want.

Basically, you have three choices for your savings program. You can make small investments, such as automatic debits from your checking account that go into mutual fund shares. You can save up for large investments, again, for example, by having deductions earmarked for your savings account. Or you can borrow to make large investments, as I did. All of these choices will work. What doesn't work is waiting to accumulate enough money some time in the vague future so that you can "be a real player." That is too dangerous. You will spend what you have now, and if you do happen to get your hands on a lot of cash—say, sizable stock options are exercised—the temptation will be to spend that, too. You need a regular discipline.

Buying whole life insurance that builds up cash value is another form of forced savings, and I've done that , too. I knew I could always borrow the cash quickly if I needed to, and the rate on policy loans in those days was very low, about 6 percent. I knew it was cheaper to buy term insurance, but I also knew my own inability to save and invest the difference between term and whole life premiums in any systematic way.

But I like my first scheme better. To borrow from a bank, buy an asset, and pay off the loan, is a far more efficient way, financially, to force yourself to build a nestegg. That is even more true today, when policy loans have gone to market rates, and there's some question about the deductibility of interest payments.

Borrowing to invest is a very simple strategy, but most people to whom I've described it have an aversion to the idea. They'll borrow money to buy a car but they won't borrow money to make an investment, even though the investment has the possibility of going up in value, but a car is worth less the minute you drive it out of the dealer's lot.

Ways to force yourself to save:

- To-the-limit participation in employer's 401(k) or other defined contribution retirement and savings plans
- Automatic checking account debits earmarked for a mutual fund
- Borrowing money from a bank, buying mutual fund shares or zero coupon Treasury bonds, or making other investments and paying back the bank
- Prepaying your mortgage
- A less desirable option: buying whole life insurance

---

8. The Thornier Paths to Wealth

All this skimping and doing without is somewhat depressing, I admit. "Isn't there an easier, quicker way to get rich?" you ask. We all hear and read about the schemes: options and commodity futures, currency and stock index futures, discounted closed-end funds, foreclosed properties. . . . The list is endless. And so is the number of gurus who peddle them.

If I knew a swift and certain path to riches, I would happily share it with you. But the only ways I know of to become wealthy are to get lucky with a lottery ticket, own your own business, or invest your savings wisely. Since most people aren't going to win a lottery and don't own their own business, that leaves investments. And the sad truth is that the only way you can compress the time line in investments is to take outsize risks.

Sure, some people do take those risks and hit it big. All investment options will, from time to time, produce extraordinary returns and make some people very wealthy. And all investment options will regress to the mean in their returns, so your timing or your luck had better be good. Most people who have accelerated the wealth accumulation process have taken risks that were symmetrical. If you want to make 30 percent a year, be prepared to walk away from your capital, because that's what the flip side is going to look like.

I know there will be witnesses to the contrary. Sometimes people take a gamble on a hunch and are lucky—"lucky" in the sense that their speculations worked. They shopped at one of the first Wal-Mart stores, said, "Hey this is terrific," and bought 300 shares of the stock. Luckier still, they held on, and a small investment turned into a very significant windfall. That happens, and a good thing, too, since that's what fuels the American dream. But rarely do they hit the right investment, or hold on to their stock long enough, or place enough money on the table to make a hit big enough to make them really rich.

Wealth by Chance

A lot of people proved exceedingly lucky in recent decades dabbling in real estate. And in most instances it *was* just plain luck. In the late 1960s and early 1970s, if you kept your money in a bank savings account you earned 5 percent. If you had a big enough account—say, $100,000—the bank might have given you more, maybe 7 percent. So these people, trying to get a higher return on their money, bought residential properties—a duplex or maybe an apartment building with six or eight rental units. They put 20 or 25 percent down and got a 10 percent or 12 percent return on their cash. They saw it that way— 12 percent instead of 5 percent or 7 percent. They hoped the buildings would appreciate in value, of course, and there were some depreciation tax advantages as well, and they knew that over time rentals would also pay off the mortgages, so that in 30 years they'd own something. But their prime motive was that 12 percent.

Then came inflation, and we all know how real estate appreciated. Between 1970 and the mid-1980s rents and the value of the properties tripled. And that's a modest estimate in some places. In some coastal areas of California rents and values went up four- and fivefold. A $100,000 investment over the years turned into $500,00. And by that time a substantial chunk of the debt had been amortized. Furthermore, some pyramided along the way. As apartments appreciated, they refinanced and put money into other real estate deals.

Having achieved wealth and status, today they'll tell you how smart they are, that they saw it all coming. The fact is, these people were not visionaries. They had never taken a real estate course in their lives and they still don't know the difference between a leasehold and a leaseback. They are basically simple folk who, in trying to get a higher return on their savings, prospered enormously. They benefited from a historical anomaly. One asset class experienced extraordinary returns. But we know what has happened to real estate values since then, and their experience is not likely to be repeated for a long, long, while.

And then there are those who claim sophistication in high-roller markets. They speculate in stock options, commodities, zero coupon bonds, or elaborate trading schemes. And though a few have made it big, most by far have lost their shirts. The probabilities of success in that kind of exercise are infinitesimally small. You are talking about tax-deductible lottery tickets. The notion that you are going to go out into complex markets populated by a world of professionals and compete successfully against them is ridiculous.

So if you think you are going to find a book—including this one—that will short-circuit the process of time and thrift, you've been misled. You've succumbed to the seduction of promotion.

Owning one's own business is different from investing. You often have to take large risks. There is a high risk when starting the business in the first place, and then, at certain times along the way, further big risks have to be faced. Those who took them probably didn't realize, at the time, the extent of the risk. Entrepreneurs are so busy getting the next big contract or developing a more advanced widget that they are not processing possible failure into their decision to forge ahead. If they didn't have that temerity, they'd never have the courage to take the necessary steps to build the business.

However, I am talking about people who were not entrepreneurs but lawyers, doctors, or company executives and who retired with a few million, and these people, with some exceptions, were very conservative when investing their savings. They probably started with money market funds or tax-exempt bonds, and then, when they decided they had enough in conservative savings to be comfortable, they put some money into an equity mutual fund or, when they had accumulated enough of a pile, hired an investment manager. They have never been very sophisticated about markets, but even the unsophisticated have some awareness of market alternatives, and they know stocks can capture a higher return over time. Also, until recently, capital gains treatment of stocks was more favorable than it was for income produced by fixed return securities.

So if you have the temperament to accept risk, you would be foolish, until you reach the age of 50, to put your money into anything but stocks. Temperament is the soft part of the equation, but the financial part is clear-cut. Dial in as much risk as you can, and if you are too uneasy, dial back the other way until you do feel comfortable.

Few who have followed that path have invested on their own. They have, as noted given their money to a mutual fund or an investment professional. They realized that they can't do as well in stocks as a pastime as can someone whose activity is totally focused on a market. It's like practicing amateur dentistry. It's not that my clients who became wealthy haven't the intellectual ability. It's merely that they don't have the time or the commitment.

9. From 40 to 55, When You Could Hit It Big

The savings habit, even compulsion, usually starts, as we've seen, when young married couples start a family and are suddenly confronted wth the realization that there is such a thing as the future to worry about. The earlier the savings start, the better, so that compounding has more years to work its magic, but the amounts that can be put aside are circumscribed, what with careers still building and families still growing. The disciplines I've suggested are admirable, but they will hurt.

It is when we reach our 40s that financial constraints begin to ease up and the savings habit becomes easier to satisfy. A very substantial disparity develops between the level of income and the level of consumption, for consumption tends to flatten while income continues to rise. It's the time of life when a substantial acquisition of assets begins.

Indeed, there is about a 15-year interval in life—between the ages of 40 and 55—when you can make real money through investments, and I don't think most people understand that. Before 40 you haven't accumulated enough of a stake, and after 55, you're shedding your appetite for risk (see Figure 2.1). Also, by the time you've reached 40 you've had enough experience in life to be able to make some well-reasoned decisions about investments. True, at 55 you have even more affluence, your skills are more finely honed, and you still have a reasonable level of energy. But because you are conflicted about taking risks, you turn into more of an observer than a participant in the parade.

I am not suggesting that if you continue along a conservative investment path—a diversified portfolio of blue-chip companies or proven mutual funds—you won't end up wealthy. You will, almost guaranteed. The saving, the compounding, the long-term returns of invested capital will live up to their promise. But I am speaking about those people who are now willing to take somewhat greater risks in the expectation of a bigger payoff. They will retire not with 1 or 2 million but maybe with 5 or 10 million.

In your 40s you are not as afraid of risk as you were when you were greener and your resources more limited or as you

(a)

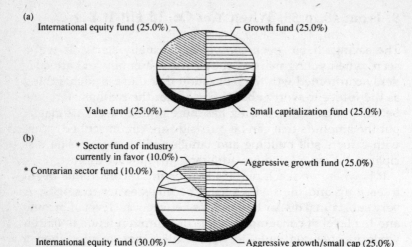

International equity fund (25.0%)   Growth fund (25.0%)

Value fund (25.0%)   Small capitalization fund (25.0%)

(b)

* Sector fund of industry
  currently in favor (10.0%)   Aggressive growth fund (25.0%)

* Contrarian sector fund (10.0%)

International equity fund (30.0%)   Aggressive growth/small cap (25.0%)

A recent in-favor example would have been a biotechnology sector fund. A contrarian sector fund is one specializing in an industry currently out of favor – – perhaps automotive or gold – – that should rebound because of the cyclical nature of the market.

(c)

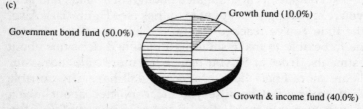

Growth fund (10.0%)

Government bond fund (50.0%)

Growth & income fund (40.0%)

Figure 2.1 Controlling risk through a diversified portfolio of mutual funds: (a) Long-term investor; medium risk; (b) Agressive investor; above-average risk; (c) Retirement portfolio; low risk.

will be when you near 60. In fact, you tend to be as confident as you were in your 20s, even to the point of deluding yourself about the possibilities. But it's a delusion built of experience, not of ignorance. In your 20s you do things with enormous conviction, but there is no basis for that conviction. It is simply the euphoria of youth. In your 40s you do have experience behind you, and you can understand and analyze your mistakes. When you take risks, the odds of your succeeding are far better.

So it's in that 40 to 55 period that you've got a chance to make your big hit, to distance yourself from your peers. And the more money that you have accumulated in your 30s, the better your chances. To the extent that you spend your 40s paying off your mortgage, funding your retirement, and shelling out college tuitions, the less likely it is that you will have enough sense of security to take the risks necessary to strike it big.

Inevitable Cycles

Although many succeed, it is never easy, even for those with a burning desire to acquire wealth through shrewd investments and the will to work hard at it. And the prime reason, in my opinion, lies in the nature of investment cycles: interest rate cycles, stock market cycles, real estate cycles, and commodity cycles. They tend to last about a decade, even longer, and few people have the skill or the luck to hit it just right. Luck helps, just as it helped those who invested in real estate and who now pride themselves on their prescience. Certainly in the 1990s it doesn't look like real estate is going to enrich many folk. A great number of people made considerable fortunes by going all out in the stock market in the 1980s. They were hardly as likely to have succeeded, at least as easily, in the 1970s, when the market peaked in 1972 and took about ten years to get back to that level. The bond market made almost as much money as the stock market for people in the 1980s, as we came out of the terrible inflation years, but it is hard to imagine that that can happen again coming out of a period of moderate inflation. Venture capital rewarded investors with fabulous returns in the 1970s, but for most of the 1980s it provided negative returns. For that matter, the stocks of small companies didn't do well in the 1980s either, even during a great bull market.

We have a very limited time frame when we have both money and courage, and we tend to invest most heavily in the market we know best. Then it's largely a matter of mere chance whether or not we've chosen the sector that will boom. We also tend to base our decisions on what we have experienced, but the past is usually not a good indicator of the future. Cycles can turn quickly or stretch out for years longer than logic says they should. The records of economists and professional investors tell us how difficult it is to forecast and time markets.

If nothing in your history suggests that you can identify cycles, then I suggest you best diversify and settle for the surer path to, albeit more modest, wealth. Scatter your chips over the board, diversify into large capitalization stocks and the stocks of smaller companies, bonds, and maybe real estate, instead of taking the bigger risk of concentration, and you will do well, you will have your million in time. Most of my clients have proved that conservative investments are all that are needed, not the risky investments that could double in two years or drop to zero.

On the other hand, while still diversifying in several markets rather than putting all your eggs into one basket, if you do want to try to weight your investments partially in favor of one sector that could provide the greatest returns, I have a suggestion that could put the probabilities on your side. We looked earlier at my asset allocation scheme for the already-rich. Let me suggest a way of allocation for those hoping to get not just rich, but *very* rich.

Go Against the Flow

My advice is, simply, "Favor the market that is most depressed at the moment." It is depressed because no one wants it, and that means you can buy it cheap. Buying cheap always puts the odds in your favor. "Buy low" is the obvious, accepted wisdom when investing. We all have been told that we should be contrarians but most people do just the oppposite. A flow-of-funds study always finds the most money heading into the sector that is currently at the top. Most people follow the crowd, buy whatever's hot, get caught up in the euphoria of the moment, and, therefore, pay top dollar.

If stocks have been doing poorly for a few years, it would be stocks you would emphasize by earmarking new investment dollars for stocks and/or shifting money out of another "asset class" that has been performing exceptionally well. If real estate is in a funk, then it would be real estate. (And my veto of real estate, remember, was for the already-rich, who don't need the admitted headaches of property management.) Real estate has certainly been in the cellar in the early years of the 1990s, and people are asking, "Will it ever come back?" Of course it will.

You buy what is out of favor. It's just a matter of statistics. If the rate of return from an investment sector has been substantially out of whack with its historical norm, chances are the pattern will correct itself and the norm will be restored, at least given enough time. In more concrete terms, if stocks have returned 10 percent for the century (as studies show that they have) and for the last ten years they've averaged 17 percent (as they did in the 1980s) the math informs you that such a bull market has a limited shelf life. You're unlikely to be able to predict cycles with a lot of precision, but at least you can buy when prices are low, relative to their norm. Price is your great indemnity.

High Yields Are the Clue

Most of the time you can tell which market is cheapest by looking at which is currently paying the highest cash return. Start with stocks, your basic investment, since you know that they provide the biggest payoff over time. When the collective expectation is that stocks, though high, are headed higher, investors don't demand much in the way of current dividend income. They think they'll make their money from appreciation. As the dividend yield of the Dow Jones Industrials falls below 3 percent, it is a sign that the market is frothy, already at or nearing a top (see Table 2.4). You are safer, and have mathematical probabilities on your side, if you avoid buying stocks at those times. Conversely, when the dividend yield of the Dow is at the high end of its historical range, above 5 percent—because investors, having little faith in earning their return through appreciation, demand current satisfaction—it is time to buy stocks. If you heed those simple signposts, the probabilities are on your side.

If stock dividends are low and prices therefore suspect, where should you put your money? Bonds are the obvious

Table 2.4   Recognizing an Overheated Stock Market: Dow Jones Indicators

Indicator	Typical Level[1]	Summer 1987 (before market crash in October)
Dividend yield	4.49	2.80
Price/earnings ratio	15.0	24.0
Price/book ratio	1.43	2.60

[1]Median since 1926; 1929 in case of dividend yields.

Source: Leuthold Group.

alternative. If stocks are yielding 2.5 percent and ten-year Treasuries are yielding 8 percent, go for the Treasuries. If Treasuries are unpromising—yields are only 5 percent or 6 percent—keep your money in money market funds until the signals are clearer.

Most of your money will go into stocks and bonds, because they provide liquidity if you need money or want to switch from one to the other when you see opportunities or great risks developing in either market. If you want to keep some of your money in real estate as well, the rules are not as simple. When demand for space is strong and developers are building right and left to meet that demand, both property prices and rentals are high. If in the next phase of the cycle the developers have built beyond demand and there is more than enough vacant space, both rents and values are under pressure. Nevertheless, it is when pessimism reigns and prices are depressed that you want to be a buyer.

This is sound advice, patently sensible, yet it is very, very hard to follow. People don't invest against the current because it is a lot easier to go with the flow, to put money in what has been working rather than what hasn't. The financial press is telling you daily that it isn't working, and quoting the professionals who predict that it probably won't for a long, long time. You could have bought 30-year Treasury bonds in 1981 that paid 15.5 percent in interest, the highest in history, and besides all the income you would have received, today those bonds would have appreciated by more than 50 percent. But inflation was 13 percent at the time and everyone was talking about the United States going the way of Latin America. What's more, every time you bought a bond from 1946 to 1981, as interest rates kept climbing, you got kicked. It is very difficult to defy 35 years' experience.

And you will seldom see your bet pay off quickly. You must have patience, for the longer you wait for the tide to turn, the more foolish you feel. The emotions get involved, and probably the biggest problem in investing stems from emotionality clashing with economics, for emotionality usually prevails. I think it's true of investments generally, that the more uncomfortable the investment, the more probable that the economics are skewed in your favor.

Time Is Your Ally

But time is on your side. What is hated and therefore cheap will eventually come back into favor. There are three components to financial success:

1. Saving, not consuming all you earn
2. Being thoughtful about how you invest so that you don't get skewered on the tip of whatever is fashionable at the moment
3. Time, which can absolve you if you mess up step 2

The passage of years will, in most instances, remedy an ill-timed investment. Poor timing will diminish the returns of your investment, but you won't come out a loser (see Table 2.5). Because you are investing regularly, the result of your saving regularly, you will have smoothed out your returns.

You'd think that people would eventually learn the lesson about buying what's out of favor, that they wouldn't repeat their mistakes and chase the latest fad only to find they'd bought at the top. But there seems to be a law of investing, and of life, that is almost as rigid as a law of physics: that which is put in motion tends to go on that way, so we are forever

Table 2.5 What a Difference Two Years Can Make

If you had bought into the stock market (S&P 500) on 12/31/72, when the market was at a high, or on 9/30/74, when the market had dropped to a recent low, your return on the following year-ends would have been as follows:

	Market High 12/31/72	Market Low 09/30/74
12/31/80	65%	187%
12/31/85	226%	468%
12/31/90	503%	953%

repeating our mistakes. As has often been said, our second wife or husband is usually like the first.

The fact that emotionality stands in the way of healthy contrarianism is another argument for hiring professionals to do your investing, whether it be a mutual fund or investment counselor you choose. The best professional investors—not all, by any means, but the best—*have* learned to discipline themselves, to be skeptical of fads, to suspect overheated markets.

The Middle Years

- Between 40 and 55 offers you the best chance to hit it big in investments.
- Much depends on whether your biggest bets coincide with investment cycles.
- To put the odds on your side, favor the market that is most depressed.
- Current yields are the clues to under- and over-valuation.
- Even if you buy during periods of over-valuation, time will bail you out.

They are more objective, even cold-blooded, about making money than are most individual investors. Some of the top investors stay fully invested at all times, but most are cautious when prices are high and bargains few. They pull back from the market and keep some money in cash or bonds for a time. Then they have the cash on hand to buy when the inevitable corrections occur. I am not talking about short-term timing, or about going 100 percent into or out of stocks. I am talking about sensible reactions to realities, and caution when caution is called for. Yes, time will bail you out if you ignore those risks and opportunities, but the highest returns are earned by those who duck the risks and seize the opportunities.

10. Can Financial Planners Help?

It is at this stage of life—between the ages of 40 and 55—that people start to contemplate consulting a financial planner. Assets are growing, options are thereby expanding, and one begins to think about the best way of ensuring that the assets will be able to sustain comfort upon retirement and of distributing those assets when one is no longer among the living. Earlier I expressed my doubts about the advantages of such a consultation.

Who are these planners? What are their qualifications to advise you on the many financial questions on your mind? *The Wall Street Journal* looked into this matter not long ago and found that all that's needed to become a certified financial planner is to pass a course given by certain community colleges or by mail from a place in Denver, which could, uncharitably, be called a diploma mill.

Most of those who take the course are salespersons of investment products, such as mutual funds, partnerships, and life insurance. They tell themselves that if they could change their credentials and put "financial planner" on their business cards, it would be far more prestigious and could prove a financial bonanza. They could charge nice fat fees for their advice, and at the same time obtain information about their clients' financial circumstances—an advisor, after all, has to ask questions—that would open all sorts of marketing opportunities. "Mr. Frost, you really need more life insurance, a long-term-care policy and some municipal unit trusts, and I can take care of all of it for you."

What a brilliant set-up! No wonder there's been an explosion in the number of financial planners. Every stockbroker and insurance salesperson in America has been eager to send a check to Denver.

Of course, with so many people becoming planners, the credentials don't have the cachet they did at the beginning. Also, some complaints have been filed with the regulators concerning investments placed through planners that turned out to be total bombs. Oh yes, in some instances the planners neglected to mention to their clients that their compensation came from the sale of products as well as from their advisory fees.

A Cure for Procrastination

I will admit that the financial planners perform one function that is very beneficial. Once people have paid a fee to a planner, they will no longer put off sitting down and working up a personal financial statement—a list of their assets, sources of income, and annual expenditures. At least some organization enters the life of the client seeking help; this is an essential first step in making any sense of one's financial status. The planners then feed all the information you have given them into a computer program they buy from a subsidiary of H&R Block, the tax return preparation people, and come up with your personal "Financial Profile," elegantly bound in genuine Taiwanese leather.

The planner, it is true, may charge you up to $3500 for that service when you could probably have had it performed for $1000 or less by your accountant. Computax, which is used for tax returns, has a similar program for financial profiles, and you could have access to it for a fraction of what you have to pay the planners.

Still, organizing who you are, financially, is admirable. But the second service the planners render is investment advice, which I am far less happy about. Are your assets properly allocated, relative to diversification requirements, relative to investment opportunities, and relative to tax consequences? (And at times, be reminded, these considerations can be in conflict.) This person, who is by training and nature a salesperson, whose experience in investments is perhaps only slightly greater than your own, is going to render allocation and investment advice involving multiple disciplines.

He or she will rely on a combination of computer modeling and intuitive skills that are as suspect as anybody else's when it comes to deciding the perfect asset mix. I know myself how difficult it is to come up with the right combination of investments, one that not only reflects the nature of markets but of the individuals who will be living with those investments. It's easy to achieve diversification. All that involves is checking a lot of boxes and you've got money all over the map. But to do it intelligently, so there isn't too much diversification and too much complication in people's lives, is a little tougher.

Also, I am skeptical of the computer programs used in making these allocation suggestions. These programs are based on historical data, and how much can you count on some of the assumptions that rest on that data? Look at real estate. It is a given, never challenged, that real estate is a hedge against inflation. Historical data has made it a truism. But I also know that there is enough real estate today, certainly on the commercial side, to take care of demand for years, maybe to the year 2000. There is no certainty that if inflation rates were to go to 10 percent, real estate would appreciate by a like amount because it has done so in the past. In order for anything to appreciate, it has to be in scarcity at the margin rather than in surplus. You could have high inflation and not make a dime on real estate for many years. Yes, if real estate is depressed, some day it will not be depressed, and patience will be rewarded. But that doesn't mean it is an automatic defense against inflation. Any time someone hands you an asset allocation based on historical relationships, you must apply a final litmus test and ask, "Is there any reason why this type of investment, which worked in the past under certain circumstances, might not work now?"

They Promise Too Much

More disturbing, most clients expect the planners not only to recommend how assets should be allocated among stocks, bonds, cash, real estate, tax shelters, and so on, but also to help them implement the program. Most financial planners are willing—nay, eager—to comply. How well do they do it? If they stick to mutual funds for their investment programs, things can't go too badly. But when they go beyond stock and bond mutual funds and suggest other investments, I get very nervous. I and my associates know what we do, how much time we spend at it, and how hard it is to keep up. I've followed the securities markets for three decades. I've been a real estate investor on my own. I'm active in a venture capital group. I come from a family with business interests in oil and gas. I feel I know more than most. Yet I do not feel qualified to cover the universe the way so many financial planners claim to do. Their reach exceeds their grasp. The world's too complicated for them to justify their promises.

I get *really* nervous when they enter the areas of estate planning, tax planning, and insurance. Planners can pull out a very, very broad menu. Each of these areas is highly complex. When I need tax advice, I go to a tax attorney. When I need estate planning, I go to an attorney who specializes in that field. When I want to know what to do about insurance, I like to talk to someone who's been in the field for many years. And for that matter, when I need investment advice, I go to an investment manager.

There are larger financial planning firms, of course, with experts in different disciplines on staff, and in that case you will receive better and more current advice on taxes or estate planning—and probably pay a good deal more than $3500 for it. But you can't be entirely certain that what is delivered to you reflects the firm's best work. In financial planning, much like investment management, the only thing that counts is who's in charge of *you*. Suppose you ask your planner, working for a large firm, "Is this your opinion, or the opinion of your tax expert? Ah, the tax man. Well, then, do you mind if I talk to him, because I have some reservations about this advice?"

If accessibility to the expert is denied you, then maybe you should consult another authority.

I know there are planners who are very bright, very clever, and very honest. I would, however, consult only those people who operate on a fee-only basis, and that means only about 10 percent of the practitioners. In other words, they should *never* receive compensation from selling you products. I would ask them not only to disclose that fact but to put it in writing. This way they have committed fraud if they said they don't receive any compensation directly or indirectly from commissions when, in fact, they do. Don't let them be vague in their response.

Be Cautious

Further, no matter how competent planners may be, you should evaluate their advice very carefully and get other opinions when you have doubts, in particular when anything in the plan has substantial financial consequences, be they from an investment standpoint, a tax standpoint, or an estate standpoint. Many of the decisions you are asked to make based on the advice rendered have extremely important economic consequences, particularly in estate planning. I believe estate planning is such a big-money issue that it should be done only by people who specialize in it. The counsel of a financial planner would never satisfy me. I'm willing to pay up, based on my belief that I will get better quality advice.

Sometimes it isn't easy to bring yourself to consult others, to have the advice you've been given confirmed someplace else. The minute you pay the planner's fee, you've vested him or her with authority. If you pay somebody $3500 for advice, your strong inclination is to follow it. But I would urge you to be cautious and diligent on your own behalf.

Financial planning was brilliant in its conception. But like many things, it often disappoints in its execution. Another reason for that shortfall is that financial planners may understand eonomic solutions, but they don't understand how human beings interact with money, how people feel about risk, about security, about the consequences of financial decisions on their families. And that's because so few of them have money themselves. One of my favorite observations about America: this is a country where the rich hire the poor to tell them what to do with their money.

11. After 55, Preservation Becomes the Priority

After 55 , few people want to take the risks necessary to make a sizable fortune through investments. Most value stability more than anything else. There are few divorces. Men and women start thinking more about diets and exercise, and they take more vacations. Mortality, you see, is on their minds. They start preparing for the end. They review their estate plans and their balance sheets. They don't want any debts and they don't want risky investments that can make their net worth bounce around. They want a tidy end to the last chapter.

It's funny that they start to ready themselves for death at 55, but they don't really start to think seriously about retirement until they are about 60. They can come to terms with their mortality but not with the end of their work lives. But at about 60 it sinks in. If someone in the family gives them a nice clock for Christmas, they wonder if they should take it to the office, because, after all, they'd only be taking it back home again soon. At 60 they start to think about winding up the job, about how people will view their careers, and about who will replace them. But many deny the need to leave their desks until it is time to clean them out. Many men—and I suppose this will become true of women, too, as the new working generation of women ages—are really more afraid of retirement than of death. Death is abstract to them and still a bit distant, but they are terrified of what their lives will be like when the office door closes behind them for the last time.

That's not true of everyone, of course. There are some people who are truly blessed. They have this inexhaustible list of interests and passions, very real ones, that lie outside their work. They are in good shape when retirement comes. They've always liked gardening; now they build a greenhouse where they potter for countless hours. They used to sail from Boston to Martha's Vineyard; now they try to make it all the way down to Florida. They've liked to go hiking on weekends; now they're off trekking through Nepal.

But these people have had these interests for years. Most of us have a list of things we think we'd like to do when the work days are over, but these have been daydreams. I have noticed that those who don't actively develop nonwork interests before retirement seldom pursue them after they've hung up their cap. You have to build on interests through a lifetime. The drive to start from scratch at 60 or 65 just isn't there anymore. If you want to have a full life when the work is done, you'd better start filling it up early on.

A Tough Transition

It is terribly important that you do so. We all know people, maybe in our own family, who found retirement only a descent into depression. The first two years or so are hard on almost everyone, including spouses. For some spouses, it's pure agony. All of a sudden they have a full-time companion. The husband and wife had been looking forward to an interesting new time in their lives—until they were confronted with reality. There are limits to compatibility, and those limits get tested if the retiree has nothing to do but mope around the house all day.

I usually hear the man's side of the story, since 95 percent of the people I deal with are men, though male domination of the financial aspects of family life is rapidly ending. These men, who have not developed interests outside their work, know they have to get out of their wives' hair, and they can't play golf every day of the year, so they socialize a lot. They look forward to putting on a suit and tie and having lunch with their old office mates or friends who are still in harness. Or they get together with other retirees. That helps for a time, but after a while, these get-togethers, too, pale. The interests you shared with business associates are largely gone. Old relationships become awkward. Even with fellow retirees, things get strained. Once you tell war stories and relive experiences, the pauses in the conversation are long.

I have noticed that many of these men, disoriented, verging on depression, start drinking far too much. It is a definite hazard of those first years of leisure. Besides the lunches in town, there will be many lunches at the club after golf. George will almost certainly have the noon drink that he passed on when he had to go back to an important 2:00 meeting at the office, and if he's at the club with cronies who are also retired and have no place special to go, they will all sit around and have a second drink, and a third. They are all in the same boat. They once had their customers, suppliers, competitors, and associates to keep their minds working, but that's all floated away. They've always drunk, but now they drink more, and it has the potential to become a serious problem. There's a sort of flirtation that goes on, a probing of what the limits are. Often friends and spouses step in and help. They remind the men that they're going over the bounds of acceptability and that the drinking is starting to get dangerous.

The transition is hardest on those who had a business of their own. Those who worked for somebody else, though certainly committed to their jobs, were not as totally involved in their work as the entrepreneurs. Employees are more likely to have developed outside interests, whereas people who own their own businesses are often too absorbed to think about anything else for long. Those who worked for a corporation or professional firm tend to say to themselves, "Well, it's over, the rat-race, goodbye and good riddance. No more commuting, and tiresome meetings, and trips to Wichita and Pittsburgh, and all the politics and nonsense. I've put up with it for all these years, but now this is a new beginning for me, and by God, I'm going to enjoy myself."

The entrepreneurs, on the other hand, don't know what to do with themselves. They were so wrapped up in their work, and often quite isolated, that they can't relax. If you are wholly focused on your work for 40 years, leaving that work behind is like jumping into a big black hole. They long ago became action junkies, and the time they now have on their hands works against them. Mere idleness is unthinkable.

These retirement syndromes have a relevance to financial matters, because these somewhat lost souls tend to start to fill the time that lies heavy on their hands looking after the money they now have responsibility for. And without experience in managing money, and impatient to make decisions as they did in their working years, they often make foolish mistakes. So those first few years of retirement, when the chips have been cashed in, are financially dangerous ones, especially for those who have never developed real hobbies and interests. Their stockpile of assets is too likely to become that hobby. And while the desire for risk has abated, perception of just how risky some investment courses are can be faulty. This is a matter we will consider again.

Add Up the Figures

Aside from investments, it is easy to prepare for retirement financially. All you have to do is to determine that you have x amount of income coming in before you retire, and whatever amount of that you consume after taxes are paid has to be replaced somehow, or there's going to be a diminishment in life-style, assuming we are talking about a sole income. So you had better figure out where that income you've been spending is going to come from, and, if there is a gap between what you need and what you can count on, how you are going to deal with it. If you haven't the ability to close the gap, then figure out where the cutbacks in your life-style are going to be made. Otherwise you *truly* step into a black hole. The emotional strain is bad enough, without the aggravation caused by not sorting out the economics of your retirement.

Yet so many people just don't seem to prepare for what future remains to them. Several years ago I had a man come into my office whom I will never forget. He was a doctor, a specialist, about 62 years old. His practice had been declining markedly, because a specialist depends heavily on referrals from other physicians, and the doctors he knew were gradually retiring or dying off. His expenses were fixed, so he had actually been losing money for some time. And he had never saved much over the years. When he was in his mid-50s he married a woman of about 30, and they had two children, so his expenses were high. I had to tell him, after he showed me his financial statement, that he was broke, and that he would be less broke if he stopped practicing medicine. He protested that it wasn't possible, that he had patients who depended on him and a nurse whom he'd had for 20 years whom he couldn't bear to turn loose. I said, "Well, you have a wife and two children who are going to be impoverished if you don't act soon."

His wife had come with him, and when she heard all this, she turned white. I don't say she didn't care for him. For one thing, he was a very handsome man, even at 62. But I suspect she had thought that, since she had married a physician with an established practice, she was going to enjoy a very comfortable life-style. Then, sitting in my office, she heard her expectations shattered. The only thing she could hope, as far as money was concerned, for herself and her children, was that when the good doctor dies—and he is of course, considerably her senior—she will be left enough insurance money to maintain her family. My guess is that he's inadequately insured as well, but I had the decency not to ask.

I would not have wanted to have dinner with that couple that night, not after I had seen that look of betrayal on her face. It was so depressing and there was nothing I could do. I told the doctor, "I am sorry, but I can't help you. You can't become a client because you have no money to invest. My guess is that, painful as it may be, you are going to have to close your office and find a job giving physicals for an insurance company or something like that to make your mortgage payments—and it may be a mortgage on smaller accommodations." When they left, the wife threw me a fierce glance. I think she wanted to kill the messenger.

The Risk-Bearing Years Are Over

The aversion to risk that those past the age of 55 feel is reasonable. I have seen it argued that if you think you are going to live another five years, stocks are still the best investment because they provide the highest return. Five years may do it, may correct a downturn, but then again, they may not. Look again at 1973–74, when the Dow Jones stocks went down 40 percent, and the average stock went down more than that. That loss wasn't recovered until 1982. Do you want to lose 40 percent of your capital two years before you retire and feel that you can no longer afford to retire but will have to continue to slave away? And what if you can't work, if retirement is mandatory or your health gives out?

A bear market is a very threatening experience, and most people will respond to a sense of threat by purging the source of the anxiety. How many retired people saw the market drop 20 percent in October 1979 and just said, "The hell with this, I want out"? So they sold at a huge loss and never benefited from the rebound. It was the human thing to do. When you feel you can't stand another sleepless night, you sell out, thus making it impossible ever to be healed. At that age, time starts to be your adversary instead of your ally, as it is for the young person who can afford to wait for the inevitable turnaround.

Forget Stocks, Unless What Happens to Them Is Irrelevant

I definitely tell people who are 60 or older not to own stocks— unless if all the stocks went to zero, it still wouldn't hurt them one bit; that is, their life-style wouldn't be affected. It's the same message to the wealthy I delivered in the last chapter. Divide your money into two pools. One is sanctuary, which is the money it takes to operate your life. The other, the risk money, which I sometimes call the "endowment," is the money you'll probably never use but will pass along to your children. Just make sure the sanctuary is taken care of first. Then if your stocks do start to sink to zero, your vanity might get hurt, but you'd live just as well. Your kids can inherit the stocks and wait out the down cycle.

And if you did put 80 percent, or 100 percent, of your money into stocks and your million turned into $2 million, you are not really going to live any better. What would you do differently? Buy a bigger car or a bigger house? As I said, in your late 50s and 60s you don't crave that kind of thing anymore.

My clients usually come around to understanding these facts of life. They see that if they defy good sense, take a flyer, and the good Lord doesn't accommodate them, they're going to have some serious problems. Maybe the people who love stocks don't come to me, because what I suggest is too passive for them. They'll be out there making their bets, looking at the stock tables every morning, and poring over their quarterly statements. As far as I am concerned, these people are not really investors. They are amusing themselves with a compulsive hobby.

Past 65? Forget it. People just want Treasuries. They've reached a point in life when they don't want to be bothered. My father always loved the stock market and he did very well over the years. It took him until he was 70, but then he was through. He put the money in government bonds and he'll keep it there for the duration. It's the rational thing to do, and for most of us, it happens earlier than it did for him. When they reach their 70s, most people develop a deep affection for the U.S. Treasury.

Prescription for the post-retirement years:

Don't own any stocks unless whatever happens to them won't affect your life-style.

3

THE SUDDEN RICH

---

1. Generation Gap

Though most affluent people accumulated their money over a lifetime of "passages," for some it has come all at once. That happy event could be the result of the sale of a business, the buyout of a company where one works or in which one owns a great deal of stock, a large divorce settlement, an inheritance, or a windfall of any kind.

Often very large sums of money are involved, sending the recipient into a kind of shock. Big money takes getting used to. If you are 50 years old and you've led a comfortable but modest life and all of a sudden you have $5 or $10 or $20 million, it creates enormous discomfort. It's like a Midwesterner who's worn Hart Schaffner & Marx suits all his life deciding to buy an Armani. He may look dashing in it, but when he glances in the mirror, it doesn't seem like him. He has to wear it a long time before it becomes natural. New wealth is like that. Somehow it doesn't fit.

It's different, however, for the second generation. Even if the children are teenagers or young adults when good fortune strikes the family, they are spontaneously comfortable with the idea of money. It is one of the problems that accompanies newly arrived affluence. The generation that acquired the wealth lived frugally most of their lives, and, as we saw in the last chapter, tend to raise their standard of living only modestly. Their kids, however, usually want to live it up, and the parents are upset. They worry that their offspring will be spoiled. The kids get the feeling that their parents sort of want to hide or deny the fact that they are now extremely well off. And that's often true; the parents simply aren't comfortable with the idea yet. The children are ready to live on a scale that is in keeping with their new affluence, but the parents keep resisting. Their Puritan ethic, or whatever it is, tells them that money not acquired by sweat is unappreciated and undeserved.

I see this all the time. The parents, disoriented by their new status, send out mixed messages. They take their teenagers to Aspen for the week and then lecture them on how they piddled away their $10 allowance on CDs. They buy $45 Polo shirts for the kids to wear to school and then chide them for wanting expensive rock concert tickets. Or they give their college-age daughter a new car and then, hit by benefactor's remorse— "My God, I just gave this kid a $15,000 car and she knows *nothing* about the value of a dollar!"—they tell her to get a job so she can pay for her gasoline. That is the only way, they tell her, that she'll learn the connection between effort expended and money.

There's nothing wrong with children working; I'm all for it. But the parents don't handle it well. There should be an agreement beforehand that the car will be a gift, but the youngster will be expected to earn the money to maintain it. But so often the announcement comes as an afterthought, the byproduct of guilt. So the kids get mixed signals all the time. They don't understand what's going on. Their parents' ambivalence about their new affluence drives them wild. And the truth is, the kids are more in sync with reality than their parents are.

There's no communication on the subject between parents and their kids. When I ask my clients if they have brought up the change in their circumstances with their children, I've found that I've raised a really provocative topic. The parents are more uneasy talking about the financial facts of life than they were about the biological. They'll say, "Well, the kids know we sold the business, of course, and made some money, but, uh, we haven't gone into any details with them." Which means they've ducked every question that could elicit a quantitative answer. ("Dad, are we rich now, yes or no?" "Well, we're okay.")

I advise people, when it comes to money and the next generation, to be direct and open, and to spell out the dollars. I say, "You are rich now and your children aren't—but they're going to be. They should find out right from the beginning what that means."

I urge the parents, too, if the kids are of at least college age, to get them involved in the process of deciding how to invest the money. The kids don't have to be there for the final decisions, but they can certainly be privy to the process. I think it's just good sense for them to begin their education about money. One of these days they are going to be consumers of investment advice; they might as well learn what that means. Some familiarity with investment jargon will save them from being intimidated when they begin to assume this responsibility for themselves.

(Parents shouldn't be surprised if their children, when they are in their 30s, lobby for new financial advisers. I used to think naively that if I did a good job for a family, when Mom and Dad are gone and the kids have the money, they'll identify me as the family advisor and I'll be retained in that capacity. I was dead wrong. The issue for children is not how well their family has been advised, but *who* did the advising. One of the rites of passage for children who inherit wealth is to break parental ties by imprinting their own authority on all matters concerning financial management. The minute they have control, they can't wait until they have systematically and methodically replaced every family advisor— lawyers, accountants, stockbrokers, and financial advisors—by people of their own choosing, usually their contemporaries.)

Late teenage or older children of the wealthy

- should be told the family's financial situation
- should be brought into the process of deciding how family money is invested

2. A New Popularity

Another problem that arises immediately for the newly wealthy is that everyone seems to know about their good fortune five minutes after they themselves have heard the news, and is at their door proffering services or seeking solicitations. It is amazing how quickly the legion of predators descends. Or maybe it isn't so amazing. After all, if you sell a business for $5 million or $10 million or whatever you get for it, it is a fairly public event. Even if the company is a private one, with all stock owned by the family or a small insider group, word of the sale gets out, because people keep track of other people's money. Lawyers and accountants are involved in the sale. People in those firms know when some colleague is working on an important transaction, so word spreads and then leaks outside the firms. Someone in the know blurts out the figures, say, to the organizers of some charity, in order to tell the committee to be sure to hit Mr. Big. You'd think, for example, that if someone sells his privately held company to a European privately held company, the price would never be widely known. In fact, it's almost always known, within a few thousand dollars, whether the selling price was $10 million or $30 million. And sometimes the man who's sold his business makes what amounts to a public announcement himself, by buying a boat, say, of a size that telegraphs there's been a big change in his circumstances.

First in line to offer congratulations will be those eager to help manage the newly arrived assets. Stockbrokers, for example, have very sensitive antennae. The large firms subscribe to what's called a *13-D service*. Anytime someone acquires more than 5 percent of a company, a 13-D form has to be filed with the Securities and Exchange Commission. The assumption is that whoever bought 5 percent of a company is planning to acquire more, to gain control, or that other people, seeing the interest in this company, will also become intrigued about what hidden values are there. The company has "been put into play." The stockbrokers easily find out who the major private shareholders are; if somebody does indeed buy the company, those people are going to be instantly enriched, as in the case of RJR Nabisco. These brokers are waiting and ready to pounce if that event transpires. And oh, yes, they will not call themselves "brokers." That might sound like they are crassly motivated by brokerage commissions. They will describe themselves, rather, as "investment managers" or "investment consultants." All very professional.

And there will be others who will call: the private banking group at your local bank, financial planners, investment managers, and people selling partnerships and other deals. There are many who feel they deserve to share in your newfound wealth.

You will soon became aware of another cadre of solicitors. People you know, even if they are not the least bit close to you, now or ever, have no reservations about asking you for money. Not long ago *The Wall Street Journal* told about a woman who won a $2.6 million lottery and started getting letters from total strangers, such as the one that stated, "I'm going blind. I need you to buy me a new pickup truck." Often people simply ask you for a loan. You would be both astounded and distressed by the number of people whom you have always regarded as friends or near-friends who now view you as their financial angel as well. The logic seems to be, "Well, Bill and Joan have millions now, and I need only a hundred thousand. Why shouldn't they help out?" It's as though, by virtue of your new circumstances, you now have an obligation to fulfill the needs of those with less.

It could be a friend with a business venture in mind who's been turned down by the banks. He's had a dream; you can now make it happen for him. Or it may be relatives with crises in their lives. Obviously, they turn to someone with money— you. People are very good at defining what is reasonable for other people. They seem to have no inhibitions about it at all, and, as a matter of fact, become bitter and resentful if their wishes aren't granted. After all, it would be no sweat off your back to peel off a few thousand.

And even when you want to help out, you don't like what's happening. Friendships are supposed to be based on shared interests and affections, not on the fact that one party can provide economic benefits to the other. An unwillingness to lend develops simply because you don't want to redefine your relationships. You want to help, but you feel almost forced to draw the line and say, "Look, I'm going to have friends and I'm going to have business relationships, and I am going to be clear about which is which."

3. All for a Good Cause

People also swoop down on the newly rich for donations. Charitable organizations, too, are highly organized these days. They make title searches of property transactions, for example, so they know who owns the major buildings in town, and are on the alert when they are sold. They search partnership filings and watch for when those partnerships are dissolved. They possess state-of-the-art research facilities, elaborate dossiers, and highly organized intelligence systems. Their files, even on those whose assets haven't been liquified as yet, are dazzlingly complete.

They know all about you, or think they do, anyway. A lot of their "information," I am afraid, is hearsay. I think most people would be appalled by the amount of supposedly confidential information, or misinformation, that is in the files of charitable institutions and foundation and endowment fundraisers. They have recorded your approximate net worth, your taste in charities, and your level of giving in the past. They know the names of your close friends and business associates, so they know whom to seat next to you at fund-raising dinners. Their mission in life is to answer the question, "How might I extract money from this person?" and the agent of extraction is preferably someone with whom you have a close social link.

Some of the college people are the worst. They have a passion about their alma mater, maybe because they haven't been as happy since they graduated from the place. They relish raising money for Yours-'n'-Mine U, and all's fair in the cause. Classmates tend to track one another's economic progress, so a bunch of the devoted will gather together and rate the affluence of every class member and arbitrarily decide what level of contribution is appropriate for each.

If you have had a fortunate event that has left you with considerable funds, be prepared to batten down the hatches, for the assault is about to begin. And the battle plans of the gatherers are clever. Suppose it's a capital-raising fund they are pushing—say, to erect a new science lab on your old campus. If you've just come into a fortune, they'll hit you right away, to catch you in your first flush of affluence, in the hope that you may be feeling just a wee bit of guilt about all that money you've come into. They stand ready to provide a conduit for the discharge of that guilt. They may ask you to foot the bill for the whole building. But if they don't judge you are quite at that level of munificence yet, they'll start out with a simple, "We'd like you to give a million." Before fortune struck, you understand, you had been in the habit of donating hundreds, maybe even a couple of thousand dollars, but a million? "It's unthinkable!" you respond. But the negotiations have started at a million, so they can wheedle you down from that level to the point where you say, "Well, all right, I suppose I can afford a few hundred thousand now," and you consider yourself lucky to have gotten off for no more.

And don't think your contributions are going to end with that one gift, big as it was. Charities tend to swap information. Most obviously, if you allow your name to be used for a steering committee or an invitation for some fund-raising dinner, you can be sure it has been duly recorded by every other charity in town. Dozens of causes will be after you, and each will find someone you know to be in charge of the solicitation.

I am not against charities, despite my cynical tone. All of these causes are wonderful. They are good uses for your money. But you can't fund them all.

The first thing I encourage people to do to help them through the transition period from modest affluence to considerable wealth is to include charities when they make up their budgets. Sit down with your spouse and say, "All right, we can afford to give away $35,000 a year now. Let's make up a list of the things we feel most strongly about. Then we'll give more to those at the top of the list and make modest gifts to the rest."

A Family Foundation

If there is enough money—$500,000 would be about the minimum you would need—I would recommend setting up a private family foundation. You'll need a lawyer who can work up the papers even before your business is sold so that all is in readiness.

A private foundation offers a number of benefits, some of which are tax-related. If you paid $300,000 for stock that is now worth $600,000, for example, you can sell the stock and use the $300,000 in appreciation to fund a foundation and avoid any tax consequences to yourself. A foundation has continuity; it is a lasting entity that can support causes dear to you after you yourself are gone from this world. And there is a certain status associated with having a foundation with your name on it, if that appeals to you.

The main advantage of a foundation, though, is that it segregates funds whose sole function will be charitable. It is an easy way, in effect, to box the issue and say, "This amount of capital will be used to generate contributions, and the contributions we will make will come from no other sources." You have isolated your commitment. The fact that solicitors have to deal with a foundation discourages you from, in moments of being pressured, making gifts you would later regret.

You can also appoint a board to assist you in making the donations, and you can put your children or other members of your family on it. That will help diffuse the assaults as well, because you can tell solicitors, "We have a family foundation, and I'll have to talk to my brother and the others about it." From a legal standpoint, decisions are vested in the board, but since the board will be chosen from family or like-minded people who will listen to your advice, from a practical standpoint you will still be in control.

The foundation must by law distribute 5 percent of its principal every year. If you want to perpetuate the effectiveness of the foundation, total return from investments—dividends, interest, and appreciation—must be something in excess of 10 percent to cover those distributions, expenses, and the impact of inflation. Stocks are the obvious investment choice, and there will be some years, when the market is off, when you will probably have to liquidate part of the principal to comply with the distribution rule. The foundation has to file its own tax return, so there are some accounting costs. You can hire someone to bear the administrative burden, but a good many communities have set up what they call a "community foundation" that will administer your private foundation for you. In other words, it will do the bookkeeping and invest the money for you, as well, but you still get to designate which causes you want to support. Communities have found it beneficial to provide central administration for a number of small foundations and nonprofit organizations with modest endowments and no staff to deal with investments and other matters, for the simple reason that they know community causes will get their share of the donations. Most of these community foundations will put 60 percent or 70 percent of the money they are asked to administer in stocks, so returns over time will be large enough to make distributions yet allow the foundations to maintain their capital and even grow.

Advantages of a family foundation:

- Segregates funds devoted to charity
- Channels solicitations and provides more rigorous examination of the worthiness of causes
- Can have tax advantages
- Will continue to support favorite causes after your death

---

4. The Rich May Get Richer

Those who have come into considerable wealth suddenly are often solicited for advice, because if you have become rich, you are obviously—at least in our society—smart. You have a nice disease that others would like to catch. They want to ask your opinion about deals they are involved in. Are they good enough that you, with your experience and wisdom, find them attractive? The richer you are, the more respect you get and the more deals you are shown.

There's a pecking order based on affluence. If Jones sold a company for $20 million and Smith sold his for $50 million, and if you could be a fly on the wall watching how the two interact when they meet at a party, I'd be willing to bet that you could tell which was Jones and which was Smith by noting who is deferential to whom. And most other people in the room will also act a little differently around the $50 million man than they will around his neighbor. The richest person present is always the center of power. The difference between a dilettante and a Renaissance man is about $10 million. And the wife shares in that status. When deals—real estate, venture capital, a hedge fund—are marketed, one of the questions always asked is, "Who else is in on this?" And if Smith has signed on, it has class and it flies.

If you are known as a person of wealth, you are perceived as having three contributions to make to other people's enterprises—your capital, your judgment, and your prestige. And if you're clever, you learn that the aura of superior judgment and prestige can be substituted for the cash. People who now respect you like crazy ask you to become a director of an interesting new company and, of course, want you to have a piece of it to sustain your interest. You may be asked for little or no money; your very presence is believed to enhance the enterprise. Many people don't believe me when I tell them about this. They can't appreciate what power they now possess. But then it happens: they are offered 5 percent of a venture without having to ante up a dime. And some of these ventures work out beautifully. These people are able to compound their wealth by leveraging their reputation rather than their money.

Wealthy older men often do especially well in identifying opportunities in the businesses where they originally prospered. They know the protocol of that business, they understand its pricing policy, its cyclicality, they have vendor contacts, and they have an intelligence network that can verify the representations being made. They can leverage off the skills they have accumulated over a lifetime in that business. I've seen those men get into deals where the odds are so skewed in their favor that the risks relative to the rewards are almost ridiculous. They've made 20 times their money on a very small investment, with little risk of loss and very modest expenditure of time and effort.

I know one man, for example, who was a builder and owner of eight to ten unit apartment buildings on small lots in Southern California. By the time he reached his 40s, he was well off but not what I would call really rich. Then a real estate boom in the area skyrocketed the price of his buildings. They went up something like 400 percent, and the rents he collected rose commensurately. So a little guy who had been happy with his 10 percent return on capital suddenly ended up with a 400 percent increase in capital—at least that, since his equity was leveraged. At that point he was probably worth $4 million. He knew his markets and the local markets knew him; he was shown properties before they were turned over to a broker for listing and he understood how to evaluate them. He sold a lot of his apartments and started acquiring commercial properties of a more substantial nature, most of them one-story buildings used as warehouses or for light manufacturing. Then the appreciation cycle repeated itself. By the time this man slowed down, in his 60s, he was probably worth $20 million to $25 million. Basically he did it by recognizing good deals in a business he knew well and letting the market compound his money for him.

These stories usually have happy endings, because they happen to seasoned businesspeople who know exactly what they are doing when they accept complex deals. But once word gets around the community that you are now rolling in considerable money, you, too, will probably be offered participations in deals, even if you were a pediatrician who just came into an inheritance, and wouldn't know a balance sheet from an income statement. It is just one more sort of solicitation you can expect, and if you are not knowledgeable about such matters, you obviously have no business getting involved. Dazzled by talk of big returns, you could jeopardize your newfound security and comfort. More on this later.

5. Why the Hurry?

Once people know they are going to come into a big chunk
of money, how to invest it is on their minds long before the
check actually arrives. I know, because I get calls. People tell
me they've just sold a business and, after the closing in three
months, they're going to have about $8 million after taxes. And
they seem to think they have to have everything in place the
day the money is in the bank. They've never had to deal with
a sum of money like that. They feel stressed, and they want
to get the problem behind them and remove the stress. People
who make a lot of money are generally the kind who like things
crossed off a list.

They are terribly worried that in their eagerness to take action, they'll make some stupid mistake or be exploited. After
all, the money represents the culmination of a lifetime's work,
and they don't want to blow it. Maybe they sense that they
can't trust themselves not to do something foolish. Quite often, you know, when people go from a comfortable economic
position to very substantial affluence, especially when it's as a
result of circumstances over which they had no control, they
feel a fair amount of guilt about it. It's hard to get used to flying
first class. (Most manage, but it's hard.) And feeling that guilt,
they often take some crazy risk very soon after the money is
theirs. Subconsciously, I suppose they are trying to give back
some of that "undeserved" money.

I remember one middle-aged gentlemen who came to me in
great distress. "I spent the first two years after the sale of my
business turning my cash into an assortment of deals," he ex-
plained. "It's frightening, what I did. I own pieces of apartments
in Texas, an electronics firm in Boston that I suspect is on the
ropes, and some land in Hawaii. I control none of these deals.
They all consume more cash and they've all declined in value. I
must have had a financial death wish." Since all his investments
were illiquid, there wasn't much I could do to help him.

If you are ever in the fortunate position of instant affluence,
my first advice would be to slow down. There is no point and
no advantage in rushing matters. And with all the changes
going on in the life of the suddenly rich, the decision about

where to put funds can wait. I would tell you, if you were the person with $8 million, when the money arrives, buy some three-month Treasury bills through your bank and then come out to my offices in San Diego and we'll talk.

People come, with their spouses about 75 percent of the time, often carrying their tax returns and net worth statements. But those I don't need. What I *do* need, as we have already discovered in an earlier chapter, is just two numbers: how much money you spend in a year, and how much money will be free for investments. With those two numbers, again, you can work out how much of your free money should be put into investments that throw off the income needed to support your newly enhanced lifestyle, and then you can decide what to do with the remainder.

I talk to people, too, about some of the changes they can expect in their lives. The money has come so suddenly that they have no idea what they are in for—like the investment gurus, institutions, and friends-in-need who will soon be knocking at their door. I suppose I am foolish to play the counselor, but I have seen so many instances of what these people will have to go through in adjusting to sudden wealth, that I cannot resist trying to prepare them a bit.

I would caution you, for example, about another fact of your new life—that you may soon sense a change in your personal and social relationships, not because wealth has made you snobbish, but because some of your friends will feel they live in different worlds now. Friends have a propensity for deciding that your sudden good fortune has put a distance between you and them. It may be regrettable, but it is common that social alliances are formed around economic strata, and the newly rich have been thrust upon a higher plateau. There is often a definite element of jealousy as well. The newly rich can immediately embrace a style of living that separates them from those who are not of similar circumstances, which is most of the world.

If you come into money, even though you are not offensive about your new affluence, your life-style does tend to change at least somewhat, and there is now a material difference between your dwelling and theirs, the vacations you take and the vacations they take—and before very long these differences suggest in the minds of your old friends that there's also a big difference in who you are and who they are. So you find that the people you went to college with, your lifelong friends, drift away, just by virtue of a change in your financial circumstances. As Logan Pearsall Smith once wrote, "It is the wretchedness of being rich that you have to live with rich people."

I am probably wasting my breath with these messages. Most of the time, people don't want to hear that sort of thing from me. In some ways, warning people what it's going to be like to be rich is like warning newlyweds about what can go wrong in a marriage. But I think it helps people to get a sense of where they are now, what the new rules are, and what they can expect ahead.

If you are lucky enough to suddenly come into a great deal of money

- Don't be hasty or rash about investing it.
- Put the money in three-month Treasury bills.
- Use those months to study your income needs and investment options.

4

FAMILIES

---

1. The Root of Unhappiness?

Money, even money newly and unexpectedly arrived, doesn't always mess up families. In fact, I am pleased to report that in my experience it adds to the happiness of most. Those times it does create misery, as might be expected, is when it accumulates in the hands of neurotics. The more neurotic, the greater the misery.

I think in particular of a family in the Midwest that asked me to help them find investment managers for their considerable wealth. The founder of the family fortune, whom I'll call Mr. Jones, was selling another big chunk of his stock in the company he had built, and he expected to realize about $50 million for himself, the trusts that he had set up for his children and his nieces, and a couple of family foundations. He was nearing 60, had a wife (his second), a son in his late 20s, a daughter in college and five nieces in their late teens to early 20s. Mr. Jones had two sisters, but one had passed away; the other was off in an ashram somewhere in India. I couldn't get a clear picture of the nieces' fathers; nobody seemed to want to talk about them. In any case, their uncle had made a commitment long ago to take care of his sisters' offspring, since nobody else seemed about to do it.

I told Mr. Jones over the phone that I would line up some investment managers I believed suitable to invest the proceeds of the stock sale and that I would ask them to appear with me at his office to be interviewed. As it happens, I selected two from my state, California, one from New York, and one from Boston. Since we were talking some $500,000 in annual management fees that somebody was going to be paid, they were delighted to fly in from their respective coasts.

I also strongly urged Mr. Jones to include his wife and children in the selection process. Just listening to the kinds of questions that would be asked would be educational for them. The money they already had and would have upon his death would be in trust for some time, but ultimately his wife, should she survive him, and certainly their children, would have responsibility for big dollars; they would be consumers of investment advice until they die, so they might as well start learning how to deal with professional investment services. All of the young people, except the son, were single, which is a better state in which to start. The minute the kids get married, their spouses will have a vote in how the money is invested, and the direct beneficiaries of Jones' wealth ought to learn enough to be able to hold their own in taking care of what he's left them. The nieces, I said, needn't be at the family meeting in his office, but I wanted to talk to them, too, since they would face similar responsibilities one day. Mr. Jones agreed to my request.

I flew to Mr. Jones' hometown on a Friday and started talking to the second generation the next day. It soon became apparent that this was not a happy family, for all its money. The nieces, far from being grateful to their uncle for his generosity, resented bitterly the way he parceled the money out. They already had some money in trust, and he was the sole trustee, so they had to go to him for everything from a new car to a new dress. Every time, they complained, they had to listen to the same lecture on how money should be spent, which reflected *his* set of values, not their mothers' and certainly not theirs. It wasn't so much that he was tight with the money; it was the way he enjoyed exercising his control that took the joy out of having it.

On Sunday I met with Mr. Jones' son. He had opened a gadget store in town, of The Sharper Image sort, but I gathered it was not doing well. I had the distinct feeling that he wasn't putting the necessary energy into the venture, that the store was more of a hobby. This was a boy, it struck me, who saw no reason to work for a living. The daughter refused to see me on her own.

On Monday I met with Mr. and Mrs. Jones and their two children in his office. The money managers waited their turn in the reception room. They had to wait a lot longer than they had counted on. Mr. Jones, without apology or explanation, showed up almost an hour late. Ten minutes after he did come in, he picked up the phone and made two lengthy calls. Then minutes after that he received one of his flunkies and fifteen minutes later he summoned another. He didn't even show the common courtesy of stepping outside to conduct his business with them; instead, we all had to sit there and be quiet until he was finished. Phone calls and consultations interrupted our proceedings the rest of the morning. At one point he ordered his secretary to bring in a bowl of popcorn. I have never seen a human being so uncomfortable when the spotlight was pointed anywhere but on him. No one else had a chance to say much. My blood pressure was rising by the minute.

By the time I left that office I had formed a strong impression of the Jones family. It was clear to me that the son hated and feared his father, hated his stepmother, and hated himself. The daughter seemed without any will of her own. She never uttered a word, looked bored, and was obviously present only by command. The children's stepmother, I am convinced, had contempt for them all. At our meeting she got in a squabble with her husband about some arrangement for later in the day—who was going to be picked up where by the limo at what time—and she rose to announce theatrically, "I can't stand any more of this, I'm leaving," and stalked out of the room. It was one of the damnedest days I've ever spent with a client. Months later, the managers were still waiting for Mr. Jones to make up his mind.

You walk out of a forum like that absolutely contemptuous of the rich and of riches. You say to yourself, "I work hard because I want to make a living for myself and my family, and maybe even to get rich myself some day and have some of the indulgences these people have. But why should I bother?

Look at them! Look at the mental condition of those children, absolutely out of touch with reality. The money brings this family no joy. It just seems to generate eternal conflict among them, particularly because dad/uncle isn't turning loose the purse strings until they bury him. And those women are all going to marry guys like him." All I could see was generations of psychiatric bills that will look like Brazil's national debt.

Money As a Cushion, Not a Shrine

Thank heaven, the Joneses are not typical—not rare, mind you, but not typical. *Most* of the rich I deal with are really lovely people. They are unaffected. They consider themselves blessed and they are humble about their success. The majority worked hard and fortune then bestowed on them economic rewards of a magnitude they never envisioned. But they view the money as a byproduct of their work, not as an end in itself. They are not obsessed with money.

Nor do they, now that they can afford it, adopt a life-style of opulence. They are not interested in making statements about their new status. They don't build a 30,000-square-foot castle, because they would be uncomfortable living in and with that kind of display. When they spend their money, it is to enrich their lives and their children's lives. Quality of life for them is defined by people, not possessions. Possessions have a human agenda. If they buy a boat, it's because they like to entertain their friends, not because they want to impress the world. They take their grandchildren to Hawaii and arrange other elaborate family trips. Even if they start to do something grand like collect art, it is because they have always had a passion for the arts that can now be fulfilled, not because a painting is just another thing to own, like a Bentley. Sure, collecting art or antique furniture means spending big dollars, but I'm more comfortable with that than with acquisitions made for no other purpose than to elicit envy from those who possess less.

On the whole, too, they are not overly obsessed with the question of what to leave their kids, with how much is too little, and how much would be too much. They just have an implicit faith in life. They know their kids are O.K., and they believe they're going to be O.K., too, about the money. If they are wrong about that, well, they'll be dead by then, so they are not going to worry about it too much. They don't try to manipulate their kids' lives; they don't have to control everything. They have faith that things usually work out for the best, and anyway, they understand that it is beyond their power to make sure that they always do.

2. Multiple Marriages and Assorted Offspring

There is one problem area, however, that I see often, and it relates not to children but to second wives. Husbands are so often just a tad suspicious of a second wife. The last thing they seem to want, for example, is for Susie to know how much money they have. At some visceral level, whatever the love between them, Charlie's got Susie pegged as having a little avarice in her heart, and maybe, just maybe, the avarice exceeds the affection. When he sets up a meeting with me to discuss an investment program, Susie is not invited. Then he can open up to me about his nagging doubts. And he *will* open up all right. Clients tell me things they wouldn't tell anyone else, unless it's their lawyer. (They generally don't talk so frankly to their accountants, and I think rightly so. I've found that leaks at accounting firms are common; the files just don't seem to be controlled.) Lawyers, almost by necessity of their trade, have to learn to keep confidences. And I, too, seem to serve as some kind of confessor, confidant, or therapist they can spill out their hearts to.

Many men, by the way, aren't much more open about their finances with their wives even if they've been married for 40 years and will never have a second. It's not out of suspicion but simple neglect. Until one day they finally realize that the money's probably going to go to her one of these days and that she won't have any idea how to look after it. These men bring their wives into our meetings, but with an air of hopelessness. "She doesn't know a thing about money," they say in front of her, "and I know she's going to outlive me. I want her to learn. That's why she's here." Well, Gladys doesn't have a clue, because Bill's never bothered to discuss anything with her during their 40 years of marriage. She doesn't know about money and, at this stage of her life, she doesn't want to know. Gladys sits there with this blank expression on her face, wishing she were elsewhere. And that is the husband's fault. He should have introduced her to financial realities years ago.

Second marriages do carry special seeds of contention. A second wife usually enters the scene at a much higher economic level than the first wife enjoyed for most of her years with her husband. The first wife was there through the formative years, the years when sacrifices were made to build for the future, and then the second wife comes in to reap the harvest—the grander house, the longer and more lavish vacations, and so on. The first wife is naturally resentful, but very often so are the children. Especially if the bonding is strongest with the mother, they object bitterly to what their stepmother is enjoying.

Children and Stepchildren

When the new wife comes into the household with her own children, the difficulties are obviously compounded. The new marriage partners want to believe that there will now be one happy expanded family, but most of the time it just ain't so. There is a finite amount of adoration, and now a subdivision of that adoration—of all resources—has to occur.

And there may be an even greater subdivision in the future. It's rare that anyone talks about it, but the kids by a first marriage are bound to wonder if their inheritance has just been pared. If the husband has three children and the new wife brings two kids of her own into the marriage, it is sure to occur to the original three that the divisor of Dad's estate has just gone from three to six, considering the portion of the surviving wife and her offspring. And if Dad leaves everything to the second wife and *she* ends up with control over the family assets, how will she distribute them? The kids can only see themselves as net losers in the transaction.

I happen to believe, and studies bear me out, that in the case of second marriages and integrated families, the most you can hope for is to learn to like and respect somebody else's children. Love of all for all is usually a fictional view of what happens when you throw unrelated people together. If the newly created couple proceed to have a child of their own, that's different: that child obviously assumes equal status in everyone's eyes, or at least in its parents'. But to expect stepchildren to like each other, that integrated families are going to be like the Brady Bunch, clashes with reality. Stepchildren are an intrusion on the life of the other children. Nobody in these families likes to talk about such matters, but very often the situation is close to a nightmare, and the conflicts often spill over into financial matters. The best you can hope for from a forced interaction is acceptance.

These may not be pleasant truths, but they are, in my observation, truths nonetheless, and perhaps there's a comfort in admitting them. There's a big gap between how people think extended families are supposed to be and how they really are, and the comfort comes from knowing that you are not selfish and unfair if you love your own child more than someone else's. That seems natural to me, despite the persistent myth that love for another adult is supposed to lead to the same affection for his or her offspring that you bear toward your own.

Facing reality helps in dealing with the economic consequences of second marriages. In my experience, as far as financial solutions are concerned, the husband makes a provision for the new wife's children, but one that is smaller than that he's left his own. If it's the woman who's brought the money into the union, she is equally protective of her own brood. And that is natural, I think, particularly for women. Indeed, the truth is that the mother is probably always going to be closer to her children than she is to her second husband. Maternal bonding is a strong adhesive. If the husband has the money, the new wife will, in some fashion, lobby, either through his will or at some other economic juncture, to ensure that her children are dealt with financially—if not on equal terms then as close to them as she can negotiate.

> *When a man with children takes a second wife with children of her own...*
>
> He usually provides for his stepchildren, but leaves more money to his own offspring.

3. Grey Hairs Over Black Sheep

Another matter about which people are frank with me and which they seldom admit within the family confines is their favoritism among their kids. Even if they don't say it outright, they make it pretty clear before long. I don't know what the dynamics are, but whether it's the kid who's the best looking, the most clever, or the best athlete, or, whether it's the daughter in a family with four sons, there always seems to be one child who gets special treatment. And so often that child—who, of course, knows he or she is favored—has learned to manipulate the situation. Why work hard when you know Mom and Dad will take care of you forever?

It can get to the point, in fact, where the favorite is absolutely incapable of earning a living. But clearly, with Mom and Dad feeling as they do, making money never has to be an option. "I have a 28-year-old adolescent," the wife says, and you can see the affection in her eyes. And her husband just nods and smiles. But you can also see that, without abandoning the beloved ne'er-do-well, they're trying to figure out how to be fair—how to reward, or at least not disadvantage, the kids who *have* gone out and achieved in the ways their parents did and *have* embraced the ethic of education and work.

It's a very difficult situation. The parents are desperate for a solution and hope that I can supply it. It's clear that *they* don't want to deal with the reality of the matter. I'll ask them, for example, about Johnny's future. Here he is, 28 years old, hasn't finished college yet, can't hold down a job, and obviously hasn't found himself. "Do you think," I ask, "that to motivate him into making some decisions, it might be wise to draw the line somewhere?"

"What do you mean?" they ask, as though no one has posed this question to them before.

"I mean, you could choose an age, say 35, and tell him that if he's not self-supporting by then, you're going to withdraw all your support. Are you willing to make a decision to do that?"

Oh, that's a fine idea, they agree; they should indeed do something exactly like that. And yes, they can deal with it and will speak plainly to the boy. Of course, Johnny's only 28 now. If I had suggested the age of 30, only two years away, that would be unthinkable. It would be too much reality for them. And I'm sitting there thinking that when Johnny's 33, they'll change their minds.

So I give up on getting them to make Johnny independent as long as they are alive, and I proceed to ask them about their wills: When they are gone, then what? If they are going to continue to take care of Johnny from beyond the grave, they are going to have to take a big chunk of money and dedicate those funds to the support of the child, because there is no evidence that he'll ever be able to support himself. "Is that what you want?" I ask.

They can't face that either. They know that it isn't fair to the other children who are working hard to make their way in the world. "We really shouldn't give Johnny any money when we die," they say. But again, I can tell they are saying one thing and their sentiments are entirely different. When I probe further about how their estate is drawn, I find they have most definitely not cut Johnny out of their will.

Clearly, they are not inclined to change the way they are going to deal with this child. Johnny's always had favored nation treatment and it is going to continue; it has been institutionalized. The best I can do is to tell them, "OK, do as you want. It is your money. Just be ready to face the resentment of the other children." I warn them that the resentment is there— even though they tell me the issue has never come up—and one day it is going to explode. "If you intend to continue with this special dispensation for Johnny, you'd better be prepared for a confrontation, especially when the kids get married and their spouses start to chime in with their opinions about the unfairness of it all."

So if you have a situation that is similar, I say, "Deal with it now." Don't run away from reality. Sit down with the other children and explain to them that it may not be fair, but it is the way you want to deal with the situation. And if they don't like it, too bad. That would be my attitude. Tell your children, "We love you, we appreciate what you are making of your lives, but it is *our* money, *we* made it, and this is what *we* want to do with it. You will have money, too, but not as much as you would have had, because it is our decision to take care of Johnny. You will be able to live better because of what we leave you, but it certainly won't be enough now for you to live on easy street, and you will have to continue to work hard and build your own fortunes."

Many parents agonize over the issue of fairness. One question I am often asked is: "I have a daughter who has three children and a son who has two children. I've been giving gifts to the grandchildren. Should I give more to each of my son's kids to keep it all equal?"

My answer is, "If your son has another child, it will be equal. Otherwise, you have no obligation to do any more for your son. Your gifts are to the grandchildren, even though the parents probably benefit, residually, from your generosity. The fact that your children have different-size families is just the reality, and don't worry about it." To me, the answer is self-evident, but people want to be reassured that they are observing the proprieties.

I think frankness with children about what they can expect for themselves and their own children in the way of an inheritance is always advisable. Parents should gather their children and tell them, "The fact that we have $5 million doesn't mean that when we pass on you'll never have to work again. There will be taxes, the money is going to be split among you, there are some charities and causes we want to remember. So don't sit around and wait. We don't think that is a good idea for you or for *your* children." If parents don't hold that kind of dialogue, some kids will live their lives as though they've won the lottery but they just don't know when the check is coming in the mail. It's a parental duty to deal with these issues. Obviously you can't do it when they are too young, but I think these matters can be discussed frankly when kids reach their mid-teens, certainly by the time they are of college age.

> **If you have a problem child who is not making his or her own way in the world**
>
> · Give that child a deadline, after which support will be wholly or gradually cut off.
> · Or, if you want to continue the support, be open about your intentions with your other children.

4. Sons-in-law, Daughters-in-law, and Inheritance Laws

In many instances, of course, parents *are* at fault when kids are not motivated to achieve because they have been so thoroughly coddled and, sometimes, emasculated. I've seen this especially with mothers and sons. These controlling mothers smother the boy when he's young. Then, when the son, with no confidence in himself, turns out to be unable to stand on his own two feet, the mother continues her control by the way she doles out money to him. When he's 30, the boy marries— usually a woman who's like his mother—and the conflict becomes terrible to behold. The daughter-in-law starts to scream, "Why do you let your mother treat you this way? Your parents are worth millions and we live like gypsies with the pittance they give us." (Never mind that the husband can't hold down a job.) And the mother cries that this vicious woman her son has married has come between a beautiful mother–son relationship.

Then the mother starts to dwell on the fact that if the boy is left a lot of money, this detested daughter-in-law is going to have a big hand in how it's spent, and she can't bear that. So she looks for ways to put all assets in the son's name, so the daughter-in-law is economically impotent. Or she is ready to truncate the son's inheritance because of her hatred of the daughter-in-law. In either case, the conflicts are just horrendous. These are issues I cannot adjudicate. I spell out the alternatives and walk away from the ugly situation.

Fathers who are equally controlling seem to be very adept at never letting their children have enough money to make serious mistakes. Mothers tend to exercise their control by the way they dole out money, fathers by the way they withhold it. While Dad's alive, no child gets his or her hands on serious money, and some fathers create trusts that make it certain that it is tied up long after they are gone.

Prenuptial Agreements

Even when parents like the mates their sons and daughters have chosen, they are aware that there is a 50–50 chance these days that any marriage will end in divorce. Many parents, therefore, would like to see their offspring sign a prenuptial agreement, to ensure that the treasure they have amassed over the years will devolve only to their own children. This is just as true if the money they have given to a son or daughter is held in trust. If the children live in a community property state and the income from the trust is commingled or a house is bought from that income, and then after several years the marriage fails, each spouse will have entitlement to half the acquired assets and half of any income that was deposited into a joint checking account. A spouse may also lay claim to alimony from future income.

Parents who are worried about such a scenario will often talk to a son or daughter about a prenuptial agreement that will keep ownership of all major assets of the couple separate. It is an awkward conversation. Trying to educate a hopelessly enamored child about the realities of the divorce tables without telegraphing disapproval of his or her love object or cynicism about love and marriage is not an easy undertaking. And success is highly problematic in any case. You can't force your kids to do it. They're in love, and your advice tends to be dismissed out of hand because of its source. They don't want statistics intruding on matters of the heart.

Still, this is an issue that comes up again and again. It seems to be part and parcel of how affluence affects many parents' relationships with their heirs. I tell my clients, bring up the topic of a prenuptial agreement with your children if you want to, but don't be surprised if your advice is abruptly dismissed.

Control Through Trusts

If you get nowhere by persuasion and you are adamant because of your mistrust of your child's intended or of the chances of eternal matrimonial bliss, you could set up a trust that makes your child the beneficiary of the income but never the beneficiary of the principal. (At some point, of course, the principal has to go somewhere—a charity, or your grandchildren, or wherever.) That way you can deny the person you view as a predatory spouse ever getting his or her hands on the principal. But that is a nasty business and I don't like to see it done. First of all, you are going to be dead when all this ugliness you foresee may happen, so I wonder if it matters, and second, you have ended up punishing your child because of the person he or she has chosen to wed.

I know of one circumstance, involving a family of great wealth, in which the parents very deliberately set up a family trust for their two sons that owned everything; that is, the trust owned the boys' houses, owned their cars, everything. The daughters-in-law never had any ownership in anything, and as a consequence, could never have entitlement to any alimony. The trust threw off enough income to support the children's lifestyles, but not enough for them to acquire any meaningful assets of their own; no community property of value was ever created. One of the sons did indeed get divorced. His wife, who had never signed a prenuptial agreement and never really understood the set-up that had been created by her in-laws, discovered that she was left with practically nothing, even though the divorce was her husband's idea and one she opposed bitterly. She was entitled to a modest amount of money, but that was all. Even though she had been married to a son of one of the wealthiest families in the community, she found that she was essentially broke.

> **If you don't like your child's choice of a spouse and you want to block that spouse's claim to family wealth, you can**
>
> · Ask the couple to sign a prenuptial agreement stating that in case of a divorce, neither will have a right to the property of the other.
>
> · Set up a trust that distributes income to the couple but keeps the principal in trust so that you can dispose of it as you wish.

5. When Should Kids Get the Money?

Those with children in their teens or of college age almost invariably ask me at what age their offspring should be empowered to control their inheritance. It's important, maybe more important than how much is given. There is an old Chinese saying: "He who waits for the shoes of a dead man often goes barefoot." When children know they are not going to be given a lot of money during their parents' lifetime, they understand that they had better go out and make it on their own. An inner voice says, "Sure, I can live like a prince when I'm 55, but I'd better do something in the meantime if I want to live decently for the next 30 years."

A parental policy of denial can raise considerable resentment, however. A son can be struggling to make ends meet and growl to his wife, "God, what a difference a few hundred thousand would make, and dad and mom have a hundred million. Why don't they lighten up a little?" The situation is not exactly conducive to a good parent-child relationship. But the alternative of giving too much too early frightens dad and mom. The boy, they fear, will have no incentive to succeed.

A middle ground is what I call "mild enrichment." While the parents are living, the kids get a house, a car, and enough income to live somewhat better. Dad, who usually makes this decision, says, "I want to see them and their families live better, sure. But I also want to see them get up and go to work in the morning. So we'll compromise."

Well-meaning parents often try to do too much for their off-spring and not only damage the children but their own financial health as well. I think of a couple who gave half of their money to help their two sons save a business in trouble. The business failed anyway, and the parents had to sell their house and move into a cheaper neighborhood. The sons at least had their youth left to comfort them.

Reined In Until 35

Most estate planning lawyers today recommend that whatever money is willed to children be kept in trust until they reach the age of at least 30, and preferably 35. By that age, in most cases, the child has become an adult and presumably has a sense of responsibility. I have no quarrel with that advice.

Generally by the age of 30, and certainly by 35, parents have a pretty clear picture of what their children's motivations in life are. If they haven't found a career, they probably won't. If they've chosen not to be educated, they're either not educable or education will never be a priority for them and its completion is not certain. The probabilities are very strong at that point that they are likely to remain adolescents forever. We can all cite examples of somebody who was a spendthrift and a cad until the age of 42, when he met this wonderful woman and settled down and built factories. But those are only the exceptions that prove the rule. Once the kids cross 30 and haven't conformed to your idea of what conformity is, the odds go up geometrically that they never will, and at 35 the odds are extremely remote.

So if you keep the money in trust until then, you have control until you make up your mind about what you want to do. If the kids are fine, you say they can have their money when they reach the age stipulated in your will. If one or more is proving a wastrel, you can decide whether you want to let him or her have the money anyway, at 35, or you want the money to stay in trust for good after you are gone, in order to protect the child from his or her own irresponsibility. Of course, if you've gone to your eternal reward before the child reaches 30 or 35, you no longer have options.

I know of one instance involving a family that was enormously wealthy. This man sold his business in the 1940s for about $40 million, which is the equivalent of several hundred million today. He had four sons and one daughter. He set up irrevocable trusts, designating the age of 35 at which each would come into his or her inheritance. But when the offspring were in their late 20s and early 30s, he realized that they were all—except for one son—hopelessly irresponsible. The rest had never earned a dime and he saw that they never would. He went to the state authorities—and I never found out how he brought this off but I suspect he ended up paying off someone—and got his irrevocable trusts revoked. His children wouldn't get their money until they were 60. I know the beneficiaries—three are now in their 60s and two in their early 70s—and I'd say he made a good call. Except for that one son, the rest have never earned a penny; they've lived off the income of the trusts. Three of the heirs, when they finally did get their hands on the money at 60, threw it away in stupid investments. That was one father who knew the worth of his own children.

Incentive Trusts

In the past couple of years a new kind of trust instrument, called an incentive trust, has evolved, and it is a very sensible way of attacking the problem of disbursing and bequeathing wealth to children without stripping them of motivation. Children receive money from the trust only when they meet specified goals, and parents have total flexibility in designating those goals. The son or daughter, for example, gets a specified amount when he or she graduates college, earns a post-graduate degree, participates in the family business, overcomes drug or alcohol dependency, or gives something back to society through charitable or community volunteer work. Also, income earned can be matched by some formula, so the children get no money if they loaf and incremental money if they toil. Obviously, dictatorial parents could use an incentive trust to control their kids' career paths, which is not exactly a loving thing to do. Parents should sit down with their children and talk about their goals in life before drafting these trusts, and, again, make sure the kids understand what Mom and Dad have in mind and why these strings are being attached to the family purse.

John L. Levy, a Mill Valley, California, consultant who specializes in providing both financial and family advice to the wealthy, has some clients who have found another solution. They divide up each child's inheritance into three, not necessarily equal, segments. Each child receives the first when fairly young, say at 21, and the other two at intervals of five to ten years, usually contingent upon the heir's demonstrating an ability to take care of the money responsibly. Levy says his clients who have adopted this plan have been pleased with the results. Giving children some money when they are young not only teaches them how to handle it, but, just as importantly, helps them develop the sense of responsibility, self-confidence, and self-esteem that the children of the wealthy so often lack.

Some options in leaving money to children:

- Limited help while they are young, and their full inheritance, if parents are deceased, when they reach 30 or 35
- An incentive trust that dispenses money only as children achieve designated goals
- One-third of an inheritance at age 21, the other two-thirds at specified stages if the child proves responsible

---

6. How Much Wealth Is Good for Children?

More troubling to most parents than the decision of *when* to give children their money is the question of *how much*. Many parents with wealth, whether they've come into money suddenly or accumulated it over a lifetime, agonize over this matter. It's the same dilemma: they want to enrich their children's lives but they don't want to ruin them with too much. After all, if each child is left $20 million, that money put out at 8 percent provides $1.5 million a year in income. That makes for mighty good living without lifting a finger.

Inheritance decisions run the gamut. In 1986 *Fortune* ran a cover story on how wealthy families were dealing with the inheritance quandary. The investor Warren Buffett, whom *Forbes* recently pegged as worth $4 billion, give or take a couple of $100 million, said he was leaving his children very little, "a few hundred thousand dollars." He is going to leave most of his money to charity, because giving children "a lifetime supply of food stamps just because they came out of the right womb" can be "harmful" to them. At the other end of the spectrum is Jackson Stephens, chairman of Stephens Inc. of Little Rock, Arkansas, the largest investment bank outside New York, whose family, along with that of his late brother, is worth nearly $1 billion. He said, "I'd rather give my money to my kids than do anything else with it. If my heirs want to clip coupons, that'll be their business. I can't control the future, and I'm not going to worry a whole bunch."

I almost invariably talk over the issues with my clients, probe for their own feelings on the matter, and try to lead them to the decision that makes them comfortable. The only guideline I suggest is that "too much" would be the threshold point that robs them of their self-esteem. Leave them enough money to allow them to live fuller lives but not so much that they won't have to go to work in the morning. They must be allowed to take pride in their own achievements.

But that number is a moving target, based on the parents' attitudes and on where the children live, how they live, and what kind of people they are. There's no precise answer. You may have a son who is proving a go-getter on his own, and how much you leave him probably won't make much difference in how he runs his life. Another son may be in the arts and making $25,000 a year—which is probably more than 95 percent of people in the arts make—and be a rousing success in his field but a failure by most economic measures. You may want to do a great deal for that son. Still another son you may feel is struggling to find himself and needs help, but not so much help that he will give up that struggle.

Worth Defined in Dollars

I do know this: parents are right to be concerned. Those who inherit considerable wealth often inherit psychological problems along with the money. It is hard for them to build self-esteem. If you have created a business and sold it for a lot of money, you feel entitled to that wealth. You can relate your money to the ethic of hard work and sacrifice and ability. If you inherit money, on the other hand, the work, sacrifice, and ability were a prior generation's. Affluence derived from good fortune isn't the same as affluence achieved through your own initiative and labor.

The inheritors of wealth are constantly reminded that nothing they do as human beings seems to carry value in the eyes of others distinct from the fact that they have money. These people are so closely identified with their affluence — "Oh yes, he inherited $20 million, didn't he?" — that they soon wonder if they have any worth aside from the ability to dispense funds.

To build self-esteem through their own achievements isn't easy either, particularly if they themselves choose the business world as their arena. If they take $20 million and turn it into $100 million, nobody gives them credit for it because of the base from which they started. People say, "Hell, with a $20 million pot to start with, I could do that, too." And often the achiever has a nagging doubt that there's a strong element of truth in that statement, that a lucky birthright provided the push that made success a downhill ride.

Not every inheritor is intimidated by such considerations. Some children decide they are going to turn big money into very big money and are indifferent about what others think. They believe they are good at business and they simply forge ahead. Some succeed and some are deluded and squander their inheritance, and what better example than two Texas families — the Hunts, for whom, by and large, it's been dust to dust, and the Basses, who have piled the wealth ever higher.

A lot of rich kids, understanding that business success will be a tough road to prestige, gravitate to the professions, whether law, medicine, or the arts. There your competence and success cannot be attributed to the size of your inheritance. The scorecard isn't kept by tallying income tax returns.

Esteemed According to Your Generosity

Another path to esteem often chosen by the sons and daughters of the rich is to use their wealth to become benefactors. They are then assured of the adoration of those associated with the cause they are supporting, be it the opera, the library, the museum, or a charity. They are invited to endless meetings, asked to sit on boards, and honored for their contributions to the noble endeavor.

However, if there is a change in circumstances—if they withdraw their support, either because of an inability to continue their funding or because of a conflict with the policies or people associated with the cause—they quickly find themselves pariahs among these same people who revered them earlier. They have betrayed the cause. The rich get a very quick lesson in the relationship between contributions and adoration when they deal with nonprofit organizations. And that is a blow, once more, to self-esteem: your worth seems to depend on your ability to write checks.

Inheritors of wealth who become benefactors know, on a visceral level, that this is true all along. They sense early on that the welcome they enjoy predominantly depends on their financial support, even if they are passionate about the cause. There are plenty of working bees who also have passion, but the people who are treasured and who make policy are those with the fat checkbooks. Even in doing God's work, there is a pecking order.

Uneasy Lies the Wealth

Because their self-esteem is so low, these inheritors of wealth who don't trust themselves often lack the ability to trust others. They are constantly confronting and changing the people who work for them, including their investment advisors. My clients who fall into this category are a real problem. They just can't believe that anybody would serve them in a sincere, nonexploitative way. And they seldom change; they tend to remain suspicious all their lives.

Their insecurity drives them constantly to ask others for advice, and they tend to believe the last person they've talked to.

There's usually been a heavy turnover in their investment advisors, as they have convinced themselves time and again that they have been victimized and that some other advisor has better answers. In most cases, their previous advisors have done an adequate job, and when I see such a pattern, I tell these people that I can't do anything for them, that they should probably stay put with the advisor they are thinking of leaving or have just left. It makes them crazy to hear that. A firm "No" from someone whom they pay is unthinkable, because that would mean they are no longer in power. They are convinced that their whole worth is wrapped up in their checkbook, and it has just been made impotent.

Such stories are not likely to have happy endings, financially. These people continually seek advice, but they don't understand the differences in the sources of that advice and they don't know how to assess the information they receive. They do whatever sounds most compelling at the moment. People who sell investments are very clever at playing to their insecurities, and because these uneasy rich, accustomed to receiving attention, like having people queued up outside the door, they buy from one vendor after another instead of turning matters over to one competent professional. The upshot is that *their* kids are probably not going to inherit as much as they did. If they get lucky, they get so much conflicting advice over the years, and become so tired of the constant turnover in advisors, that they just throw in the towel and keep their money in tax-exempts. Inflation will take its toll, but at least they don't end up impoverished.

How much money should you leave your children?

Enough to enrich their lives but not so much that they are no longer motivated to achieve

---

7. The Midas Curse

People open up to me, as I've said, because they feel there is no one else to talk to about money-related matters, and there are times when these beneficiaries of ancestral entrepreneurship tell me they would happily repudiate their good fortune. Like everybody else, they yearn for what they don't have, and in their case it's the ideal of having a job where there is a high correlation between input and output. What they are really yearning for is not to be thought of as apart. They want to be a person, instead of a "person with $20 million." So even though there are very few people who actually do reject an inheritance—as a matter of fact, quite a few people have killed for one—many truly suffer because of their "good fortune."

I've seen many with inherited millions try to hide their wealth from the world in order to escape social isolation. These closet rich live on a scale that belies their affluence, because it is easier for them to deny themselves the benefits of the affluence than it is to face what they think would be the envy and resentment of friends and acquaintances. That is particularly true when the source of the inheritance is obscure. If they live in a small community where everyone knows their family has money, they could hardly hide their wealth. But if they live in Chicago and Grandpa in Cincinnati dies and leaves them millions, it can be done. It turns out that Grandpa, who everybody thought was just a successful dentist, had quietly acquired a few buildings in downtown Cincinnati that are worth a fortune, but certainly nobody in Chicago has heard about it. So the beneficiaries of this bonanza spend a lifetime hiding their affluence for fear of being judged "different" by the people around them.

Others, fearing ostracism or feeling guilt about the enormous advantage in life they did nothing to create, work hard at getting rid of the money. They spend lavishly, beyond even their considerable means. Or they make stupid investments, telling themselves they will prove their worth by increasing their wealth many times over, while in truth they are working their way toward bankruptcy as a way to expunge their guilt. Or they give it away; philanthropies are the beneficiaries of their penitence.

These are people who are constantly at odds with who they are because of what they were given. They end up in the unenviable position of being financially blessed, yet emotionally cursed. Suffering from a kind of schizophrenia, they cannot enjoy their good fortune. Peter Collier and David Horowitz, in their book *The Rockefellers*, traced a number of the descendants of John D. and found many who are miserable because of their money, their misery intensified by the name they bear. "Most of the fourth Rockefeller generation," say the authors, "have spent long years with psychiatrists in their efforts to grapple with the money and the family. . . . To some degree, they are all princes and princesses yearning to be paupers" (pp. 506–507).

With each succeeding generation, the problem compounds itself, because, in effect, you become an economic aristocrat in a country where you feel isolated and uncomfortable if you are outside the ranks of the middle class. Americans tend to revere wealth, are curious about it, and like to associate with it, but they still think of the rich as very much apart from the mainstream. Feeling their estrangement, the children of the Rockefellers and Vanderbilts often view themselves as poor little rich kids.

We came out of the Reagan years with a raft of people of enormous, fresh-minted wealth, creating a host of new dynasties. Europe is full of such dynasties. As a matter of fact, Europe, because of the kind of tax avoidance that is still possible there, has fortunes that make our rich look like rank amateurs at amassing money. Fortunes tend to stay intact over there. This is true of South America and the Middle East as well. Dynastic wealth in other societies is familiar and accepted. In this country it is viewed as a deviation from the norm, almost immoral.

To Thine Own Self

When I am consulted by those who have inherited a great deal of money and I see they are torn apart by ambivalence toward it, I tell them that they would almost assuredly be far better off if they just went ahead and lived in a way that reflects their affluence rather than trying to disguise it or rid themselves of it. In one case you end up going through life feeling a fraud and an imposter, and in the other, you end up unpleasantly broke. If their social alliances change as a result of living honestly—and it's not certain but it *is* likely—then they must accept that.

Not every inheritor of millions is doomed to discontent, of course. Many manage to lick the curse and find a way to be happy on their own terms. I think of one man I know who has third-generation wealth. He decided to live in a small town, because in his case it was where he felt he could achieve anonymity. His name was not instantly recognizable, but it would be more readily known in big cities. He bought a nice house in the suburbs, the kind of neighborhood where successful doctors and lawyers live. It was a very comfortable house, but far less opulent than he could have afforded; this pretty much defines his total life-style. I asked him what he does for a living.

"I don't do anything, and I don't intend to do anything. I look after my investments, I spend time with my family, with my children. I want to live that way and I'm perfectly content doing it. I don't need to prove anything. I don't want to prove anything. I just want to live my life."

He's uninvolved with any charitable organization, but not because he lacks compassion; he makes substantial charitable gifts, but anonymously. He doesn't want to be in the limelight and he doesn't want constant solicitation and harassment.

I consider him a success as an heir. He doesn't seem the least bit neurotic. He's self-contained, absolutely at ease with who and what he is. His pleasures come from his family, not from consumption and status. In a way, he is an imposter, because there's a big difference between the way he lives and who he is financially. But he seems to have bridged that gap successfully.

There are others I've known who have compromised, but also with considerable success. They live more luxuriously than the fellow just described but not as lavishly as they could. Having come from socially prominent families, they also feel a sense of duty to carry on a legacy of public service, of supporting charities, and of being involved in their communities. They, too, would prefer to live out of the limelight, but they feel almost forced to carry on a tradition. However, they draw the line. They find one or two causes they truly care about and become deeply involved in, but they don't sit on a dozen boards.

A Healthy Division

Dynastic wealth—fortunes of one hundred or several hundred million dollars—is one thing; succeeding generations have a hard time dissipating that much money. But in other, more modest cases, the problems of inherited wealth are often self-correcting. The children of the middling rich are likely to have the opposite problem than the one the parents have suffered from.

Let's say a couple has inherited $5 million and they have three children. The $5 million was put out to earn interest, so the family's income was supplemented by $400,000 a year, obviously ensuring that they dwell in great comfort. The parents die and that income, after a 50 percent inheritance tax and a three-way division of the remainder, is one-sixth of what it had been. So the children, expecting to live at the same level they have been accustomed to, quickly and decisively are brought to a far lower level of incremental income, about $65,000 a year for each. That's not peanuts, but there's clearly been a generational degradation of life-style. But the kids don't get it. They've never thought it through. Their reality is substantial affluence, and telling them to enjoy their adolescence because their adulthood is going to be materially different is pretty tough to sell. It just isn't believed until it's experienced.

Maybe that's healthier. Maybe that supplies the motivation that's missing when too much money is handed to the next generation. But just try to convince the kids of that.

8. The Trouble with Parents

It isn't just relationships that parents have with their children that create money conflicts; there are conflicts, too, in the relationships children have with aging parents. I get a lot of calls from men and women who say, "My father just died and my mother, who's 75, inherited $2 million. I'd like your help in talking some sense to her about how to invest that money." What I usually find out the caller means by "talking sense" is that he or she is thinking, "Mom'll live another maybe ten years, and that $2 million could be $4 million if we put it into stocks." But stocks are the last thing Mom has on her mind. At her age she doesn't need growth. She's going to be a lot happier if all the money's in Treasury bonds throwing off $150,000 a year. It's safe, it's trouble-free, it's income, and that's what she needs. So if I meet with her, that's exactly what I tell her to do—put the money in Treasuries, or certificates of deposit at 20 different banks, if that's what makes her comfortable. And I tell the sons or daughters, "Don't interfere, because if your mother puts the money into the stock market and the market takes a plunge like it did in October 1987 or October 1989 or August 1990, and scares the daylights out of her, what you will first be the beneficiary of is her anxiety. She will make your life miserable. No amount of money can compensate you for how her life—and as a consequence, your life—would be turned upside down."

The older people are—and it's as true of men as of women—the more important it is that the money is placed where it involves the least amount of discomfort and looking after and the highest degree of certainty. Older people are terrified that they will outdistance their capital, and it does no good to demonstrate to them that they could go through $100,000 a year and not run out of money until they are 105; they simply don't care. Another common issue is their fear of abandonment: as long as they have money to dispense, either currently or in the future, they feel assured they will have the attention of those around them.

In my experience, a widow is much more likely to solicit financial advice from her children than a widower is from his. But that may be a generational difference, and will probably change as working women become more familiar with money matters and feel they can handle their own financial affairs when their spouses are gone. Though older people are generally ultra-conservative, occasionally a widower will take it into his head to do things that drive his offspring up the wall. If the surviving women are too timid for their children, the men, to judge by some of the calls I get, can be just the opposite: "My father is 82 years old and he is a financial madman," I hear on the phone. "What can I do?" The answer is, short of having the courts declare him incompetent, nothing.

The other terror for children is that Daddy will find some sweet young thing who's pushing 60. It happens all the time. And when he does, he indulges her in ways in which their mother was never indulged. That hurts the children, who see this intrusion in their lives getting jewelry and trips to the Orient that their mother never had. If Dad decides to marry her, and especially if she has children, they are terrified there's going to be nothing left for them. They call me, and my guess is that they call anybody they think has the remotest possibility of providing a solution more in line with their self-interest. They are desperate. They have lost control of the old man.

I refuse to get in the middle of a situation like that. I guess I subscribe to the Oriental belief that if you're old enough, you get to do any damn thing you want.

5

THE RISK COMPONENT

1. The Uncommon Attraction of Common Stocks

We have already determined that common stocks are the risk investment of preference. After a retired person's sanctuary assets are set aside and invested in Treasuries to ensure the income that will in turn ensure a desired life-style, whatever money is left can go into stocks. Stocks can make your money grow, or take a dive, but as long as the life-style-supporting capital is sacrosanct, that risk can be borne.

There is nothing magical about stocks. They are simply another place to put money. I don't maintain that stocks are superior to real estate, precious metals, coins, Chinese porcelain, or anything else you can invest in. Over long periods of time the alternatives will probably generate comparable returns, if they entail comparable risk. The principal virtue of stocks is their liquidity. You can sell stocks and have your money by noon, which is hardly true of an office building. Stocks pay a dividend along the way, which gold and porcelain do not. Stocks are easier to manage than, say, real estate. Most people of wealth have made the decision, rightly in my estimation, that stocks represent the most sensible way to make money passively.

How much money? What returns *can* you expect from stocks? When I ask people that question, more often than not, I am appalled by what I hear.

People have numbers in their head, numbers that come from the media, including advertising. They read a story in *Barron's* or *Forbes* about some manager who has been a star for the last three years, or they come across an ad for the Magellan Fund or some other big winner, so they see a lot in print that has 20s in it. They think they should get, at a minimum, 20 percent a year from their stocks. Maybe they'll settle for the high teens. And, of course, I am supposed to know the very gurus who can do it for them. The rich tend to see this kind of reward for their money as their entitlement.

Rarely do the editorial features, much less the ads, explain that such returns are way beyond historical norms, and though managers can have a couple of great years, nobody brings in that kind of money forever. How many times have you bought into a mutual fund because some magazine's ranking showed it was the Number One performer, up 42 percent, the year before, only to find that in the year when you plunked down your money, the manager tanked and ended up near the bottom of the ranking? Peter Lynch, the investment genius who ran Magellan until he retired a couple of years ago at the age of 46, said openly that there was no way he could continue to bring in the kind of numbers he had in the past.

Historical Returns

So I often have to explain the financial facts of life to folks. I point out that over the long term—and I mean 65 years of history—the return on stocks, including dividends, has been between 10 and 11 percent a year (see Figure 5.1). Treasury bonds have returned about 5 percent and stocks give you more, as compensation for the extra risk. But it's still 10 percent, not 20 percent.

As we moved into the last decade of this century, investors enjoyed an extraordinary bull market that really commenced in 1974, so 20 percent returns were indeed captured by a few managers over a considerable roll. But that is a historical anomaly, and there will be a couple of years out there when the math will be reconciled. It's generally not a good

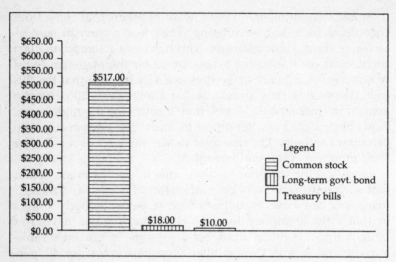

Figure 5.1 65-year history of asset classes (value of $1 invested, 12/31/25–12/31/90).
Source: Stocks, Bonds, Bills, & Inflation, *1991 Yearbook,* Ibbotson Associates, Chicago.

idea to argue with probabilities, because they have a way of reasserting themselves. That is particularly true if there's a lot of history behind the figures, and 65 years is a good chunk of stock market history.

You can make a case for a grimmer scenario if you want, because we're in an environment where inflation rates are trending down and tax rates are relatively low, and since the world is a pretty rational place, returns might adjust down even further. It can happen fairly quickly. For the ten years from 1980 through the end of 1989, the Standard & Poor's 500 index turned in a very handsome annual average return of 17.3 percent. But then the market dropped, modestly, in 1990, and for the ten years through the end of that year, the annual average return of the S&P 500 dropped to 15.3 percent. One can see how a few disappointing, negative years in this decade can restore the historical average handily. Rarely are there long periods when money falls out of the sky.

Rational Expectations

That doesn't mean we all have to settle for 10 percent as our long-term goal. If you tell me, "The average isn't good enough for me," I would answer, "I agree." I am not suggesting you put your money into an index fund—and there are mutual funds that replicate the market—and thereby earn market returns. I am in the business of searching for the gifted managers who can bring in an increment to that return, who can, in the jargon of the trade, "add value."

How much value? If you can find managers who can earn 20 percent to 50 percent better than the market—anywhere from 12 percent to 15 percent a year over long periods of time—you've got a lot to be happy about. Look at Table 5.1. It shows you what a difference 2, 3, 4, or 5 percentage points more than the average can do for your money, and the difference becomes increasingly dramatic the longer your money is invested. On a pretax basis, 10 percent compounded doubles your money in a little more than seven years, 15 percent in about five.

Is even 15 percent—50 percent better than the market—likely over longer periods of time? Frankly, no. But it is possible. If you settle for 12 percent or 13 percent as the number you are shooting for, then you have quite a reasonable chance of gratification. When you look for 15 percent, you're pushing at the edge. Don't forget, every manager is pitted against every other manager, and there are very few people who manage money

Table 5.1   The Difference a Percentage Point of Annual Return Makes (the value of $100,000 earning the following percentages, compounded)

Percent	10 Years	20 Years	30 Years
10%	$259,374	$672,750	$1,744,940
11%	283,942	806,231	2,289,230
12%	310,585	964,629	2,995,992
13%	339,457	1,152,309	3,911,590
14%	370,722	1,374,349	5,095,016
15%	404,556	1,636,654	6,621,177

who have poor SAT scores. This is a world dominated by very bright, well-educated, highly competitive people. When it comes to intelligence and education, it's a fairly level playing field. When it come to intuitive skills, it stops being level. But there are ranges of excellence beyond which you cannot expect to go.

Also don't forget that I've been talking about pretax returns. Unfortunately, taxes are another reality that has to be faced. If we apply an arbitrary tax rate of 40 percent—federal, state, and local—then a 15 percent return will allow you to keep 9 percent. If you generate a 9 percent after-tax return, compounded quarterly, you'll double your money at about eight-year intervals. Live sixteen years and your $1 million will turn into $4 million.

But that, I again emphasize, is the upper range of expectation. It is very well grounded in history. Of course, there will always be plenty of people around who will promise better, far better, returns, particularly as we came out of the generous 1980s. I think of Charles Givens' enormously successful *Wealth Without Risk*, which promised its readers "20 percent per year safely." I believe that statement is irresponsible. If you expect 20 percent "safely," disappointment is virtually guaranteed.

> The average annual return from an unmanaged portfolio of representative common stocks: 10 percent
>
> A realistic long-term goal from a professionally managed portfolio: 12 to 15 percent

2. Do It on Your Own?

Before considering the best way to approach the stock market, a couple of questions need to be asked. You have to be sensitive to the kind of person you are before you get involved in a risk market. We all tend to share similarities in our tolerance toward risk that reflect our age, but temperaments do make a difference.

If someone tells me she has never owned a stock in her life, for example, I'm not going to advise her to begin at the age of 60. Throughout her life she must have considered stocks as a place to park some of her money, and dismissed the idea. I don't want to impose changes that might be good economic solutions but that will rachet up the anxiety quotient. Again, that's exactly what wealth shouldn't do. There are clients whom I advise to keep *all* their money in Treasuries because they simply have *no* appetite for risk, and you may be just such a person.

I am very frank with these people. I say, "Look, you're 60 years old, and it's not as though you've never had any capital. You have an IRA, for example, and you didn't put it into stocks. You've looked at the options over your adult life and you have systematically rejected the stock market as a place for your money. Well, I don't think you should start the learning process at this stage in your life."

I lost a very big account with such words not long ago. The man, in his 60s, had owned real estate and cash . . . period. But he was trying to tell me that he had enough cash, enough real estate, and that he'd like to diversify into stocks. I said, "O.K., maybe, but before we do anything, I still think you ought to go back and reflect on this for a couple of days." I offended him. He didn't want to be lectured to. He ended up going to someone else. But I believe I was right. To change after 60 is a stretch, and I wonder how happy he is with his decision. At that age your tolerance for risk certainly hasn't increased.

What's Your Record?

If there *has* been a history of involvement in stocks, I want to know what sort of stocks have been owned. If you are someone who has held General Motors, IBM, and Coca-Cola, you are not going to be happy with mutual funds or investment advisors who specialize in the Genentechs and Price Clubs of the world. Did you buy the stocks on your own or did you rely on a broker? How did you decide on the stocks you picked? How long, generally, did you hang on to them? You have to understand your own investment profile when you go looking for a mutual fund or investment counselor.

And how's your record been? I send home some people who come to see me to help them find managers. It's clear they don't need an investment counselor—or me. They do just fine on their own. Their records are as good as the professionals'. Usually, the only reason they've come to see me is that they are in their mid-60s and worried about the future. "I've been investing in the market for years," they'll say, "and I think I've done a pretty good job. But one of these days, you know, I'll be going to my reward, and I don't want all my money in Treasury bills when I die. My wife has no interest in this stuff. So I thought maybe I ought to let someone else start to run the stocks, and I just kind of wanted to get a sense of what it is you do."

Stock-picking Successes

What sort of people *are* good at investing in the stock market?

For one thing, they care, passionately, about investing. They have been very serious about it, almost all their lives. They devote considerable time to their portfolios. They read *The Wall Street Journal, Barron's, Forbes, Fortune,* and *Business Week.* They watch "Wall Street Week." They know exactly what they've invested in and precisely how they've done. There are no delusions, no "I-bought-XYZ-at-10-and-now-it's-100" stuff. They'll tell you about their losers as well as their winners, and can state, in percentage terms, what their rates of return have been.

Usually they are good businesspeople with a honed sense of what a good business is. They recognize a well-managed and well-positioned company, and they buy its stock because they want to own a piece of it. Sometimes they see a company in their own industry with a new product or process that excites them—"They're going to eat everybody else's lunch"—but they are more likely to invest in other industries. People have this peculiar quirk of believing other businesses are infinitely easier and more rewarding than their own.

They don't follow any one style, the way professionals do. One day they'll buy a stock because they think it's a bargain and the next pay up for a very high-priced stock because they have decided the company has it all over the competition. They are just financial eclectics and opportunists.

They'll own 15, maybe 20, stocks, most of them large, well-known companies. The process isn't very complicated for them. They'll go out to buy a cellular phone, be impressed with Motorola's product—particularly because it seemed better than the Japanese-made phones—and they'll write the company for an annual report. They'll read a bit more about the company at the library and in brokerage reports, and decide "it's a hell of a company," and that's that. Or on a trip to Atlanta a friend tells them about a new Home Depot store and they'll go take a look. "There was a traffic jam out front of the place. I spent more than an hour in the store and was very impressed. My friend says they're killing everybody else in that business. So I bought 500 shares." Or they bought SmithKlein when it came out with Tagamet "because everybody I know is flirting with an ulcer these days. That one was as sure as sliced bread."

They'll study SmithKlein's annual report and maybe look up the company in *The Value Line Investment Survey*. They might ask for their broker's opinion, but it isn't likely. Their broker is usually a nephew or somebody they like, so they give him the business, but they don't rely on him for ideas. They don't bone up on Federal Drug Administration policy or look at ten pharmaceutical companies before buying SmithKlein. Do they know the company's return on equity? No. Do they know what return on equity is? Yes, they know. But businessmen tend not to think in those terms. Because unless you have a publicly traded company, all you are interested in is the bottom line. Am I going to make $1 million this year or $3 million? If the return on equity is 17 percent, that's all very interesting, but it isn't as relevant as what's going in their own pockets. They aren't shackled, as many of us are, by too much Hamlet-like analysis and caution. And they don't trade much. They sell a stock when they think the idea has run its course—say, four other companies come out with products that compete with Tagamet.

They are not likely to sell because they think the market has become too pricey either—though they may hold back from buying when they think euphoria has taken over. I believe their insensitivity to the general market is their one failing. To earn really superior returns you have not only to find good investments but also to match your buying with market cycles. I don't mean short-term trading, but there are times when the market is so high it's only good sense to scale back or not play for a while. But these people are relatively indifferent to the market. They have an implicit faith that the market works and that equity works. And they have an implicit faith, too, in their own skills.

To such people I simply say, "You've done a great job. You know what you're doing, and what's more important, you like doing it." One thing wealth makes possible is the pursuit of one's interests. I would tell you, if you are such a person, to keep on running your own money even if you weren't doing as well as you are, because if you pay someone else to do it, it would create a big hole in your life. If you are 67 years old and you've got a lot of dough and you love investing, what difference does it make, when they cash you out, if you are worth $12 million or $14 million or $9 million? Besides, you probably wouldn't be a good client of an investment counselor. You know too much about investments. It would be very hard for you to be passive.

As for your wife after you are gone, I say, "My advice is to tell your wife that when you die, she should sell the stock and put the money into Treasury bills. Yes, I know that's not the way to make money grow. But she can live well and not have to bother about annual reports and days when stocks fall 10 percent. She's going to be 75 years old and alone, and the last thing she needs to worry about is the Dow Jones Industrial Average."

3. Hodgepodge Portfolios

The usual pattern, however, is far different from the example of someone who has proved his or her ability to deal with the stock market. Most people have tried investing in stocks, usually with the help of a broker, and have decided that they don't have the interest, time, resources, or skills to make a success of it.

The stories I hear are pretty predictable. "I've been working with a broker for about ten years now"—and they usually add that they consider him or her "a dear friend"—"but I just haven't had the results I want." Some have lost money, most haven't made much, and it has dawned on them that they should be doing better, that it is probably easier to find a good professional money manager than it is to find good stocks. Or the stakes have simply become too high. They have started out with a little money in the market, but now they realize they are dealing with hundreds of thousands, or even millions, of dollars, and trying to run the money themselves is truly like high-stakes amateur night at the Follies.

Many who have done a lousy job of investing won't admit it for quite some time. Their egos won't allow that. So they'll just keep hitting their heads against the wall until they are finally ready to say, "I'm no good at this. I'm more confused all the time by the noise out there. I want professional help."

They also feel that with the market increasingly dominated by institutions—80 percent of the trading reflects institutional decisions, often distorted by program trading—they need to be on the institutional side themselves. They decide they had damn well better join the enemy rather than stand in the way and get mowed down.

Some got caught up in a speculative binge, trading wildly, buying on margin, and chasing the hot stocks of tiny companies that run into trouble the minute they are no longer tiny. But these people have finally come to their senses. They are fed up with losing and with the frenetic quality of the game.

Random Recommendations

The amateurs also come to realize the senselessness of what they are doing. When I look at portfolios, for the most part I see a potpourri of broker ideas. You know how it works. The broker has a new stock to pitch and rings you up. You bite or you don't, depending on whether you are in town or tied up in meetings, the amount of free cash on hand, and your mood at the time. If you are having a good day, and there's money in the bank, and the broker has what sounds like a reasonable story, your response is, "O.K., buy 300." If you're having a bad day, you say, "Not now. Call back on Monday." And if you're having a *really* bad day, you don't even take the call and probably save yourself some money for a change. It is that random, really. So you end up with a hodgepodge for a portfolio. Rarely, with a broker-managed or broker-involved portfolio, do you see any rhyme, reason, or cohesiveness to the holdings. There's no underlying approach, no discipline, and no balance. You generally see gross overweighting in one or two positions the broker or client, or both, have become enamored of.

You also tend to see a pattern: long-term capital losses and short-term gains. All I have to do is to look at the tax returns of people to get an idea of their inadequacies as investors. The usual is 15 percent to 20 percent short-term gains, and long-term losses that are three times that amount. What happens is that the minute a person's stock goes below the price paid for it, the belief becomes fixed in his or her mind that it will come back. "I'll just wait it out until it crosses the line again." So no decision is required. Then, later, when the stock just sits below the line month after month, or sinks lower, the person can't stand it anymore and sells.

It's when these people have a *profit* that they worry about the stock day and night. Nothing is as disquieting as a profit, particularly if it was quickly achieved. "Should I sell it, and take my gain? But it looks so strong—maybe I should hold for a bit longer." Brokers know how to play on that anxiety. "Look, let's sell it, then," they say, "and we'll look for something else." The broker's compensation schedule assists him or her in delivering this wisdom.

These people fool themselves. More than half the time, unlike those who are good at investing, they don't even know what their real returns have been, much less make the rudimentary comparisons between their returns and those of the Dow Jones Industrial Average, the Standard & Poor's 500 index, or mutual funds that have goals similar to theirs. Most of the time when you ask people how they've done in the market, they simply tote up all their successes and conveniently forget to factor in the bombs. Selective memory seems to be part of the human condition.

Emotions Rule

Another common danger for those who invest on their own is that they fall in love with their stocks. Investors who defend their decision to run their own portfolio will say, "I don't speculate and I'm not a trader. I just buy blue-chip companies and put them in the vault." That sounds admirably responsible, but the fact is that companies change, and their stocks may have to be sold. IBM is the perfect example. A blue-chip company, certainly, but in recent years also a mediocre company. Its shareholders have fared poorly. But selling IBM, so much a part of our culture, for most people is akin to an abdication of faith in America. A professional investor is more likely to be dispassionate about selling decisions.

Often people blame their broker if their investment record has been less than impressive, forgetting that they have enormous complicity in the outcome of their investments. And I don't say that there aren't competent brokers. Of course there are. I understand that the people who come to see me tend to be those investors who have had the incompetents. Another group of investors that I am not likely to see are those who are so hooked on the whole process they feel they could never relinquish control to somebody else. But unlike those who *do* succeed in the market, making money is really secondary for these people. They are action junkies. They, and not their brokers, are responsible for the constant turmoil in their portfolios. But brokers know how to play to this craving for action, to create a sense that things are moving quickly, that new pieces of information have come up that require immediate responses. They foster the frenetic quality of the process. So you have the doctor who leaves the operating room to ring up his broker, that sort of thing. It's a form of entertainment. And some people are perfectly happy to pay the price for that entertainment.

But even they can tire of the gambling and its stresses. They are ready to give it all up to someone who spends full time at it, who is more dispassionate, and who is, presumably, a trained, experienced, and competent professional. After all, it isn't play money that is being squandered. The decision is made to buy investment talent.

Why most people do poorly investing in stocks on their own:

- They don't devote enough time to the process.
- They don't have the necessary training and skills.
- They take their cues from a broker, who is probably more interested in commissions than long-term results.
- They let their emotions sway their judgment.
- They hold on to losses, in order to "get even," and sell their winners too soon.
- They trade too often, because they like the "action."
- They have no system, discipline, or consistent approach.

---

4. Don't Knock Mutual Funds

If you are not going to deal with the stock market on your own but have decided to turn the job over to a professional, how do you find the talent most likely to bring in that incremental 2 percent to 5 percent return?

For someone who cares about nothing but the outcome and is not interested in the process, mutual funds are hard to beat.

One of the first questions people ask me, when they find out I help investors place money with investment advisors, is why anybody needs his or her own manager. Why not just go with mutual funds? And my answer is that if they find a fund with a manager who has a good long-term investment record, and they know that that individual has for sure been the person responsible for that record and that he or she is still in charge of the fund (and the Securities and Exchange

Commission is working on a way to mandate that the name of the person in charge be disclosed at all times), there is no reason whatsoever not to place their money in that fund. If the record is long enough—ten years would be best, because the manager has run the fund not just through a bull market like that of 1982–1989 but in a bear environment as well—you have seen a resume of the person you are considering. If the record is a good one, hire him.

An Ideal Product

In fact, mutual funds are probably the best engineered product ever created for people who want to invest money. Most have minimums of $1000, which makes it possible for those starting to build or still building their fortunes to access some of the country's finest investment talent. To hire an investment counselor, you need at least $250,000, and many of the best demand $1 million or more. With the funds' small minimums, you can diversify and have a portfolio of managers with different strengths and styles. You can hire them at your leisure by calling an 800 number and can terminate them at your leisure with equal simplicity. The accounting is uncomplicated. Every month you receive a crisp statement and at year-end a statement you can take to your accountant. The progress of your money is documented in the daily newspaper. And the financial press provides multiple and inexpensive sources of information about which managers have done well and for how long.

In a number of cases, as a matter of fact, a firm manages both mutual funds and separate accounts for individual investors, and the types of portfolios usually look roughly the same. Mario Gabelli is considered one of the best managers of our day, and he will run your money on a segregated basis—if you have a million dollars to give him—or in his mutual funds. What you are really searching for is the best investment talent, and if that talent is running a mutual fund, you should seriously consider that option, even if you do have a million to invest.

Many magazines—*Forbes, Business Week, Money, Financial World*—publish mutual fund directories and rankings. Philosophically, I like the funds that *Forbes* rates A in down markets and B in up markets (rarely does a fund deserve an A in both). The mathematics suggest that if you have negative returns that are deep or sustained, you have undermined the advantages of compounding. If you are down 50 percent, you have then to be up 100 percent just to get even.

Forbes also publishes an annual Honor Roll of funds with good long-term records and reveals how long the managers have been running the funds. I wouldn't buy a fund whose manager hasn't been responsible for its record for at least five years—unless I know of his ability in a previous position—and ten years is probably not twice but four times as important as five years. Any manager can have a run of luck for a couple of years, and even the most distinguished can have a few difficult years; generally it has more to do with his or her style being out of favor than with a loss of skill. Those who have the gift seldom lose it. The prospectus will not tell you how long the current manager has been in charge of the fund. Either ask when you call the 800 number, or, to be sure you are getting the right information, write to the president of the fund and ask for the answer to that vital question.

I recommend systematic investments into funds because these end up creating a dollar-cost-averaging program. That is, if the fund's shares drop in price, the investor will be buying more shares when they are cheaper—a good discipline to enhance long-term returns. But that fact is almost incidental. What is important is that the money gets socked away religiously, providing the benefits of compounding. The thrift ethic is what makes you rich eventually.

It is hard, even frightening, to keep buying when values are falling. Most people, when they see a decline in their investments, want to sell and get out of the market. If you can buy an asset for 80 cents that would have cost you $1 a month ago, it would seem an attractive deal, but, again, psychology confronts rationality. The fact that the odds have improved encourages people not to make another bet but to leave the game. But the discipline of regular commitments, regardless of the emotions of the moment, is the way to make money. It may seem risky to buy when all the negatives are in the headlines, but in the end, stocks are the safest, not the riskiest, investments. In the long run they always move higher, and they are the best way to hedge against inflation.

Diversify Your Funds

I also recommend owning a portfolio of funds rather than one fund, no matter how good its manager. Styles go in and out of favor, and one should own funds following different styles. I would have a combination of three to five equity funds, with relatively equal weightings. If you own three, I would suggest one growth fund, one value fund, and one international fund—and we'll look more closely at these styles shortly. If you have five funds, I would have a large-capitalization growth fund, a small-capitalization growth fund (in other words, growth funds that specialize in large, household-name companies and growth funds that concentrate on smaller, less-well-known companies), a large-capitalization value fund, a small-capitalization value fund, and an international fund.

I am not particularly enamored of balanced funds or growth-and-income funds. My argument is the same as the one presented when we looked at sanctuary and risk in an earlier chapter. You buy stocks for appreciation and you buy bonds to produce income, and these funds that do both are, to me, a bastardization of the investment process. So I would prefer buying an equity fund in concert with a fixed-income fund whenever an investor is looking to mutual funds for exposure to both types of assets. However, I realize the convenience of a pre-mixed balanced or growth-and-income fund is attractive: hence the inclusion of such funds in my asset allocation recommendations in Figure 2.1(c).

I would keep the weightings of the equity funds equal. That is, if your small-capitalization growth fund manager falls behind, because smaller companies have been out of favor, then new money should be allocated to that fund to bring its dollar-value level up to that of the other funds. It's a kind of averaging again, knowing that styles out of favor will rebound, and you are simply buying shares when they are cheapest. If a fund is worth holding, it's worth rebalancing your portfolio.

If you have lost faith in the fund, because the manager has left or seems to have indeed lost his or her ability—and we will discuss reviews of investment managers in a later chapter—that is a different matter. Then you need to switch funds, and to fire that manager and hire another. But as long as you believe in the manager, and think the fund's faltering performance is not evidence of the manager's loss of skills but stems rather from a temporary swing in the preference of the market and the investment public, then it is just smart to double-up.

Pay Up for Talent

No-load funds are the obvious preference, since no one wants to pay an unnecessary entrance fee, but I would not hesitate to buy a load fund if the manager is one of the three to five I would like to run my money. If you want the talent, you pay the price. Very few funds still charge an $8\frac{1}{2}$ percent load; most loads are closer to 5 percent. If you were in a personal-injury suit and you could get someone like Melvin Belli to handle your case, you wouldn't quibble if he charged you 35 percent instead of 30 percent of your settlement. And if you needed surgery, a 5 percent difference in a celebrated surgeon's fee compared to that of most others wouldn't discourage you from going to that doctor. To say you wouldn't hire an outstanding manager because his fund charges 5 percent to become a shareholder would be naive and counterproductive.

Most people think one reason to choose mutual funds over investment managers is that they are cheaper, but that is not true. Investment counseling firms typically charge 1 percent of assets as their fee, paid quarterly, sometimes in advance of the quarter, sometimes at the end of the quarter. Some firms have a lower minimum account size, but also charge a minimum fee; that is, you would pay 1 percent on a $1 million account but 2 percent if you had only one-half million to turn over to the manager. Mutual fund management fees run at about the same level, but you are not aware of it unless you read the prospectus carefully. In fact, a fund can charge as much as $2\frac{1}{4}$ percent; that is the limit in most states. But in most instances the total fees will run between 1 percent and $1\frac{1}{2}$ percent, which includes investment management, custodial charges, and all shareholder services. And that is in addition to any sales charge, if you buy a load fund. So you don't go into mutual funds to save on management costs.

People often focus on fees because it is a tangible matter that leads to ready comparisons. It is easier to compare the fee of Manager A with the fee of Manager B than it is to compare the investment style of Manager A and Manager B. As in any business, there is a lot of jargon thrown around in the investment world, and it intimidates people. They also want to know, if they hire a manager instead of a fund, who has custody of the securities—usually a bank with whom the investment manager has an arrangement—and what the additional fee is for that. It generally runs about 0.3 percent.

Something else to keep in mind is that your professional manager, as an institutional investor buying investment services in volume, pays a lot less to buy and sell stocks than you do when you trade as an individual. An investment counselor generally pays no more than ten cents a share for a trade, and if you see you are being charged more than ten cents for trades in your account, it should certainly raise the question in your mind of whether or not this manager is sensitive to your costs. By all means raise the issue with your manager.

While we are on the subject of fees, some investment managers are also brokers, members of the New York Stock Exchange, and some mutual fund families are run by organizations affiliated with member firms. Most of these are in New York, simply because a number of firms there started as stockbrokers and later expanded into investment management for clients who wanted the service. People worry that, because these firms earn commissions on some trades, as well as management fees, they will have an incentive to churn the account. It is true that there is a potential conflict of interest, but the fact is that there's no cause for worry. The firms place trades with many brokerage houses to gain access to their research. But even for the trades handled internally, the firms know that it would be poor business policy as well as a breach of ethics to exploit the situation. It has been my experience that these firms are very sensitive to the question and seldom do anything that could justify criticism of their handling of trades.

Why a mutual fund?

- Access to some of the industry's best talent
- Records and other information about funds readily available
- Low minimum investment requirements
- Can own several funds with different styles
- Easy access and exit
- Regular, easy-to-understand statements
- Daily newspaper reporting on progress
- Simplifies dollar-cost-averaging
- Reasonable costs and fees

---

5. The Pros for Hiring Your Own Pro

If there are mutual funds run by people who have proved themselves over time, why, then, would anyone want an investment counselor?

To be honest, vanity is a major factor. People with a million dollars or more to pass out understandably feel that they deserve and can afford their own, segregated account and their own personal list of stocks. They don't want to be just one more shareholder among thousands. They don't want to commingle with the masses.

But there is more to it than that. They are interested in the process as well as the outcome. They want, in addition to a talented manager, someone to interact with. They want a dialogue. You can't, after all, call up your mutual fund's manager and ask questions. Also, they want to feel that they are putting their own imprint on the process through that dialogue. They want a closer identification with the people making the decisions. Perhaps more important than talking to the managers periodically is knowing that they can. In some ways, availability of access is as important as the access itself, because the truth is that they usually don't have that many discussions with their investment managers. The usual, after the first year, is two or three times a year.

Curbing Harmful Impulses

These dialogues suggest another very important reason some people might be better off with a counselor than with a mutual fund. Beyond performance, you have to consider how human beings react to heavy losses during market declines. If your money is in a fund, you still control the decision of whether or not to stay in the market, and you can't call up your fund manager to talk the matter over.

The longer a bear market lasts and the greater the sense of threat, the more probable it is that the mutual fund shareholder will panic, reach for the phone, switch to a money market fund near the bottom, and then not be around for the upside of the battle. It isn't easy to resist that urge; even professionals can succumb to it.

The longer a bear market persists, the more the media buys into the proposition that we're flirting with a depression. The economic news becomes more and more frightening. Negatives get underscored and projected into the future. The poor, confused person whose capital is diminished by 20 percent is led to believe by the vast majority of the opinion he or she is reading that 20 percent will prove a cheap hit because before long it's going to be 40 percent or 50 percent. The anxiety becomes unbearable. The investor, most humanly, needs to remove the stress from his or her life and says, "The hell with the stock market; it's no place for me."

That's what bottoms are all about. It isn't very complicated: the math tells you that the further down the market goes, the better the probabilities that you'll make money from that point. So the greater the pain, the closer you are to the bottom. But people can't stand that pain. And they have different thresholds. Some people get to theirs after a 10 percent drop. Investing is this constant battle between rationality and emotionality. For many, many individuals, the emotionality will prevail.

So if you suspect that is how you are likely to behave—that you will get out of stocks at a time when you probably should be buying them instead—then mutual funds probably shouldn't be your first choice. If you have enough money to hire a counselor, you'd better do it. A good investment counselor—partly because it is your money and not his and partly because of his training and experience—is better at curbing emotions and maintaining rationality and objectivity. And he or she can talk some sense to clients, give them some perspective, calm them down. If you do *not* have enough investable money to interest a counselor, and mutual funds are your only option, then you'd better learn to discipline yourself. Make up your mind when you go into a fund that if the fund manager performs well—and that doesn't mean that if the market is down, he or she won't be down, too— you will stick with him or her for the long haul. Let reason, not emotion, rule your decisions.

Greater Portfolio Flexibility

There are two other advantages an investment counselor may have over a mutual fund. If a mutual fund has a good record and keeps growing and growing, the manager will have to own a much broader list of issues. What you essentially want from your manager is his or her best ideas, to discriminate among the thousands of stocks, and distill the list down to 20 or 30. If someone has to buy 100 stocks, instead of 30, the probability is that the level of passion for the 70 add-ons is lower than for the 30. Investment counselors can get "too big," too, of course, but it tends to happen faster with mutual funds, because press publicity can bring in a flood of money in a matter of months. At one point the Magellan Fund owned more than 1000 stocks.

Another factor can put mutual funds at a disadvantage: because emotionally driven shareholders can make switches over the phone, flows of money into and out of the fund tend to come at difficult times. In the jargon of the trade, the money comes in on spikes in the market and goes out on troughs. So the manager has to put money to work when the market is expensive and liquidate some stocks in advance of expected redemptions, or liquidate into a declining market to raise money for those cashing out. He usually has to keep 5 percent or 10 percent of his money in cash, in case of redemptions, even when he would rather be fully invested. Good mutual fund managers have shown that they can handle these exigencies reasonably well, but the manager of a segregated account doesn't have to deal with that pressure.

> ### Advantages of a separate account with an investment counselor:
>
> - Your own personal portfolio
> - Ability to communicate with your manager
> - Manager is less likely to abandon stocks during periods of market weakness
> - Manager has more freedom in portfolio structure, stock selection, and cash position

6. Starting the Search

If you have decided that you would prefer your own investment manager, how do you go about it?

It is not easy. My associates and I have seen some 4000 managers, and there are probably that many again out there. The precise number is difficult to come by, because so many securities brokers and financial planners have registered as investment advisors. All it takes to call yourself a registered investment advisor is to mail $150 to the Securities and Exchange Commission and attest that you have never been convicted of a felony. In the city of New York it is easier to find an investment counselor than it is a working pay telephone.

Twenty years ago the banks had most of the counseling business, sharing it with a handful of national firms such as Scudder, Stevens, & Clark; Loomis Sayles; Stein, Roe, & Farnham; and—a firm now defunct—Lionel D. Edie. Then came low-cost computing, which allowed anybody who wanted to manage money to get into the business for a pittance; he or she could track thousands of stocks from data banks and easily handle all of the administrative burdens. At the same time small businesses and professional corporations were setting up pension plans, creating an enticing local institutional market. So the number of counseling firms grew from hundreds to thousands. They were helped, too, by the horrendous performance records at the banks, particularly in the bear market of the early 1970s. And, of course, the number of mutual funds exploded as well, especially during the prolonged bull market of the 1980s. There are now more mutual funds than there are stocks listed on the New York Stock Exchange.

When you have that large a universe of managers, most are going to cluster around the average. The average may be better than you've done on your own, but you'd like to think you can find somebody who will do *better* than 10 percent a year.

Your first problem in finding those who are above average in generating returns is that, as I've mentioned, you may not have enough money to interest them. Those who have proved they are good over many years have everybody knocking on their doors. Most of the managers I work with have at least $1 million minimums. Some investment managers have created partnership mechanisms to allow, say, four unrelated parties to kick in one-quarter million each to create a $1 million pool that will meet the account minimum. It will be treated as a single account, with the understanding that the participants will have a lower level of communication than the client who has $1 million on his or her own. You may want to ask a manager in whom you are interested if such an arrangement is possible, and if so, you can then look for partners.

Your choices are many when you have a million, but when you don't, they narrow considerably: you either have to go with a manager who seems good but doesn't have as long and outstanding a track record and so is still willing to accept less, or pool your money with others, either to meet a counselor's minimum or through a mutual fund.

Wrap Accounts

There is one other possibility. In just the last few years brokerage firms have set up what are generically called wraparound, or wrap, accounts; each firm will have its own name for its own product. The minimum you need to get into one of these programs is $100,000. The firm has screened a large number of money managers and selected several for each major style. You, the client, are evaluated by a customer's representative, aided by a questionnaire you fill out, who helps you decide which style and which manager from the list are best for you.

Since your money is pooled with that of other investors, you have access to managers with high minimums whom you could not approach on your own. You can feel you have gained entry to top talent usually reserved for the very rich. For this privilege you pay an annual fee of 3 percent, which covers the manager's fee, all commission costs for trades, and the broker's fee for the initial work and continual monitoring of your account and of the managers on the approved list.

My main objection to wrap accounts is that there is no interaction between the investor and the investment manager. If you want to talk to someone, you call the brokerage representative, which just isn't the same. You have given up what's special about an investment management relationship, in a noneconomic sense, but you are paying a high price, high enough to suggest that you *are* getting those benefits. It seems to me that you have bought a mutual fund, a pooled account, at a higher price. You don't have the comfort of dialogues with your own manager that might, for example, get you through some rough times. You might as well put your money in mutual funds and pocket the savings.

One Manager, or Two or Three?

Another issue to be considered is whether it is wiser, even with a million, to give all your money to one manager, no matter how glowing his or her reputation, or, instead, to break up the pot and go for a couple of managers with different styles. If you have just a million for the market, these would have to be managers with lesser minimums, and probably, therefore, a lower level of experience. Or you could pull back from the notion of having your own counselor and split your money among several mutual funds with different approaches to the market.

The virtue of diversification is the same with counselors as it is with mutual funds. Managers have different approaches to the market, and those approaches go in and out of investor favor. So if you have one manager, and, therefore, one style, the time will come when no one cares about that style for two or three years, and you are going to be very aggravated by second-rate performance. If you have two managers, with different styles, your returns from year to year will be more consistent; this makes the market a happier place.

Some people simply don't want multiple managers, no matter how much money they have, because they don't want to bother with multiple relationships. Often I have clients who have started with a modest amount of money which grows to the point where I suggest splitting the account and hiring a second manager, and they'll think about it and say, "No, I'm happy where I am. I'm going to leave it alone." For one thing, they feel bad taking money away from someone who's made a lot of it for them, though managers have come to accept the wisdom of the practice. And they have become comfortable with that person; a new manager would be an unknown.

Another deterrent is that if you really believe in one approach to the market—you are, say, a value investor—and then force yourself to commit funds to a different approach— probably growth investing—it goes against the grain and makes you very uneasy. You could end up owning stocks that are 180 degrees away from your comfort zone. I can appreciate the anxiety that creates. But I still believe it would be a wise measure to take, and that if you don't have enough money for two investment counseling firms, you should use several mutual funds instead. Diversification is worth the compromise, whether among counselors or mutual funds.

If you are one of those fortunates who have $2 million to put into stocks, then I would definitely suggest two managers— one growth manager and one value manager. Definitions are not as precise as some textbooks suggest, but essentially a growth manager is what the name suggests: someone who buys companies whose earnings are growing at a rate significantly higher than that at other companies—usually pegged at about 15 percent for bigger companies and 20 percent or more for smaller companies. Since these companies' ability to grow is well recognized, their stock prices relative to their trailing 12 months' earnings are high. But growth managers are willing to pay up for these stocks, with the justification that earnings are almost sure to be higher next year and the year after that, so that the current price will look cheap before long.

The second million I'd give to a value buyer. Value investors generally shun high P/E (price/earnings) stocks as too expensive. They want bargains, and the most common tool used in digging for bargains is a low P/E. Investors have shunned the stock, and driven down its price-to-earnings multiple, because profits have been disappointing, the industry is cyclical, or there are some specific troubles at the company. The value buyer takes a contrary view. He or she says the stock has been hammered down too far, is now cheap, and will move up one of these days, when other investors start to understand the company's true worth..

The value game of the 1980s, when there were so many acquisitions and leveraged buyouts, was to look for companies whose private market valuations—if you took the companies apart and sold off the pieces—would be higher than the public market valuation. The investor who found such a company stood a good chance of seeing it either sold or restructured so that he or she would realize the underlying value. That's obviously a different focus than earnings growth. Another value situation is a company whose cash flows are high relative to its price; the cash flows could stay high but not move higher, so there isn't necessarily growth in earnings. But such companies in the last ten years or so have used their cash to become active repurchasers of their own shares, and this normally drives up the price of the stock.

With the first million placed with a growth investor and the second million with a value buyer, if there's money left over after that, I'd suggest hiring a third manager, someone I'd just call an opportunist. He'll buy growth, value, bankruptcies, foreign stocks, junk bonds, or whatever looks like it might go up. He is basically looking for trading opportunities. That sounds risky, but these opportunists are usually very wary buyers who tend not to get killed in down markets because they move out of disappointing situations quickly.

Most of us, of course, don't have multiple millions to scatter among a gaggle of investment counselors. That's the beauty of mutual funds. You can gain the same diversification of styles with even modest amounts of money.

Your investment management options:

Under $100,000: mutual funds

$100,000: wrap accounts, mutual funds

$250,000: own account at some investment firms, pooled account with other investors to meet a $1 million minimum at other firms, wrap accounts; mutual funds

$1,000,000 or more: own account at almost any investment firm, mutual funds, wrap accounts

---

7. Hedge Funds

So-called hedge funds are perhaps the ultimate opportunists, and they can be a sensible repository for the high-risk portion of the total portfolio of the very wealthy. Hedge fund managers are very aggressive seekers of capital gains, and the funds are only for those affluent enough to bear the risks the managers take to achieve those gains.

In fact, hedge funds are often called millionaires' clubs, because that's what they are. To be a partner in one—they are virtually all set up as limited partnerships—you must have a net worth in excess of $1 million, exclusive of your home, or, as an alternate test, a household income of at least $200,000 a year. Such folk are known as Regulation D investors by the Securities and Exchange Commission: they are presumed wealthy enough to afford big risks and knowledgeable enough about money, given they have so much of it, to make sophisticated investment judgments that lesser mortals cannot. Hedge fund managers do not have to be registered investment advisers, for the same reason: their participants don't need SEC protection.

I happen to have a pet peeve about Reg D. The SEC, in its infinite wisdom and caring, is trying to protect the poor or, more accurately, those of only modest affluence. It has set up a barrier that prevents those people from closing the distance between being moderately rich and filthy rich. Those with less than the minimums are denied access to some of the best talent in the investment business, people who might multiply their assets. The government's paternalism, designed to protect wealth, is inhibiting its creation.

On the Short Side

Hedge funds go back to 1955, when one A. W. Jones mused upon the fact that every day there are stocks that go up and stocks that go down; so why not, he asked himself, try to exploit both opportunities simultaneously? Why not be short the stocks you think are overpriced as well as long those that look underpriced? If you were both long and short stocks at the same time, you stood a chance of making money in both bull and bear periods. And there would be less risk than if you were only long or only short. That was the "hedge." But the manager generally had a bias—more long than short, or vice versa, according to his or her view of the market's direction. And then, of course, you could pick the wrong stocks for either strategy. So you were never really hedged. Your money was certainly still at risk.

A. W. Jones was quite successful with his new notion and more hedge funds sprang up. By the late 1960s they had pro-liferated, but growth stopped abruptly with the 1973–74 bear market. For those of you who are not market historians, the av-erage stock went down about 45 percent, and a number of mu-tual funds were down 70 percent and 80 percent. Many hedge funds disappeared. Even if they held up during the crash, their investors simply soured on the equity market and decided they had better uses for their money. A few of the old funds are still around, however. Two of the best known today are Steinhardt Partners, which grew out of the earlier firm of Steinhardt, Fine, & Berkowitz, and Cumberland Partners, which is now being run by the second generation of managers.

As the bull market that began in 1982 gained momentum, hedge funds caught on again. There are something like 200 of them today. The word *hedge* doesn't mean much anymore though. Most of the managers do short stocks, but only when they see overpricing opportunities rather than as any kind of offsetting mechanism. A *hedge fund* has come to be a term for a pool of money that gives its managers almost total freedom and pays them an incentive fee. Hedge fund managers are a kind of professional speculator legally allowed—since few are registered with the SEC—to use every device known to humankind to enhance returns. They concentrate in just a few stocks, they trade constantly, they use leverage, and, in addition to shorting, they buy and sell options and currencies. (But they don't trade soybeans and other like commodities; that's a separate category of professional speculator.) Some specialize—they only short, they do risk arbitrage, they concentrate on convertible hedging, or follow other, more obscure disciplines.

20 Percent Off the Top

The usual incentive compensation scheme stipulates that the manager, the general partner, gets to keep 20 percent of the profits. If the manager has a negative year, he or she has to get even again before sharing in subsequent appreciation. In some cases, if the partnership makes nothing, the manager gets paid nothing; in other arrangements, the manager earns a minimum fee, usually 1 percent, no matter how badly the portfolio is clobbered.

Now consider: if you manage a $100 million partnership and the account appreciates 40 percent in a year, you make $8 million. If you were managing $100 million for the 1 percent fee that investment firms usually charge, your gross income would be $1 million. And in all probability, as a registered investment advisor rather than a one-man band, you would need more personnel and office space—for dealing with clients, if nothing else—and you might end up with $800,000 for yourself. So the hedge fund manager can make ten times as much as someone else performing basically the same function.

Slight wonder, then, that hedge funds attract many of the best people in the money management business. These are people willing to shake hands on no-upside, no-pay; they live by their wits and welcome the challenge. And many, certainly not all, thrive and prosper. One could say that the crème de la crème in money management are running hedge funds.

By the same token, however, many who are mere aspirants to membership in the money management elite have been lured by the prospects of fabulous compensation. In recent years a number of people edged out of an ailing Wall Street have decided to take their severance money and look for partners to join them in a hedge fund. They may one day prove their worth, but if I were sharing in the kinds of risks these managers take on, I would be looking for someone with a proven record.

The hedge fund structure itself encourages better performance. These people are very independent; they want it understood from the beginning that there will be no interaction with clients. So they aren't inhibited by anyone's looking over their shoulder. They don't have to conform to anybody's notion of how money should be managed, the way, say, a manager at a large outfit always has to answer to a committee or chief investment officer. Their ability to use any kind of investment style, to employ leverage, and to concentrate—to be in one-half dozen stocks instead of ten times that number—gives them total flexibility. They can cross boundaries and asset classes, be long bonds one day and short Portugal the next. They can trade ferociously. Some use leverage infrequently; others use it extensively, amplifying results, upside or downside. They don't need much capital or much staff, so they have eliminated factors that intrude on time and attention. An operational purity reigns that is diluted in your usual investment management environment, where you have to worry about administration, marketing, and client service, some of which duties require considerable travel.

There is another important plus: a substantial portion, if not all, of the general partner's net worth is invested in the fund. After all, what else would these stock jockeys do with their own money but keep it in the market, and who else would they trust to manage it? So their money is at risk right alongside yours. Their fees *and* their capital depend on their performance. They know that their clients are paying high prices to have high expectations gratified and will be quick to leave if they aren't. A couple of bad years would be a disaster for their business and their bankroll, a real hemorrhage. This is as close an alignment of economic interests between manager and client as you can hope to achieve.

Locked In for a Year

Some hedge fund managers have done extraordinary jobs, averaging twice the 15 percent a year most of us would settle for, so investors don't mind the 20 percent haircut. Why else would you let somebody have a call on one-fifth of your money? Or give up liquidity—because most of the funds allow you to put money in quarterly but only take it out once a year, typically on December 31, with at least 30 days' written notice? And you wouldn't get all your money right away either, not until the annual audit is completed. Many hedge funds have emergency provisions, but most, on advice of counsel, adhere to the letter of the documents.

So lack of liquidity is a definite negative; you have to be certain you won't need the money. And understand that you can't back out if you are terrified by events like the one that occurred on October 19, 1987.

The second negative is that 20 percent incentive fee. Is performance going to be so terrific that after handing over 20 percent of profits you will still come out ahead of a more conventional arrangement, paying 1 percent of principal? To justify such an arrangement you will have to agree to risk levels that could in time diminish or eliminate that advantage. Because of the limited history of the industry—the phenomenon may date back to the mid-1950s, but few people have been on-line for more than a decade—there's no way to find out statistically whether or not hedge funds are a bargain. There have been few disasters, but then again, most of the present-day funds were launched after 1982 and never experienced a prolonged down market.

If you do travel with the hedge funds, eager to arrive at El Dorado, know that the ride can be a wild one. I think of a manager I know who, as I write this, was down 21 percent the past quarter. But I don't worry, because I know last year the same guy was up 55 percent. When you have concentration and leverage, you can have big swings like that, but this fellow is just off-the-wall when it comes to volatility. He obviously isn't for everyone, no matter how rich they are, and it would be devastating to wander into such a situation not knowing what to expect. That is one reason I think investors looking for entry into this strange world should use a consultant as a guide.

Most hedge fund managers don't mind the volatility at all. For them, that's just the nature of the game. We tend to use the word in a pejorative sense. If your account is up 30 percent, that's performance. If it goes down 30 percent, that's volatility. If you try, you can squeeze the volatility out of your account, but you'll never make any money. Stocks have to go up—and down—if managers are going to find stocks they can sell at a higher price than they paid for them.

Still another drawback is that, though most of the partnerships are audited annually—and if one you are considering is not, I wouldn't buy in—you receive minimal reporting along the way. The most you typically get is a quarterly letter telling you what your interest is worth and the manager's view of the world at that moment in time, and maybe the names of a couple of stocks he is long or short. In most cases, you will never see a complete list of securities or a record of the transactions during the year. You won't know how concentrated you are, what you own, and what the turnover has been. You have no damage control; you don't get a statement at the end of the month that says you're down 10 percent, but you might get a statement at the end of the quarter that says you're down 22 percent. And even then, you can't get out until the end of the year.

All partnership agreements have a provision that allows you to show up at the office and go through the books and records, but as a practical matter, nobody ever does. So you fly blind between audit dates. If the operator is prone to fraud, there is a long period when oversight is severely limited.

Hedge funds, therefore, do require an abdication of control in favor of just plain faith.

Difficult to Enlist

There is another, very big hitch. The best known hedge fund managers are almost impossible to invest with now. You often have to wait until somebody dies or drops out, because the funds can't have more than 99 partners or they would have to register with the SEC. Another detail: to get these superstars when an opening does occur, you will need $2 million or $3 million to command their attention. Even managers who are not yet such eminences, and have lower minimums—the most common threshold is one-half million, but they range from $250,000 to a million—usually adopt a cocky attitude. They want to look you over to decide whether or not they want you as a partner; it helps if they think you will be totally passive and never, never bother them. They might even waive their minimums for you if you pass their smell test. Investors are sometimes welcomed for the information they themselves can bring to the game—say, a knowledge of leading-edge technology companies.

It's even hard to find hedge fund managers. Most aren't registered, remember. And the lawyers tell all of them it is better if they are not too visible, so that the SEC doesn't think they are trying to lure the unsophisticated. They seem, moreover, to revel in their obscurity. It is as though they are in charge of exclusive clubs, and it's up to you to find the right address and enter with introduction or referral in hand. Retail brokers are aware of their existence but most haven't a clue as to where they are. You really need a consultant who has kept track of them, and there are only a handful of firms that have—mine being one of them.

Another real concern is that if they get too big—either through successful investing that compounds the assets or an inflow of money from satisfied customers and of new clients up to the limit allowed—performance can sag. Partnerships of partnerships have already been created; that is, the assets of one manager have been farmed out to other select hedge fund managers, and the client is charged $1\frac{1}{2}$ percent for the oversight service, on top of the 20 percent of profits. Again, the managers had better produce, because the word Darwinian comes to mind: if investors like the outcome of these partnerships of partnerships, they'll stay, but if they don't, they're gone at year end.

But the most threatening development, in regard to size, is that some pension funds have overcome their reluctance to pay incentive fees, much less such high fees, and have been sending money the managers' way. They have been drawn by the obvious talent. The danger is not just that the funds will get loaded down with too much money, but that the pension funds will demand more attention than private clients have been accorded. If people give you $50 million, you have to treat them a little better. So that could raise the very problems the concept originally eliminated—servicing, visits, distractions, maybe even some over-the-shoulder pressure. But it's hard to turn your back on $50 million.

Not for Widows and Orphans

There is another reason hedge funds are a millionaires' club, at least as far as I am concerned. As has been stated forcefully, I believe these funds are an addenda, to be approached only after the sanctuary and the more conventional equity managers are in place. Hedge funds can make sense if you still have one-half million or more to play with after the necessaries are taken care of. But don't kid yourself: when you go for higher returns, you are getting higher risk. The short positions do create some hedging, and your manager, with his money alongside yours, is going to think twice before trying to shoot the lights out. But no matter what the past record of a hedge fund manager has been, you know the possibility is always there that you will lose a very high percentage of your money.

Hedge fund managers are a special breed. Most good money managers tend to be "different" than the rest of the population, but hedge fund managers are even more so. They are a wild bunch, more single-minded, more isolated, more competitive. They are middle-of-the-road about almost nothing. They are financially ruthless. I don't mean they are unethical, but they are interested in nothing that blurs their focus. Investing has nothing to do with apple pie and motherhood. It has everything to do with turning money into more money.

Not bad people to have on your side—if you find the right one and can afford him or her. But it has to be the right one. Remember, if a manager is going to be on the far end of the risk spectrum, he or she has to produce big rewards, and the usual target you will hear from the hedge fund crew is 20 percent a year. For you to earn 20 percent, the manager must earn 25 percent, since he or she takes a 20 percent haircut. Now, 25 percent a year is about twice what we decided is a reasonable return. Given the risk these people take, it can be done—by a few. *Very* few. God didn't intend everyone to be rich.

Hedge fund pluses:

· Managed by some of the very best investment talent.

· Possibility of exceptionally high returns.

· Managers have total freedom to seize opportunities.

· Managers are not encumbered with administration and marketing, can concentrate on investments.

· Managers' money invested alongside yours; a confluence of interests.

Hedge fund minuses:

· Minimum investment very high—many require $1 million or more.

· Ultra-high-risk investors; suitable only after conventional managers in place.

· Illiquidity; you can get your money out only once a year.

· Performance is usually highly volatile.

· Managers take 20 percent of profits.

· Minimal reporting; you don't know how your money is invested.

· Little information about the managers; it is difficult to locate them and be accepted as a partner.

· Successful managers attract large sums, which can hurt future performance.

---

8. The Myth of Computer Power

For the core equities, the growth and value portfolios, I am not much for quantitative managers, those who run portfolios by relying on computer-driven models. These models screen the universe of stocks on a myriad of criteria, rank them by attractiveness, and then indicate how portfolios should be constructed from the top-rankers. "We buy only companies that do this, at these moments in history, at these prices," the quantitative managers will tell you. "We rely on discipline, not intuition."

If you aren't experienced in investments, that sounds very seductive. It would seem as though the manager has broken the code. In this vast and often incomprehensible process, here is a firm that has taken years of data and distilled it down to this simplistic approach that is bound to perform better than those working without benefit of the same touchstones. Here at last is a system you can understand, take notes on, and explain to your spouse.

There is another reason more mechanical methods appeal to some. If you are past 40, your educational experience—if you had any in the field of investments—was based on Graham and Dodd, the investment textbook that stressed a close analysis of the fundamentals of companies. Investment professionals were trained to talk to management, study balance sheets and income statements, and make judgments about the company's prospects. Quantitative managers see no need to visit the companies and apply subjective analysis; they just crunch the numbers in a computer. And in recent years quantitative techniques have been emphasized in many business schools like Stanford and the University of Chicago. People who attended such schools naturally carry their biases forward. They are predisposed to quantitatively oriented managers. What is threatening to someone of 50 comforts someone who's 30.

Most quantitative techniques might work reasonably well if left alone, but they are not left alone, because they are based on probabilities. Such and such happens, and then this will be the outcome, and 80 percent of the time that will be true. It's that 20 percent that upsets the apple cart. When the uncertain 20 percent pops up, these managers, not used to dealing with non-quantifiable uncertainties, tend to panic, and even trash the 80 percent that works.

The models are based on historical relationships, and in my experience, when you look to history for guidance, you soon find that enough twists occur—that damn 20 percent—to derail the formulae. Cause-and-effect relationships don't occur with enough precision to allow you to rely on mechanical methods. I have the same reservations about so-called market timers— those who move from stock to cash to stock according to where *their* models tell them the market's heading.

Talent Over Systems

In my opinion, computer power is a myth. Though computers are useful tools, of course, intellectual and judgmental skills are the *only* sustainable edge in this or any other business. All these model-dependent people care about is their *systems;* they hardly know what the companies whose stocks they own do to make a profit. I like managers who care about *stocks,* who have a passion for the investment process, and who relish grilling managements and tearing apart financial statements.

One product of the mathematical types is indexing—simply buying a portfolio that replicates the Standard & Poor's 500 Index, in light of the thesis that few will beat the market so you might as well join it. This approach has won wide acceptance among pension funds, and maybe if you have $20 billion in the market to worry about, indexing does make considerable sense. As noted earlier, individuals can also index, through a couple of mutual funds.

Entrepreneurs, those who have owned their own businesses, find the indexing concept laughable. There is no way to improve the outcome of your investments using intellectual skills? You have to settle for the average? That idea goes against their life experience. They've beaten their competitors, often with the odds against them, and prospered, simply because they've been smart. They've looked for opportunities and exploited them. They have made better decisions than the people they've competed against. Why that can't happen in money management is beyond them. And I happen to agree. There is just no field of human endeavor in which some people don't manage to excel.

9. "Should I Invest in Foreign Stocks?"

This question is rapidly becoming irrelevant. The big United States companies get half or more of their revenues from abroad, and the big foreign companies have operations in the United States or export to it. We are all going to feel soon that there are just "stocks," whether the companies happen to be based in the Unites States, Europe, the Far East, South America, or anyplace else in the world. Here is one cliché—that economies are becoming global—that happens to be true. If you think about what is going to happen when the European community becomes a reality, and consider the creation of a North American trading bloc through the lowering of trade barriers, you see that it can only get truer.

Whatever evolves, even today an investor should be indifferent to borders. That means that you don't say, as many pension funds as well as individuals do, "I'll set aside 20 percent of my money for Europe and maybe 10 percent for the Pacific Rim and leave a few bucks, too, for emerging markets." That way of looking at markets is passé and flawed, because you really have to start thinking in terms of a global stock market. You want to invest your money in those industries and/or companies where you can make the most money, wherever they happen to be located. It could be the United States, Germany, Thailand, or Brazil. You own Sony because Sony is a good buy; the fact that it is a Japanese company has no relevance.

It's no more complicated than that. If globalization of economies and markets becomes ever more of a fact, companies are what you should care about, not their country of domicile. Any other approach is naive in a world where, from an economic standpoint, Germany will no longer have a border with France, and, more important, it won't have a border with Poland or Czechoslovakia.

Fifteen years ago the capitalization of U.S. companies was 60 percent of the world's; today it's 30 percent. In the last 15

**Table 5.2   Value of $100 Invested in
Different Countries from 12/31/75 to 12/31/90,
with Dividends Reinvested**

Country	Value
Austria	$722.50
Belgium	$1,026.00
Canada	$422.90
Denmark	$710.30
France	$728.00
Germany	$589.70
Hong Kong	$979.70
Italy	$559.00
Japan	$1,467.70
Netherlands	$1,237.70
Norway	$809.00
Singapore/Malaysia	$573.20
Spain	$186.30
Sweden	$1,042.60
Switzerland	$486.40
United Kingdom	$1,147.00
United States	$554.40

Source: Morgan Stanley Capital International.

years the U.S. stock market has never been the world's best-performing. Other economies are growing faster than ours, their exchanges are maturing, their listings are growing, and their liquidity is steadily improving. It keeps getting easier to invest abroad, and more important to think that way (see Table 5.2). The economic pecking order has been radically altered in the world.

Alien Concerns

Still, how do you go about investing in non-U.S. stocks? You pretty well understand General Motors and Coca-Cola and General Electric; you read about them in the financial pages and your broker can send you a fistful of material on them. But you are not so comfortable about Siemens, Matsushita, and Norsk Hydro. And understandably. An investor venturing abroad faces formidable decisions:

- Which countries do you want to be in at any given time? What's the relative merit this year of Spain versus Italy, or Thailand versus Malaysia?

- Aside from the country's economy, how's the currency likely to stack up against the dollar? After all, whatever money you make over there is going to be translated back into dollars.

- What kind of information are you getting? Trying to compare companies in different countries is daunting, because disclosure is sparse in some places and accounting methods differ widely.

- What's the political environment? Do you have to worry about government confiscation of the companies you invest in? It happened in Britain, it happened in France, so we're not talking only about secondary markets where radicals seize control. Are the labor unions passive or aggressive? How about tax policies? Trade barriers? Inflation and interest rates, which so often are reflections of government policies? Brazil's government once decided inflation had to be dealt with once and for all and took draconian measures that sent the country's market down 50 percent in a week.

- How tough is it going to be to buy and sell securities? Even in several European countries, it takes not days but weeks before trades are settled. Often, trading volume has simply outstripped the systems available to process the trades. And there are countries that limit foreign ownership of shares, so in those instances you're forced into country funds, many of which are highly volatile: they get bid up to prices that have no relationship to their net asset value, and then plummet. I am not enamored of country funds, anyway. They are akin to wanting to load up on Wyoming. There are very few countries—Germany and Japan might be exceptions—whose economies are so separate from those of other countries that such a fund would merit anything other than a trading position. I've been to

Thailand twice and have only the vaguest sense of how the place works, so for the dentist in Cedar Rapids to decide Thailand's a good bet and load up on a Thailand Fund seems ridiculous to me.

- Many of these countries' regulatory levels are comical. Few have anything comparable to the SEC. So there's a good chance you will be victimized from time to time. There were scandals in Singapore that forced the closing of the exchange for a month. Investors were stuck. There have been other major scandals in Japan, Thailand, Hong Kong, Brazil, and just about everywhere else. (Not that the good old U.S.A. has been squeaky clean either.)

In short, you face layer upon layer of complexity when you move beyond your own borders. Things will be better in Europe after the European Economic Community is a reality. Policies will be more aligned, country to country. But it will still be no easy trick. You have to pick stocks, after all, and in many ways it's going to be tougher for companies in Europe once all the governmental protections—trade barriers, subsidies—have been removed. Companies won't have a guaranteed domestic franchise anymore.

The world is forever changing, and changes have their impact on industries and companies. A number of Asian countries, whose economies depend on the export of products made with cheap labor, might find that the opening up of Eastern Europe, where labor is also cheap, is going to hurt them. It is easier for a manufacturer in France to buy parts from Hungary than from Taiwan, if the quality is comparable. Pacific Rim countries could lose their competitive edge. If you invest in export economies, you have to be cautious, because the music can stop overnight.

It is not easy for the person who dabbles in the U.S. market to try his or her hand overseas. I believe the wiser course is either to buy U.S. companies that are global in their scope, stick to American Depository Receipts (the surrogate securities of foreign companies that trade on U.S. exchanges), or, better yet, turn to the professionals at a mutual fund or investment counseling firm. They have access to information, a global reach, that you can't hope to develop. As said earlier, one of your mutual funds should be an international fund. And if you have chosen a counseling firm that is weak in international expertise, supplement that account with an international mutual fund.

The truth is, the money management industry has been a bit slow in accepting the new realities, but it is happening. As Roger Engemann, who manages about $1 billion out of Pasadena, has said, "For most U.S. managers, our education in international investing has been like learning to shave using our clients' faces." But the expertise is coming along. Some management firms are ahead of others, but stock portfolios look increasingly international. That is the way it is going to be, and a good thing, too. Just that many more opportunities to make money.

Do I Need a Foreign Manager?

If a manager needs a global perspective, aren't you more likely to find such a manager overseas, whether it be a foreign counseling firm or a mutual fund run out of Europe? How about, say, a British manager? The British had an empire. They are used to thinking in terms of different cultures, currencies, and political systems. Or perhaps a Swiss manager. The "gnomes of Zurich" are supposed to possess the ultimate savvy in spreading money around the globe.

The answer is, in some cases it might be useful to have an overseas manager making overseas investments, but not for the reasons that you probably think. And there really is no need. There are money managers in Minneapolis who will do just as well for you investing overseas as managers in London, Zurich, Amsterdam, Tokyo, or anywhere else.

As an example, look more closely at the United Kingdom. London is still the world's leading financial center, so it would seem a probable place to find a sage global manager. But if you examine how the British have invested internationally, you find they've kept most of their overseas money in the United States, along with a few mining shares in Australia, Canada, and South Africa. There has been very little interest in other markets, including continental Europe. The Far East was largely ignored until only about a decade ago. The British are indeed an insular lot.

As for the Swiss, they will certainly tell you that because of the nature of their clientele, they have insights into countries and regions not afforded to others. If you believe them, there's no need to fly over to Zurich to sign up. The leading Swiss banks have representative offices in the United States that will be only too happy to accommodate you. Of course, in that case you would have a "Swiss bank account," but not the kind that most of us think about when we hear the term—the kind where you walk into a bank on the Bahnhofstrasse, whisper a number, and visit your funds.

I've called on maybe 40 Swiss banks in recent years. Their investment departments are structured very much the way such departments are set up at U.S. banks. They are just banks that happen to be domiciled in Switzerland, and big institutions, dominated by committee-think, have never struck me as repositories of investment genius. Indeed, now that the Swiss can no longer sell themselves on the basis of bank secrecy laws and have to compete on the basis of performance alone, they have been losing business.

I happen to know, in fact, that some of the Swiss banks have been farming out investment management responsibilities—at least in the United States. They hire a U.S. manager, add their fee on top of the manager's, and the U.S. client gets a statement that never indicates who is really managing the money or who is getting paid for what. The Swiss are great businessmen. They are smart and tough, and have no reservation about charging prices that would have the SEC standing on its head. And another thing: transaction costs are far higher in Switzerland than in the Unted States, and the banks over there also serve as brokers, so they collect brokerage fees on trades as well.

The European Touch

As you can tell, I haven't been overly impressed with European money management. That isn't to say there aren't good people in Europe—more in London than in Switzerland, in my experience—who have had fine records investing internationally. My own firm has been working to identify them the last couple of years, just the kind of talent hunt we do in the United

States. And we are bothering with this search not because the Europeans necessarily have more ability than U.S. managers or an innate global sense, but because they do happen to possess a few advantageous attributes.

Europeans are generally better at handling currency matters; they make currency translations in their heads because that's something they've done all their lives. The accounting standards are different over there, so familiarity with those differences—between Swiss, German, and U.K. practices—is helpful. They are more likely to know if a company is understating earnings, why it's understating earnings, and the tax implications of not understating earnings.

Many Europeans are multilingual, which most U.S. investors are not. It's only when you really know the language that your antennae can function when you talk to people. Also, when you are familiar with the culture, you know what to look for. To some degree, too, they have developed analytic networks in Europe—brokers, other managers—they can share ideas with.

Because so many of their domestic markets haven't the depth, breadth, or economic growth to make them interesting, some European investors have had a broader appetite for cross-border investments than we have had. And when you've been to see 50 German companies, you have a context within which to judge the truth when talking to the fifty-first.

Most important, someone in the United Kingdom or on the continent is only an hour or two away, instead of five to ten hours away, from a European company he wants to explore or revisit, just as United States managers are only five hours away from any company in the United States they want to see. (Europe and the United States are about equidistant from Asian capital markets.) There are geographical advantages that have nothing to do with demonstrated investment skills.

Provincial Biases

On the other hand, Europeans suffer one major disadvantage: the prejudices embedded in their societies. I hear revealing comments when I visit money managers abroad. Those in the north of Europe make snide remarks about the "Garlic Belt," referring to the Mediterranean countries. Several times I've heard a sneering jibe at Spain as a country "that has finally joined the nineteenth century." People are open about such cracks: "You have to be careful in Italy, because the Italians will steal you blind." "Turkey? It's nothing more than an Arabian trading bazaar." I seldom hear anything positive about other nationals. Europeans have such a strong "them" and "us" mentality that I wonder how they can approach Asian markets at all.

I worry that all these prejudices get in the way of their economic decisions. They are trapped by their biases. There is an unwillingness to dignify certain countries as promising industrially because of contempt for other cultures. It is akin to the difficulty many Americans have legitimizing Mexico as an economic power.

In spite of the advantages that the British, the Swiss, the Dutch, or whoever in Europe may have in investing in their own backyard, it is still my perception that they are not appreciably better equipped, by training or experience, to invest internationally than are we in the United States. I question the aura they have enjoyed. Global investing is basically a new business for almost everybody, anyway, so I don't think history puts the United States at a disadvantage. Table 5.3 lists 20 good international mutual funds.

In my opinion, then, you can be comfortable with your U.S. manager. Just make sure he or she thinks globally.

Table 5.3   20 Good International Mutual Funds

DFA Continental Small Company	Janus Worldwide
Dreyfus Strategic World Investing	Merrill Lynch Pacific A
EuroPacific Growth	New Prospective Fund
Fenimore International Equity	Oppenheimer Global
First Investors Global	Scudder Global
G.T. World Wide Growth	Scudder International
G.T. International Growth	SoGen International
GAM International	Templeton Foreign
Harbor International	T. Rowe Price International Stock
Ivy International	Trustee's Commingled International

Advantages of European managers when investing in non-U.S. stocks:

- Are more experienced in investing outside their national borders.

- Analysts and managers are physically close to portfolio companies.

- Many are multilingual and familiar with currency translations.

- Are more accustomed to foreign accounting methods.

- Have developed local networks of information.

Disadvantages of European managers:

- Have insular prejudices that distort judgment of national economies.

- Are no closer to Pacific Rim markets than U.S. managers.

- Committee-dominated institutions are primary investment managers.

- Have a bias for growth stocks; US managers are more savvy about identifying value.

---

10. How About a Swiss Bank Account?

When people bring up the matter of a Swiss bank account— and we're not talking about an investment account, which we've dealt with above—I always ask them, "What is it you are trying to accomplish?"

And he or she will say, "Well, if the dollar goes to hell, it would be good to have some of my assets denominated in Swiss francs."

To that I reply, "If you're trying to deal with currency risk, you don't need a Swiss bank account. You can go out and buy Swiss francs, yen, or deutsche marks. You can buy American Express Travelers Cheques denominated in the currency of your choice. You can own gold, which is, to a degree, a world currency—though, of course, you have other risks with gold. And there are a number of other things you can do to hedge against currency risk. You don't need a Swiss bank account for that."

"All right," they'll say, "but how about confiscatory government policies?"

"Ah, that's an entirely different agenda," I tell them. "It happens in the world, of course. Most recently, Brazil and Argentina, trying to deal with runaway inflation, froze bank accounts. If you had more than a modest amount of money in an Argentinean or Brazilian bank, it in essence became a government bond that you couldn't redeem. And the authorities got the idea, I might add, from U.S.-trained economists. Now, if you think something like that is going to happen in the United States some day, then you *should* have money or assets in other countries."

If you have that concern, you can certainly send your money to Switzerland. The United States, unlike most countries, has no currency controls. What we *do* have, however, is a kind of de facto control, because you have to report it if you take more than $5000 out of the country. So even though we don't have the controls, somebody's obviously very curious about who's taking money out, and how much and where.

So if you don't want the authorities to know that you have money offshore—if that's why you are thinking of a Swiss bank account—that puts you in the position of violating the law. Because you are very definitely required to report money you are exporting, which gives the authorities precisely the knowledge you probably don't want them to have. And in these days of computerization—we live in an almost Orwellian environment—it is extremely hard to keep secrets from the government. Furthermore, if the Federal authorities ever take a serious interest in you, the veil of secrecy of a Swiss account can be quickly lifted these days. If it didn't work for Imelda Marcos, don't think for a second that it is going to work for you.

Not only is it against the law to hide assets, you need co-conspirators—one of whom, by the way, if I am your advisor, I have no interest in becoming. If you use a numbered account, someone in the family, or a very trusted friend, has to be aware of it. So you are inviting that person to share complicity in a criminal act. Then if, for some reason, you and your wife no longer see eye-to-eye, or you and your son have a tiff, someone who was once an ally has become an adversary, and you have a certain vulnerability. Those are the ground rules.

Does that answer your question about a Swiss bank account?

11. Some Fundamental Considerations

A few housekeeping matters should be cleared up if you are shopping for an investment counselor. Where you live, for example. If you live in New York City, that's easy; there are investment managers on every corner. But if you are from Fresno, and you would like an investment advisor in that city whom you can drop in on for a chat about how your portfolio's doing, I might have to tell you there is no one in your town that I can recommend. You can try to find one on your own, of course. People have to be satisfied with their financial *and* human relationships when they link up with an advisor.

One woman who came to see me decided that she had to have a woman manage her money. I know several very able women money managers, but the ones that I can recommend have established $5 million as their minimum account size (their clientele is almost entirely institutional), and this person didn't qualify.

Are there stocks you own to which you have strong emotional attachments? I don't mean the stock you bought at 35 that is now 20 to which you have sworn total loyalty until it returns to 35 and thereby proves itself worthy of your initial confidence. I mean stocks bought long ago, by your parents or grandparents, that have a sentimental, far more than monetary, value. Or the stock may have been issued by a family-owned business. If you hire an investment counselor, you must be prepared to let go of that stock and pay whatever tax is due, for most certainly the investment advisor is going to sell it to raise cash for the stocks on his or her own buy list. If there is such stock, you can just hold on to it, of course, rather than turn it over to an adviser.

Fraud naturally worries people. I guess Wall Street has earned itself a reputation in recent years as the venue of thieves with MBAs. But the investment-custodial process should be reassuring. The investment manager has to reconcile all statements with the custodial bank that holds your money. If my office gets involved, we get the statements, too. And there are other safeguards. It isn't easy to defraud anyone in this business.

And yet, it can happen. You've got to realize that if someone is committed to fraud and if he or she is psychopathic, there's no way you can eliminate every conceivable manner of his or her cheating you. Nothing is totally bulletproof in this business. If somebody hadn't got mad at Ivan Boesky, he'd no doubt still be at his tricks. Probably your best defense is using managers who have been in the business for a good long while, because people who are criminally inclined tend to be a little impatient. And the system has really been remarkable. The number of known fraudulent investment advisors is amazingly small.

Matchmaking

People who come to see me find out that I am very narrow in my approach. If someone wants a more aggressive investment program than I recommend, because he or she believes 20 percent a year is a cinch if you get the right advisor, they will have to seek support elsewhere. Sure, some managers can do it, at least for a few years, but they take risks I don't believe the already-wealthy need to take.

About half the time the decision that I am not right for a prospective client is unilateral, and it is my own. Some people have considerable money, but it's tied up, and I need investable funds to be of help. Others, as has been mentioned, have never been in the stock market, and the way they talk about it, you feel as though getting them involved would be like taking people on safari who are terrified of animals. Others, as has also been noted, are good enough investors on their own that they don't need professional advice.

I have clients who made their money in all kinds of businesses—truck trailer manufacturing, newspaper publishing, radio stations, oil, newsletters, and savings and loans that were actually run as legitimate banks. I have doctors and lawyers, of course, and, living in southern California as I do, some actors, directors, and screen writers. But I seldom have clients who have built their fortunes in real estate. Real estate people are terrible stock market investors, especially the developers. They are such hands-on managers, so controlling, so convinced they are in charge of their own destiny, that they are almost temperamentally incapable of yielding control to somebody else—that is, to an investment manager. Another problem is that they are so in love with real estate that when they hear of an attractive property or development opportunity, they can't wait to transfer their money out of the market into the deal.

Engineers also tend to be difficult, because they believe everything can be quantified. The stock market is an eternal source of frustration to them, for it just doesn't lend itself to quantification. You can do all sorts of statistical studies on the market—and heaven knows enough people do—but they aren't reliable in predicting future behavior, because trends don't repeat themselves in precisely the same way. It annoys the engineers, then, that their intellectual prowess, their study of mathematically driven cause and effect relationships, simply doesn't work in the stock market. So I often end up telling the engineers and real estate developers that the market is probably not going to be a happy place for them, and that, before they get serious about it and spend a lot of time and money on it, they should consider the fact that the market generally doesn't work the way they'd like it to. And, as I say, I don't have many engineer or developer clients.

Of the women clients I have had, a number were quite edgy about the market when they started out. These were women who had been dependent on others in financial matters, and when they were finally on their own, they naturally tended to lack confidence in their ability to deal with money decisions. So when things went wrong in the market for a time, they felt absolutely lost and frightened, and required considerable hand-holding. Women also don't seem to establish a bond with their investment advisors to the extent that men do, so they didn't have faith in the advisors' ability to pull out of slumps and they didn't respond to the manager's reassurances.

But as time went on and they gained a measure of confidence, many became extremely astute investors. In some ways, women are more skeptical, hard-nosed, and results-oriented about investments than men. The fact that they don't get caught up in the dynamics of the relationship with an advisor gives them judgmental perspective. And they don't have to "prove" their own investment genius. After that initial insecurity, they look at their portfolios with a cold and rational eye. I've known many women investors, after they've passed the learning period, who have ended up with an excellent understanding of the investment process and superb long-term returns. So to those women who are shy about becoming involved in the market because of inexperience and fear about inadequacy, I say, give yourself a chance. In time you are likely to find that you will make out very well and enjoy the game thoroughly.

At times I have rejected people as clients simply because I didn't like them very much and didn't think we could work together. A few lawyers have come to me who have made big bucks in settling personal injury cases, and I can see they are aggressively confrontational. I'm uncomfortable with them from the minute they sit down and start to talk. In other instances I suspected the sources of the money I was being asked to augment.

So to many I say, "You're terrific people, but this is not the place for you." (Sometimes that only heightens their interest in getting my services.) Basically, I look for anything that can bollix up a relationship, because rapport is hard enough to maintain when markets do well, and they happen to go to hell with fair regularity.

Stop Racing; You Have Already Arrived

If the prospective client and I do think we can get along and that I can do him or her some good, I have some final words of advice about their investment program. I want them to understand that with some of their money in bonds and some in stocks, they will enjoy certain protections. If there's a recession, for example, the stocks may be doing poorly but the bonds should be climbing in value. That's the beautiful part of diversification. But there's a flip side, and it's one that people tend to forget. It means that part of your money is also in the *wrong* place 100 percent of the time. That's the price paid for reducing risk.

Some people, I can see, think that too much risk has been squeezed out of the process. They still have a hankering to speculate a bit, to try making some big hits. All I can do is to urge them to forget about options, futures, commodities leverage, shorting, and the other exciting promises of high returns. People who are wealthy simply don't need that anymore. They have money now. There is no need to take outsize risks to make it. If you are worth a million dollars and you make another $10,000, or even $25,000—money that will be taxed—what difference does it make? And in most instances, those still struggling to become rich don't need to take those risks either—unless they are in such a hurry to get there that they want to jeopardize the possibility of making it at all.

Money is meant to enrich people's lives, not complicate them. You have to manage your money, of course, but you mustn't let your money manage you. Just because you now have many options, you don't need to pursue them all and try to become a financial and investment whiz. You should have a sense of sanctuary; you are now invulnerable to economic malaise, and that safety should be preserved.

In a perfect world, when they bury you there should be cash, marketable securities, cars, and household possessions. That's it. There should be no debt on your balance sheet, for example. Wealth affords an advantage that few realize: you are now able to reduce the number of items that complicate your life financially.

6

THE SEARCH FOR INVESTMENT TALENT

1. Why Not Your Bank?

You have a million or more to invest in stocks and you have decided that you have graduated from mutual funds. You want your very own investment counselor.

You have asked your lawyer, your accountant, and a couple of friends if they know anyone you could talk to, and a short list is on your desk. Stockbrokers, with their SWAT teams who follow transactions that might have enriched anyone in the populace, have been on the phone pushing their investment advisory services—either the firm's own or those of outside managers. Aside from the wrap accounts discussed in the last chapter, brokers assemble lists of managers who will throw them most of the commission business (often at the highest end of the rate scale) for any account referred to them. Your bank has probably let you know about its Private Banking service, which includes money management. Owners of money are being very aggressively marketed to these days, as are the intermediaries such as the very lawyer and accountant you called for advice.

So you have some names and you can begin the screening process. A lot of people won't bother. They just settle for the one recommendation that sounds most appealing. Sometimes they get lucky, sometimes they don't.

Often they turn to their bank because it is so familiar and comfortable. It's been there all your life, it's where you have your checking and savings accounts, and you know a lot of the people inside it. These Private Banking services are very pleasant: special offices with leather couches, VIP treatment, a ready credit line if you decide to add a tennis court to your grounds, and grey-haired counselors to chat with you over coffee. Where else can you make one telephone call and transfer funds, find a domestic (yes, some banks will do this), and arrange bail for your son? Also, banks are by definition supposed to be "conservative," even though the records I've seen would suggest that they are no more conservative than anybody else. A true advantage is that they offer perpetuity—that is, if there is an estate issue and you're trying to create a mechanism that will allow your money to be managed beyond your life, you know that the bank will be there. (Never mind that the Federal Deposit Insurance Corporation may be operating it).

Not all banks are bad money managers. They're like any other institution, like a mutual fund—as good as the people managing the money at the time they're given the responsibility. And that's what bothers me about banks: they're subject to more personnel changes than entrepreneurially driven firms. Banks are so often just a training ground. If people are good, they get offers for far more money from private firms and they are gone. And nobody sends you an announcement of that fact.

Then, too, partly because the bank's officers know good managers leave so frequently, a committee approach to investing is often adopted. There will be an approved list of stocks and a model portfolio so that the individual manager has less responsibility, and the bank can tell you that if your manager leaves it doesn't matter, because you are getting the institution's product and not an individual's. When you have consensus investing like that, you can't find out who is critical in the process. There are always one or two people who unduly influence the outcome of meetings, but you won't know who they are, and if and when they might walk out. The larger the cast, the harder it is to identify the key actors.

If there *isn't* committee and consensus investing, then there are a large number of portfolio managers who have autonomy, a dozen or more people all going their own way. Then you have to know who is going to run your money and if he or she is going to stick around. Furthermore, the way responsibilities are divided at banks, you're never really sure just who is managing your money; it may not be the person you talked to when you signed up. It's perfectly possible that the person or persons who attracted you to that institution have left, and you will not be aware of it unless you happen to make an inquiry.

It isn't just banks where you run up against such problems. Any very large organization is likely to be difficult to puzzle out. You want purity in the decision-making process, to eliminate as much noise as possible. The only way you can identify talent is if you can attribute the contribution of each manager to the output of the firm.

It must be pretty obvious that I am not fond of institutional products. I certainly don't like the anonymous nature of committee management. I like to find individual managers with proven talent, and to know they are in charge of my money and are going to stick around because they own a chunk of the firm. I confess I have adopted as my definition of mediocrity the median return on bank-managed funds.

Banks as investment managers

Pros:

- The institution and its personnel are familiar and comfortable.
- Banks can offer the special services of Private Banking.
- A few banks have good performance records.
- The bank, as trustee, can continue to manage your money after your death.

Cons:

- You are likely to get a committee-driven product that produces mediocre investment results.
- You often can't be sure who is actually responsible for your portfolio.
- The best people tend to leave the bank for higher-paying positions at counseling firms.
- They lack entrepreneurial spirit.

2. It's All a Matter of Shopping

If you bypass your bank, then, and decide that you are going to interview at least some of the independent counselors whose names you've been given, what are you looking for? I've been doing it for 20 years, so I have the advantage of knowing all sorts of things to look for. But you can do a perfectly adequate job on your own. The process isn't all that complex and doesn't demand a ton of special knowledge. Mainly it requires some fundamental business skills, common sense, and a modicum of work. As I said earlier, evaluating prospective managers is easier than evaluating prospective stocks.

It does take a healthy sense of cynicism, however. What I mean by that is that if you consider the dynamics of the situation, what the investment manager is holding out is the ability to grow your capital at 15 percent a year while you work on lowering your golf handicap. It sounds great: what could be better than your doing what you like while your money, through no effort of your own, generates substantial amounts of capital for you? You, the consumer, want to believe. And the marketers of the investment counseling firms understand that dynamic. The situation, then, right off the bat, conspires against you.

You defend yourself by, first of all, understanding and acknowledging that dynamic, and then, to the limits of your endurance, creating as much contrast as you can. As you see several firms, and each makes its lavish promises, your cynicism grows. The first one sounds great, and the second one sounds great, but keep going, and you'll quickly get the knack of differentiating.

It's exactly like interviewing prospective employees. You begin to define differences by the contrasts you see. The greater the number of applicants, the more probable it is that you will find someone who's outstanding to fill a position. And essentially that is what you are doing: hiring an employee. You're paying him or her real money, even though it may be charged through your account rather than your writing a check, and the work is done at his or her office rather than your own. But you are, nevertheless, putting an employee on your payroll.

So what you are interested in at all the firms you see are the same sorts of things you would try to find out about a prospective employee: some evidence of their ability from past records, some evidence of their integrity, and some evidence of their administrative skills.

Interviewing money managers is an educational process. You become "educated" in the sense that you demystify the investment business. You become familiar with the vocabulary of the trade so that you are no longer intimidated by the jargon. On a visceral level, you are absorbing how different people invest, what their logic path is, what methodologies they employ, how they arrived at those methodologies, and how consistently they employ them. You are listening to people and saying to yourself, "This makes sense," or "This doesn't strike me as rational. The reasoning is inconsistent. I can't discern any intellectual pattern to the decision making."

For sure, you'll become inured to the clichés. Investment management is a business littered with clichés. As one example, the value managers tell you, "We like to buy a dollar's worth of assets for 50 cents." Sounds like an attractive idea. There may even be periods of history that accommodate that trick, but the world really doesn't make it easy to acquire a buck for half a buck. You may buy the assets cheap, but turning them into gold is another matter entirely. The fact that the balance sheet indicates a disparity in pricing between public and private valuation doesn't mean the higher value can be harvested—especially in the 1990s, when junk bonds and liberal bank lending are no longer around to provide the financing sources that made it happen in the 1980s.

What you are looking for in an investment firm:

· A superior performance record
· Integrity
· Administrative skills

3. The Search Begins

You start by taking out your list of names, probably all in your community if you live in a city of any size, and call them up. They'll send brochures, which should include performance numbers. Most people focus on the numbers for the last three years or so, go see the two or three firms—maybe as many as five, tops—with the best records, pick one of them, and that will be the end of it.

It's not the worst approach. At least you've seen from two to five managers, instead of just one, and you stand a good chance of picking a decent outfit. But I would urge you to see more than five firms, the more the better. That's the only way to make the educational process work. If you see only one or two firms, you are all too likely to hire a firm that provides a mirror image of your own philosophy of how money should be invested, even if you are a chronic loser in the market. See more firms and you begin to pick up on differences in philosophies and approaches and to gain a new perspective. It's your money, and if money is any kind of priority, you have to make the effort. Especially if you don't live in a big city, you should go beyond your own community, because there are obviously people who provide this service in every town. The search takes time and it involves some expense, but the more people you talk to and the more comparisons you make, the more likely that you will make an enlightened judgment. It seems absurd, but most people spend more time picking an automobile than they do choosing an investment counselor.

So just what is it you are seeking? The answer, in a word, is talent.

At least I hope that is what you are seeking. A survey recently conducted by a New York market research firm revealed that most wealthy people picking an investment counselor are more concerned about the reputation of the firm and its ability to be discreet than they are about performance. They want to find firms their friends will approve of. Prestige and privacy mean more to them than making money. That is hardly my agenda, and I trust that it is not yours either.

The fact that a firm has a lot of people, a large research budget, a gaggle of analysts, and high-powered computers is fine, but when push comes to shove, it's pretty much of a level playing field among firms. Be aware of your own prejudices in that regard. It is easy to find comfort with a large organization. People tend to equate a big office and staff with better output. In this business the only sustainable advantages are intellectual and judgmental. Rarely are more than a handful of people critical to the investment process. There's little evidence that a firm with 20 analysts produces better results than a firm with no analysts. The firms that emerge with regularity as outstanding performers tend to be populated with fewer, rather than larger, numbers of people. Managing money is fundamentally an entrepreneurial skill and doesn't thrive, as I've just suggested, when institutionalized. The larger the cast, the sooner you regress to the mean.

Choosing investment managers has more in common with handicapping horses or jockeys than it does with the hard sciences, because there are few cause-effect relationships. Here, nevertheless, in summary form, are the most important of the components you need to look at (most of them we'll consider in some depth shortly):

. The investment record, obviously.

. The longevity of that record.

. The veracity of that record. Has there been any statistical manipulation?

. The continuity of the personnel. Add or take away one person who's been in a decision-making capacity, and you have a new variable in sustaining that record.

. The backgrounds of the principals.

. The recent environment. Has the firm done well lately only because the landscape has been favorable for its style? Has everyone practicing that style prospered equally, or has this firm demonstrated superior skills?

. The mix of clients. Does the firm have some pension money as well as private investors? Some people are more com-

fortable knowing a firm handles only individuals like themselves. They suspect that $20 million clients overshadow
$1 million clients, or at least command the firm's best man-
agers. It is indeed a matter of considerable concern if the
accounts are managed differently and assigned to different
portfolio managers. Your account manager could be part of
the training program.

- The size of the biggest account. Even if the firm's business
  is all retail, is one account so big—say, $30 million—that it
  gets most of the attention?

- The number of different investment styles offered by the
  firm. Focus and concentration generally correlate positively
  with good results.

- The size of the firm. Has it grown to a point where future
  results might not resemble past results?

- Any other factors that might suggest the past will not be
  replicated. For example, is the person who started the firm
  at 37 now 67, which could suggest that his appetite for risk
  may have waned?

- How administration is handled. Are money managers suf-
  ficiently segregated from the burdens of client communication and marketing to allow them to concentrate on
  their portfolios? The bigger the firm, the bigger the problem.

- Manager attitudes. Are the managers passionate about investments, or was this just a business created by people
  who saw a money-making opportunity? In the latter case,
  any product would have done for them. As in most professions, the level of passion is one of the principal con-
  tributors to excellence.

Such are the factors you will consider—at least the most important of them. Some are quantitative, but most are qualita-
tive, and you need to use judgment as well as computational
analysis in deciding whether or not this is a horse you want
to bet on.

Ask for an ADV II

You don't have to walk in the door with the above list in your hand. When you call the firm and ask to be sent a brochure, ask, too, for what is called a Form ADV II, information that has to be filed with the SEC. It's rarely offered—what is usually handed out is just the brochure, which is, of course, a selling document—but you're entitled to a copy of the more objective firm description. The two pieces of literature will tell you all of the above about the firm—its resources and its style of management—and answer a whole host of questions you won't have to bother bringing up when you meet with the principals.

Compare the ADV II with the brochure. The brochure may say that the three principals have a total of 44 years' investment experience, but then you find out from the ADV II that one principal has 38 years and the others have 3 years each. That would suggest that if the guy with 38 years under his belt leaves, you might want to do the same. More than that, it would be a low-level red flag that this firm is not above manipulating information, however amateurishly.

As you go through the material, look for any fuzzy areas that should be cleared up. As one example that has happened to me several times, I wonder why a firm has as many managers as it does. It runs $500 million but has seven investment professionals, and that strikes me as far more than is required. The firm may have a very good reason. It may have a large number of little accounts, perhaps taken on when the firm was just starting up, and needs seven managers for client handholding. But some firms don't have a good answer. They don't seem to have thought through the economics of their own organization. It's as though they don't care about making money. I think firms should try to maximize their own profits as well as their clients'. The two are not, by any means, mutually exclusive. People who like to make money for their clients like to make money for themselves as well. Running other people's assets is not an altruistic exercise. Greed, however well disguised, is an important characteristic of successful money managers.

4. Performance Is the Bottom Line, and Yet...

The first thing you'll probably, and rightly, want to look at is the performance numbers. A sheet with updates of performance results is usually slipped into the brochure. If the firm says, "We do not provide performance figures," then you say, "Goodbye." Without a record, you can't make a judgment. In this business, ignorance is not bliss; it is suicide.

Most people think the numbers alone are all they need. After all, isn't that the bottom line? If the firm has made money for people in the past, what else do you need to know?

A lot of things. Most obviously, if the same people aren't there, the numbers may not be repeated. If the same people are there, but their ardor for the game has waned, ditto. If size gets in the way, there may be a problem. So many firms have fantastic results when they start small. Their record attracts more and more business. It is a lot easier to run $50 million than $5 billion. By the time they have reached that sum, they are personally in clover, earning huge fees, but their clients are getting average performance.

The last three years may look great, but then you have to consider how other managers who follow the same style did. Maybe it is the style that was in favor, and this manager showed no particular excellence. Maybe she even did less well than her peers. Or she might have had a terrific couple of years because she caught a theme that was hot for a time—cable and cellular stocks, media stocks, or the oils. But was she clever or just lucky? You can't know until you look at more history. In any case, if a manager's numbers have been off the chart for the last three years, the probabilities are high that her numbers will move toward the trend line in the subsequent three years. Investment styles simply do not shine in all seasons.

Conversely, returns for the last three years may be anemic, but only because that manager's style was out of sync with investor preferences. One of the traps investors set for themselves is their refusal to talk to anyone who hasn't done well *recently.* A manager's ten-year record has been great but the last three have been disappointing, and although it may be true that his skills have diminished, it is more likely, again, that blame can be laid on rotational patterns in the market. But it is very tough to convince people of that fact. There is a natural tendency to overweight recent history.

The moral: you have to look at a long-term record. Don't look at just the last one, two, or three years; go back at least five and, preferably, if the firm has been around long enough, ten years. Five years will usually include a down period, but not always; from 1982 to 1990 stocks mostly went up. And you always want to pay close attention to down periods, because they will happen to you. It's not an *if*, it's a *when*, because they haven't suspended cycles. It is so much easier to make money if you don't give up in bad years a big chunk of what you made in good years.

Consider the Ups and Downs

Look at performance year by year. Long-term is what counts, yes, but could you live with a manager who is up 32 percent one year, down 27 percent the next, and up 42 percent the next? Could you stand the anxiety of the unpleasant years? And what if you put your money into the firm just after the up-32-percent year, only to see the value of your account drop by 27 percent in your first year with the firm? Most of us will settle for more modest, but more consistent, returns.

Even calendar year by calendar year isn't enough. You should look at results quarter by quarter. A firm should supply them, if asked. Again, you want to see how big the swings were. A firm could have been up 5 percent for all of 1987, but maybe it was up 40 percent in August, when the market peaked. You could have hired the firm in the early fall, based on that great number, just in time for the roller coaster plunge down. You can say you don't care, as long as the end result is good, but almost all people say they can bear volatility until they have to live with it. Most people I know are also philosophical about death, but when they get 102-degree temperatures, they want to be rushed to the emergency room.

So if you see a lot of quarters when the manager was down 7 percent, down 12 percent, and a number of them with similar results are back to back, it is important to consider how you might behave in a clinch. Most people, when their feet are held to the fire, scream to get out.

It's that same pronounced human tendency to project recent events into perpetuity. We've all found ourselves, after a big rise in the market, projecting that good fortune into very large numbers, and contemplating the beach houses, cars, and world tours we will be shopping for in the near future. Well, the corollary is that when your investments decline 15 percent or 20 percent, you begin to wonder what it's like to be a migrant farm worker. It's interesting, because you get a chance to examine how much of your self-esteem is linked to your affluence. Poverty does not seem in the least romantic. "My god," you say, "I've lost 15 percent in four months. All of the money I worked so hard to earn and paid taxes on is going to turn to dust. I am not going to be able to buy that Porsche. As a matter of fact, I am not going to be able to replace the tires on the car I have." The imagination runs wild, and it doesn't help that at the same time the financial reporters are flipping through their Rolodexes to call for quotes from every known doomsayer to amplify the arguments for impending collapse.

If that sounds like you, you'd better take a good look at those quarterly swings. Compare them to the Standard & Poor's 500 index to see if this manager is even more volatile than the market. It's bad enough when the market's down 10 percent, but a lot worse if you're down 17 percent. I know, that's a lot of quarterly statistics to look at. It may be that too much information is going to confuse you. But it's a sure bet that too little information is going to destroy you.

If you can live with volatility, and you see that there's been a payoff for bearing it, that the willingness to accept declines has rewarded the firm's clients with higher peaks, fine. But when you think about it, assume that your experience will be worst case, that you will enter the market at precisely the wrong time and that your stockpile of assets will drop out from under you. As you look at the historical record, imagine how you would have borne those periods of pain. If you decide that you can come to terms with the worst cases, you're probably going to be all right.

Since I've seen how frightened people become in a difficult market, I can make a strong case for more conservative management—for trading off return on the upside for more stability on the downside. For then you are not forced into those gut-wrenching decisions that get so many people out of the market at precisely the wrong time. The price you will pay for conservatism is that you are not going to fully exploit the really hot markets that pay big bucks to those who take big risks.

Some things to look for in a firm's performance record:

· What is the longer-term—preferably ten-year—record?

· Did the firm do much better when it was smaller?

· Has the same manager been in charge for the period under consideration?

· How does the record compare to those of managers following the same approach to the market?

· How did the firm do in bear markets?

· How much volatility has there been in quarter-to-quarter and year-to-year returns?

---

5. A Consumer's Guide to Trickery

Can you believe the numbers the firms show you? For the most part, yes. Most firms by far are highly ethical. If a firm did claim performance that was a fantasy, other clients of the firm would sooner or later get wind of it and howl that *their* accounts didn't earn those kinds of returns. Also, any firm that is not scrupulous knows that the SEC, understaffed as it is, does come around. It could be this year, it could be next, but they're coming. There are restraints against out-and-out fabrication. I know that I have found few examples of gimmicked numbers over the years.

Some firms have their figures audited, so you would assume those numbers are rock solid. But those who wanted to cheat could probably get away with the chicanery for a time, because all the accounting firms do is audit the numbers given them. Most of the people doing the auditing—often just six months out of college, because the senior people aren't going to bother with this stuff—aren't aware of the nuances and statistical games someone in the business could play to alter outcomes. So even a major accounting firm's stamp of approval doesn't necessarily mean all is kosher.

But it's not honesty that is your big concern. Even numbers that are honest can be misleading. We all know how statistics can be manipulated. It sometimes seems that every manager you visit can tell you he was in the top 25 percent of managers for the last x number of years, and 100 percent of managers cannot be above the average, much less in the top quartile. So how can such claims be possible? Because one firm compares itself to balanced managers, another to equity managers only, another to equity managers that specialize in growth stocks, another to those who concentrate on small capitalization stocks, another shows results for the last three years (if it were five years, they would look very different), this firm compares itself to only those firms managing more than $1 billion, that firm reports on a risk-adjusted basis, and so on and on. It's like the car manufacturers that all seem able to advertise that they came out ahead on one consumer survey or another. So you have to be skeptical and probing.

Representative, Not Selective, Accounts

You are bound to wonder, "What numbers are they showing me, anyway? Have they simply pulled out the results of the best account in the house?" You want the average of all accounts, or a composite of representative accounts. Admittedly, the firm can still do picking and choosing in putting together that composite, which you can't know about, but try to get a sense, by the way the principals present their tables, of whether or not you are getting a fair representation.

As a matter of practical fact, I don't worry too much about the selectivity of accounts, because the truth is that most firms run most of their money in much the same way, so all of their equity accounts look about the same. One thing I do worry about, however, is the self-purging nature of accounts. If an account came in during 1980, had lousy results, and left in 1984, does the firm erase that account's numbers out of its long-term record? That is a definite statistical opportunity to manipulate data. More and more, firms footnote how they treat such accounts. If not, ask. If the firm manages mutual funds as well, you have a public record you can compare with the numbers you have been submitted. An excellent source of information on mutual funds is the monthly *Mutual Fund Performance Report*, published by Morningstar in Chicago. A subscription is $125 a year.

Another concern is the time frame you are shown. You would certainly be suspicious if the firm gave you a five-year investment record when it's been in business ten years. An easy check is to read the ADV II before you look at the record, so you know how old the firm is and how long the principals have been there. You want to know if you are being shown the results of the same people who would be responsible for your money. It can make a big difference in results if a firm cherry-picks its time periods. I remember firms that showed their five-year records from 1975 to 1980, choosing to hide the fact that they went into the tank in the bear market of 1973–74. You want the full history of the firm.

Be sure you are comparing apples and apples. If last year was a bad one for stocks, don't let the firm show you the results of its balanced accounts, where the bond component softened the blow to equity markets. If last year was a good year for stocks and the firm tells you, "Our stocks were up 28 percent," ask, "Does that include cash?" Maybe the firm picked stocks well but couldn't find enough of them and kept 20 percent of its accounts' assets in the cash market. If you had an account with that firm, it would not have been up 28 percent but more like 23 percent.

Time-weighted Returns

Be sure your manager is using the time-weighting method in stating results, which smooths out the distortions caused by the fact that money comes in and goes out of different accounts at different times of the year. To gauge the ability of managers and compare their performance to that of other managers, you need to account for contributions and withdrawals over which they have no control. Managers have been known to use another method of reporting if it shows them in a better light.

Table 6.1 Dollar Weighting Affects Manager Performance

Account	Market Value	Percentage Return (1 Year)
A	$1,500,000	10%
B	$1,200,000	11%
C	$1,200,000	7%
D	$1,400,000	8%
E	$10,000,000	15%
Composite—accounts dollar weighted		12.9%
Composite—accounts equally weighted		10.2%

The firm's reported results look far better when the largest account, which outperformed the others, is given a weighting in the composite proportionate to its size.

Dollar weighting of accounts is another factor to be wary of: If the firm gives a $5 million account five times the weight of a $1 million account in arriving at the firm's performance composite, ask to see the performance of smaller accounts. Table 6.1 is an example of a firm that seems to have given a very large account more attention, so that it performed far better than other accounts at the firm. A dollar-weighted reporting method would distort the results experienced by the firm's smaller clients.

Such considerations may seem overwhelming, suggesting that you need to bring an accountant in the door with you. Your best protection against underhanded games being played is a firm that is long established and with a good reputation. If a firm's been around a while, it is far more likely to be honorable and straightforward, because dishonesty and distortions are revealed in time. Sociopaths have a short gratification schedule.

Another factor on your side is not being in a hurry. If you take your time in making a choice of firms, so that you see a number of them, you will begin to appreciate full disclosure and fairness in discussing performance, and to spot the deceits or the people capable of them. But you have to listen to a lot of this stuff before you know what sounds responsible and what sounds phony.

I have an advantage over most investors when it comes to judging the character and integrity of managers, for, though disreputable sorts might fool the public, they can seldom fool their peers. I am constantly checking with other money managers who may say of some guy, "I just don't trust him." But you will probably be able to sense that on your own after you've seen a few firms. As they say, anything that sounds too good to be true, probably is. Anyone who makes big claims, thrown at you as though someone were pitching a product on TV, is suspect.

Be wary of manipulated performance numbers:

- Is the record you are shown truly representative of the firm's accounts or has the firm cherry-picked its best accounts?

- Have poor-performing accounts that have left the firm been included in calculating performance?

- Has the time frame presented been selected to show the firm in the best light?

- Is the cash component of portfolios included?

- Are you being shown balanced-account or equity results?

- Has the time-weighted method been used in calculating results?

---

6. The Imponderables

From the ADV II and brochure you will have all the nuts and bolts about the firm, and I wish I could give you a checklist of what is desirable and what is not. But generalizations aren't easy in this business.

Take the size of the firm. What is too big? Or too small?

I've always felt too little isn't an issue. In some ways the perfect firm is two people who have recently left a large outfit, where they had substantial responsibility and great records, because they feel they are ready to go out on their own. You will have their optimum productivity and incentive, and minimal distractions. They will have a rebirth of energy, and not a lot of money or clients to deal with. Experience without impediments is an appealing combination.

But that raises the problem of the firm's not having the five-year track record that I have said is mandatory. What you will have is the track record the principals racked up for their previous employer. But how can you be certain that that record was the result of their own work and not a reflection, at least in part, of the contribution of their colleagues at their former post? I might know the managers personally or be able to call someone to check out how good they are. Because I like entrepreneurial management situations, I will make that effort. A five-year record is one of my general rules, but I'm trying to buy talent, and I'm not going to let the rules get in the way of access to talent. You, on the other hand, would have to make a judgment about the principals' integrity and ability on your own, and hire them somewhat on trust. If you feel strongly that these are good people you want to be associated with, go ahead. But if you don't feel comfortable about making that decision, you would be better off looking for people with a five-year record as an independent firm.

As far as too big is concerned, that's partly a function of a firm's style. If it buys the Coca-Colas of the world, it doesn't matter if it has to buy 1 million shares or 2 million; it's an easy execution. But if it specializes in small companies, with small market capitalizations, you worry when the firm gets too big. If it likes a small company but has so much money to invest that it would have to gobble up 5 percent of that company's stock to get its clients involved, it will be marking up the price on the way in and decimating it on the way out. You have to keep a constant eye out on the size of firms with that specialty. They may be alright for now, but people tend to forget that if a firm is able to grow its assets at 12 percent a year, it'll be doubling its size in six years even if it doesn't attract a single new client.

Less Is More

I happen to prefer smaller firms, those with no more than four or five principals, because I feel that when firms grow larger than that, they become cumbersome, harder to control, and decisions that come out of a large group tend to gravitate toward the mean— which is my quarrel with banks. At a smaller firm, too, you feel you are more important as a client and won't get lost in the shuffle. Still, some firms with billions have managed to keep attracting top-notch professionals who can give new clients excellent results. Ask your prospective manager how many clients he or she has. I always look carefully at the person's face when he or she answers. If I see a pained expression, I worry. Then I ask, "What do you think your capacity is?" What I like to get is a smile and the answer, "I don't know. I suppose I'll know when I surpass it."

One manager who has mostly passive clients can have 100 of them and it isn't a problem. Another, who spends a lot of time communicating with clients, can hit his or her limit at 40. It's like a health club, which keeps selling memberships and it all works fine as long as everybody doesn't show up on the same afternoon. Some firms have a policy: "We think we can each effectively handle about 65 clients, and after that we hire more managers." That 65 is an arbitrary number, but at least it shows the firm is working off a business plan.

What bothers me most is a firm that spends too much time talking to clients and not enough time running its portfolios. I want to see money management be more important than service. There's a huge difference in the mentality and psychic energy of firms with different orientations. I like people who are really stock junkies.

Another often-asked question I can't answer concerns the amount of trading a manager does. The more the portfolio turns over, the greater the transaction costs, of course, but I have to say that I really don't know what a "proper" turnover level is. One manager's style will dictate more trading than another's. I concentrate on the returns and the volatility incurred in getting those returns. The results, after all, are net of trading costs.

The age of managers is another matter that invites no easy generalizations. Some managers retain their enthusiasm and drive until death drives them from the market, and others seem to lose interest over the years. Maybe they've done the task too long. It happens with surgeons and tax lawyers, and, I suppose, with bakers and shoemakers, anybody that does the same repetitive thing for decades. It stops giving them a buzz. And no doubt over the years they've put together a decent pile of money for themselves, so the motivation to hit hard just isn't there any more.

I've found it useful, in trying to gauge how much ambition is left in a manager, to get off the topic of investments and just ask, casually, something like, "Lot of pressure in your business, I can see that. What do you do to unwind?" The manager will relax a bit then. It's easier to talk about a subject on which he doesn't think he's being graded. Suppose that he says he likes to sail. "I don't have much time for it, but if I had a choice, I'd sail 100 percent of the time." I would listen closely to a statement like that. Sometimes, when a manager talks about his passions outside the business, you get the sense that he is tired, that he doesn't care about the business very much any more, that he would rather be doing something else. That's not good. The best managers are obsessive about making money, and if they've lost that drive and are revaluating what's important in life, you have to wonder if you didn't get there too late. They may still have the right stuff, but their agenda has shifted. The firm won't be a terrible place to be, but there are probably better.

The Age Factor

It could be argued, in any case, that this is simply a young person's game. It is extraordinarily stressful. Half the things you can invest in today didn't exist 15 years ago. There's a sense of the world's changing too fast and of being incapable of adapting to all the change. I saw what October 19, 1987, when the market fell 20 percent in one day, did to some managers. It scared everybody to death, but the older you were, the more scared you were likely to be. It demonstrated that all of your experience had little value, because you could never have predicted anything like that. For most people in the business, their net worth and their income are determined by the same forces; their fees come from managing money and most of their own wealth is in the stock market. So they watched 20 percent of their capital disappear, as well as 20 percent of the assets upon which their fees were based, and they were terrified. If the market didn't bounce back, their clients would disappear along with their net worth.

If that happens to you when you are 35, you can get over it. It leaves a scar, but it doesn't prevent you from continuing a productive life. But I think many older people were rendered incapable of ever again taking the level of risk that is required to distinguish yourself in this business.

On the other hand, wealthy people looking for investment advisors are usually 50 or older themselves, and they feel far more comfortable with a mature manager than they would turning their money over to "kids" in their 30s. They would be giving responsibility to those who are of the same vintage as their own children. For most middle-aged people, that's a reach. Your children may be 35, successful, and self-sufficient, but you still question their judgment. They are still children in the eyes of their parents. So it's hard to give serious amounts of money to managers that age. They haven't lived enough, experienced enough, and suffered enough, you suspect, to be truly trustworthy.

So you are likely to end up giving your money to people closer to your own age. The consequence, in many cases, is that they will not exploit opportunities as effectively as people 20 years their junior. A lot of older people understand that, and they accept the trade-off. They would like a higher return, of course, but they're willing to take less to be able to feel their money is in more seasoned hands.

7. Poking Through the Process

The firm should have, and be able to explain, an investment process that's been thought through and follows a coherent logical path. Then you can probe around the edges to see if the firm thinks about all the issues that could impinge on that process. You may be a novice in investment matters, but once you see a few firms, you'll get a sense of where to dig. Much of it is just common sense.

For example, there are those who will tell you they are top-down managers, who start with the economic and business environment, then decide which industries should prosper in that environment, and finally which companies are the best in those industries. And there are bottom-up managers, who tend to concentrate on just plain stock picking. But make top-down managers tell you more about how they choose their individual stocks, and ask the bottom-up investors if they pay any attention to the effect of interest rates on their companies.

Then, as an extra toss-in, see if either of them consider global issues. "Do you think what's happening to the Japanese stock market will effect our own?" If they don't care about macroeconomic and global issues—"We just try to find companies that are doing well and we gave up trying to forecast the economy long ago"— that's all right; but if they do, you'll want to see how intelligently they talk about the bigger picture.

What you are trying to do, however limited your own knowledge, is to create questions that will allow you to see if you get thoughtful or at least candid responses. If they know what they don't know and they've made a decision that they're going to operate within a narrow framework, that's alright. What I don't like is pretense, answers that very clearly show that they are just winging it. When you can see that they don't know and they don't know how to say that they don't know, it would be suicidal to hire such a firm, because if that inability to deal with gaps in knowledge carries into their investment process, you're gone.

I also like firms that follow fairly simple investment strategies. I am wary of very complex systems. If their approach is simple, they should be able to articulate it and you should be able to understand it. Otherwise you are never going to be comfortable with the firm you've hired. You wouldn't hire an attorney whom you can't talk to, regardless of how clever you thought he or she was. I don't think the investment professional you hire should be any different. You shouldn't be asked to hand over your $1 million—and you had to make $1.6 million before you paid taxes—without understanding what's going to happen to it. So don't be shy about asking questions, even if you suspect you may be asking dumb ones. What are you supposed to do—say, "O.K. I don't get it, but my faith is in you. Here's my million. Just do good, baby!"?

In-house and External Research

Ask the managers you're interviewing where they get their ideas. I don't think it's important that they have an internal research staff, which is why a smaller firm doesn't bother me. There are plenty of outside sources for good research that their commission dollars will buy. But then I want to know if they follow through on those sources. I like it, for example, when managers tell me they try to visit every company that they hear about that sounds promising. I think that kind of old-fashioned commitment makes a big difference.

I know that if you go see one of the big, well-researched companies, an IBM, for example, you're probably going to talk to some third vice president in finance and you're not going to come away knowing much more than you did before you went. But it's hard for me to believe that you won't come away with *something* incremental. Just the fact that you took the trouble to get in the car and spend a couple of hours driving to Armonk, an inconvenience—or that you flew out from Chicago, an expense as well as an inconvenience—demonstrates to me a willingness to spend resources in doing the best job you can. The world is full of bright people and there are only two ways to achieve a sustainable edge: one is work and the other is judgment, and the two generally operate in tandem.

One of the questions that is part of the ritual at these meetings is, "Are you always fully invested? What encourages you to cut back and go into cash?" They'll say, "When stocks get a little pricey," or "When we don't like the market." Pin them down. "What do you mean by pricey?" "At what point don't you like the market?" You want to find out if there is some thought-out discipline about when they cut back their exposure to the

market—presuming they are not always 100 percent invested—
be it related to interest rates, multiples of earnings, book values,
whatever. Do they have criteria for identifying overvaluation
and acting on them? Ask them, "When was the last time you
owned a serious amount of cash?" They'll name a date, and
you follow up: "What got you there?" What you are doing is
searching for any gaps in their approach or logic. Try to gauge
whether these are tough questions for them. Maybe the whole
process of investing is tough for them. Press them when you
have a sense that there's something wrong. Part of the way you
can tell is by watching how much they squirm in their chairs.

What are their sell disciplines when it comes to individual
stocks? Some say they'll hold until there is an earnings disappointment or some other change in fundamentals, and some
say they sell when a stock breaks down on their technical
charts. Others sell a stock when it reaches the price they had
in mind when they bought it, which I don't like very much,
because in this business you often make your money when a
stock you thought was going to 30 goes to 50 in short order. I'd
rather hear, "When it gets to 30, we'll look at it again." Things
can change.

Evaluating the firm's investment process:

- Is the process clear, logical, and understandable?
- Is it fairly straightforward or off-puttingly complex?
- Where does the firm get its investment ideas?
- How does it follow through on those ideas?
- If the firm is not always fully invested, what factors
  does it consider in cutting back on stocks?
- Is there a stock sell discipline?

---

8. Gathering Impressions

Much of what you are trying to do when you evaluate a firm
is get a sense of the people and the place. It isn't all numbers
and process. That's why you have to visit a manager in his or

her working environment, rather than have someone from the firm stop by your office after work.

So keep your eyes open. How do the principals interact with their employees—do they treat them like dirt or with dignity? Are the phones busy or not busy? Does everyone seem frantic? Are the people you see prepared for the meeting? You want a sense of the rhythm of the enterprise; does it strike you as a firm that would run your money the way you'd like it run?

Does it look like an office where people work, or a stage set? I love the firms that are six months old and have Chippendale knockoffs and paneled walls, everything to make them look like they've been in business for 150 years. Sure, they've hired a decorator, but they signed off on the plans and paid for the Chippendale. The decisions they made telegraph their personality, reveal what kind of firm they think they are and what kind of clients they are aiming for. That helps you to judge whether or not you belong there.

I've had people tell me they were pleased that a firm had a small, almost shabby office in an older building with modest rents. For them, this was a firm that didn't spend money frivolously, and this jibed with the way they themselves think. Everybody would like to clone themselves, so the more touchstones of familiarity there are—age, education, religion, ethnic background, and family situation—the more comfortable you feel with the environment of the firm.

I always ask people, after they've visited a few firms and reported on those they favored, "And what did you see that you *didn't* like?" Negative reactions vary all over the lot and can be far more interesting than the positives. One man told me, "Well, the guy I met was really smart, I'll give him that. But he was wearing this thousand-dollar Italian suit. He was also distracted, trying to do ten things at once, but it was really that flashy suit that bugged me. I don't think I could ever be comfortable with anybody in an outfit like that."

You obviously can't let totally irrelevant factors stand in the way of the right hire. Any firm is going to have its dark side, especially when it comes to personalities. There has to be a trade-off between making money and personal comfort. So you have to go back and forth a bit to zone in on where the lines cross most efficiently.

At many firms it's a marketing or client-relations person who comes out to talk to you. That can be a real put-off. Many have spent time with a marketing consultant who has helped them whip up a canned spiel. They answer your questions in a slick manner, as though they had memorized a stack of response cards.

I particularly hate it when they use flip charts, and they read to you what the charts are already declaring in four-inch print. "Our first concern is preservation of capital." Really? You would hardly expect it to be loss of capital. "We buy only undervalued securities." Indeed. I often wonder who buys the overvalued securities. "We buy only the finest companies." "We invest only when the economic environment is favorable." "It's not how much money you make, it's how much you keep that counts." It sure is cliché time again. The one that drives me up the wall is: "Every client here is unique." There might be five different kinds of clients, if you consider objectives, but every client is *not* unique. If the firm has 100 clients and each one is unique, each with a differentiated portfolio, the firm would need an intimate awareness of thousands of companies.

There are times when it's hard to keep a straight face at these meetings. You don't want to hire a hackneyed firm. When you hear stuff like that, don't accept it. Try to ask questions that get beyond such pap, but if they're adamant about sticking to the boilerplate, then I'd just close up and move on.

Talk to Mohammed

It's all right for a marketing person to do a warm-up act, I suppose—though most of them are like wind-up dolls—but the only way you are going to capture the essence of the firm, and the way your money will be managed, is by talking to the portfolio manager who will be running your account. Insist upon seeing that person. You want to know who is Mohammed. Sometimes there is no Mohammed. There are firms in which the money is run, essentially, externally. Two or three analysts feed the firm all of its ideas and are very handsomely compensated in commissions. But that is not what you are looking for. You want the people you are paying to run your money really to run your money. If they depend on an analyst at Goldman Sachs and he or she decides to go to Tibet for two years, you would be in deep trouble and not even know it.

If the person whom you are paying a fee to run your money can't find the time to talk to you, then maybe you should go somewhere else. You are going to be laying out 1 percent of $1 million, or $10,000, a year to somebody, and you have enough experience in life to make some judgments about that person's abilities. If the firm won't offer you access to that person when you're a prospective client, it gives you some idea as to how much dialogue you're going to have in the future if you sign on.

Clues that would make you suspicious about a firm:

- Offices that are flashy and pretentious
- Disorganized, frenetic offices and people
- Principals who seem overwhelmed rather than in control
- Presentations that are mechanical and superficial
- Portfolio managers who refuse to meet with you

---

9. The Breed Called Money Managers

When you do meet with the money manager, be prepared for a surprise, maybe several surprises.

One that I've had, several times, is visiting the offices of a firm with extraordinary numbers and finding that the people who run the money seem extraordinarily stupid. I don't think you have to talk to people who aren't very bright very long to pick up on it. You just can't square the intellect with the performance. Either somebody was feeding the firm its ideas—probably outside analysts, as in the example above—or they just got lucky as hell. If the people are also arrogant, it's a dead giveaway that something is wrong. It's often true that people who have been lucky begin to think they've been anointed. Always beware of arrogant managers. The old pros know the market can humble them at any moment. The good managers know they are good, but their confidence is tempered with humility, because they know, too, how much is luck and how luck can go either way. There are three things my firm considers mandatory to justify hiring a manager, and one of them is humility. The other two are humor and a passion for his or her work. So ask managers about their mistakes. If they can't think of one, skepticism is the proper response.

At other firms you may find the people are obviously bright, but you begin to suspect they don't care very much about the business they are in. Or maybe they are lazy. But when you ask them about some stocks they like, they don't seem to know much. There isn't enough detail. They appear merely to be parroting what some analyst or stock salesperson told them. They don't have a passion about the companies they like. You can discern this not only in their narrative but in their tone. You ask a growth stock manager about his names and he'll say Wal-Mart—they all own Wal-Mart—and one guy will give you a shrug and a sentence or two, while another guy will start in, with real animation, about the ten new Sam's Clubs that Wal-Mart opened last year, how much they did per square foot compared to Wal-Mart's regular stores, how many new stores are planned for which cities over the next three years, and he'll get going until it's hard to stop him. He's excited about what he's doing and he's full of information. You want that love of the business in a manager.

Total Dedication

All the good managers are passionate about the investment process, and certainly about the outcome, but they are dispassionate about investment decisions. Most of us, as investors, get emotionally involved in those decisions, but not the good managers. Stocks are pieces of paper, no more. The only reason to own one is to sell it to somebody else at a higher price—preferably, at the highest price in recorded history just before it plummets 40 percent. They get a certain sinister joy in not only extracting the last penny but in punishing those less astute than they.

They are an intensely competitive bunch—in everything they do. They are competitive tennis players and bridge players, for example, and if they can't win most of the time, they won't play. I'm not sure whether they love winning or find losing too painful to bear. And if you run money, of course, the numbers tell the score at the end of every day.

The whole idea is to turn capital into more capital. The issue is to win. You don't hear these people talking about what a wonderful company IBM is. They talk about what a wonderful investment it has or hasn't been. There are great companies and there are great stocks, and the two are not necessarily the same. Only the great stocks matter to this breed.

In search of such stocks, they are information gluttons with an insatiable need to know. Even though most of the information is noise and unworthy of a decision, it still has to be processed. In the absence of information flow, they tend to become erratic in their behavior, because they feel disoriented, out of touch, left behind. They are workaholics, of course, but they hate vacations mostly because they might miss some piece of information. They are voracious readers. They are voracious listeners, as long as they think what they are hearing might be useful somehow. They tend to be relatively apolitical but they eagerly follow anything political that might relate to their investments.

They love to have lunch or dinner with other money managers in order to talk stocks and pick up more information. The agenda for the meeting is to make money for all parties present. But the hidden agenda is to make more than the other people around the table. There will be honest, unencumbered information-sharing, with no effort to sandbag. But when the parties are back in their own offices, each is on his or her own. If you sell a stock on Thursday that you were touting over lunch on Tuesday because a new piece of information has made you change your mind, there is no compulsion to call and tell the others. Collaboration has its limits, and the lines are drawn when something might stand in the way of your outstripping your peers.

Ask the manager what other managers he or she admires. "Who are some of your role models in the business? Who do you talk to that you think is smart?" If they just throw out the name of Peter Lynch or Warren Buffett, or say, "Gee, I don't talk to anybody," that's a bad sign. Most people at the top in this profession are very curious about what the other people they respect are doing. The lunches and the exchange of ideas over the phone are important in helping them make up their minds about what to buy and when to sell. They know some of the big names personally or are at least very aware of what they are up to. If they are unaware or indifferent, I would want to know why. There are some extreme loners who are good, of course, but that's not typical in this business. It's part of the humility thing: you know you can be wrong, so you like to check out your opinions with others you respect.

To Excel, You Have to Think Independently

But all are loners in one sense. They have to be, being as competitive as they are. They'll get everyone's opinion, be curious about the consensus, and then go their own way. If you are to differentiate yourself, in the matter of performance, from your peers, you have to take stands that are absolutely at odds with the consensus. You have to be more or less invested than the rest of the world, or more or less concentrated than the rest of the world, or your numbers are going to be identical to those of the rest of the world. Everyone gets pretty much the same information in these days of on-line data flow, so the differentiating factor is how you process it. It's like a poker game, where some information is known but a certain amount is speculative, and you're making decisions based on the importance of what's known and supposed, while calculating how others might act on the information that's known and supposed. It's quite an intellectual game.

It's fascinating to see the minds of the good ones at work at this game. They have the ability to think both globally and specifically. Some of their skill is intuitive and some acquired through experience. Tell them there will soon be an abundance of natural gas and they will quickly rattle off which industries and companies will be influenced both positively and negatively, and to what extent, by the price change that will follow. Talk of some pending piece of legislation and they will know how it will impact any industry that will be touched by it, and which companies will lose and which gain market share. Whereas most of us would take a piece of information and say,

"Hmm," and leave it at that, they are six steps down the road figuring out all the economic consequences. Those who are good do it on their own; the mediocre depend on Wall Street analysts to interpret events for them.

They can be wonderful at thematic plays. There is one extraordinarily skillful manager who, about five years ago, read about the demographic changes ahead for the country, in particular, the aging of our population. He asked what it would all mean, and one answer he came up with is a higher savings rate. He couldn't invest in banks, since most were already in the process of being discredited, so he bought mutual fund management companies. He loaded up on all the public companies, long before anybody else cared. Most of us don't think that way. For him it was a statistical certainty. You hear a lot of people talking about mutual fund management companies today, but he already has his triple in these stocks.

There's another manager who, back in 1983 and 1984, was buying the stocks of Scandinavian companies that own tankers that carry crude oil. He had learned from a European contact that few of these ships had been built for several years because there had been a glut of them. Some had been scrapped and many were obsolete. The shipping business is like the apartment business; once you're full up, prices go through the roof. Unlike the apartment business, the oil tanker business is very much of an auction market, and prices zoom way above the roof when there's a shortage of capacity. He probably made seven or eight times his money in those shipping companies.

So one of the things I like to hear when I'm running around talking to investment companies is some original thinking. The people who are good recognize change and identify how to exploit it. Investing may not be an art form, but this ability to make money is undoubtedly a talent. There is a reason that a Harry Helmsley or a Laurence Tisch, though not infallible, are very, very rich. Over a lifetime they have had the ability to make a series of important decisions that proved correct. When you find people like that with long-term patterns of success, there's a fair assumption that you can vest in their superior judgment. I think of one money manager who told me a year before the market meltdown in October 1987 that it would happen, what would precipitate it, and how it would unfold. He couldn't tell me when, but he said it was a virtual certainty, and he was 70 percent in cash when the market cracked.

Not only did he identify what would happen; he acted on it. We have all had times when we knew interest rates were going down or pork bellies were going up, but we didn't do anything about it, which is to say that we really didn't have much conviction about what we were saying. But these people have both the clarity and the courage to act. They won't always be right, of course, but far more often than not they are. That manager's been running money for 20 years and he's never had a down year.

I think you can find example after example of people who are intellectually framed in a way that encourages them to make money. You might be able to find a hundred investment opportunities that are compelling, but they'll be able to pick out the five that are the *most* compelling, and demonstrate why. They have the ability to assemble a huge array of little pieces of information in slightly different ways than other people, and those ways prove more rewarding than other assemblages. It's a fascinating gift.

And, I think, recognizable. If you talk to enough investment people, you can spot those who have it. Certainly, the dolts stick out like a sore thumb, the people who are distinguished by how undistinguished they are.

The best professional money managers

- Are passionate about investing
- Have humility about the process
- Admit their mistakes
- Are extremely competitive
- Are fanatical information gatherers
- Find patterns and investment themes in that information
- Know what other respected managers are up to
- But remain original thinkers

10. Disturbing Profiles

You'll recognize the talent, but you may not care much for the people who possess it. The exceptional managers tend to have some of the eccentricities of the artist, and their behavior can be strange. Words you picked up in Psychology 1, like *obsessive, compulsive,* and *pathological,* come to mind. They are rarely self-destructive people; you won't find them on drugs or with drinking problems. But they are prickly. They are in constant discord with their partners. Since they are egocentric, they believe whatever good happens in the world has entirely to do with them, and whatever bad happens in the world probably stems from conspirators; this quirk accounts for a lot of busted partnerships. There's a fair amount of employee turnover, because they tend to view those who work for them as commodities, nonessential to the outcome of the process, and easily replaceable. They are difficult at home, too, of course. When you spend your daytime hours making decisions autonomously, you are not very good at making decisions jointly at home. Their spouses, if consulted, might even call them autocratic and oppressive.

Many are totally underdeveloped socially and hide behind their quote machines because they don't know how to deal with other human beings. You can fall asleep during a conversation, and they'll just keep on talking. They're not clued in to how other people respond. Reading body language is an alien concept to them. They don't know when they have an audience and when, or how, they've lost it. They are habitually impatient. Unless it's something they are keenly interested in talking about, you have the feeling you've intruded on their time. Unless the topic is investments, they have the attention span of a hummingbird. They're always thinking about something else, usually the market, and often appear impatient and patronizing, which, in fact, they are, although it is not their intention to telegraph it. They live in their heads and, to a large extent, are oblivious to the world around them. They create victims—their employees, their families, and their partners. But you are not paying them for charm-school gloss.

Money management is still largely a male-dominated world, full of men who are, by nature and temperament, chauvinistic and oppressive. So women money managers—and there aren't that many yet who have been at it very long—have to be tough. Those who survive the environment are terrific. Women are the new immigrants: they will work harder, work longer, and make greater sacrifices to succeed.

Driven to Compensate

You wonder what made dyed-in-the-wool money managers the way they are. I've always suspected the need to make a lot of money for themselves and their clients is compensation for something they think is missing, or has been missed, in their lives. They are compelled to strive to make up for some lack— whether it was that they were ugly, short, or bad at sports when that mattered. They need to win, they need to acquire, and they need adoration. They have insatiable appetites for praise and recognition.

Also because they are egocentric, some would almost rather be right than be rich, which is something the shopper for investment services has to be aware of. I don't like to hear too much dogma from these folk. If they have very rigid views and have to be proved right, they'll become trapped in a notion of how the world should operate, and if it chooses to operate otherwise, it can be very painful for their clients.

The good ones aren't like that. They would rather be rich than right. In fact, they very much want to be rich. If you hire someone who doesn't care about making money, you've made a grievous error. If they can't make money for themselves, they are not likely to make it for you. The good ones are definitely motivated by profit, and they like to make their profit in stocks. If I find out that somebody running stocks puts his own wealth in real estate, it isn't likely I am going to be interested in him to manage my money. Because he's something of an imposter. He is signaling that he is distrustful of what he does for a living. He may say he does it for the sake of diversification, but I will suspect that he doubts his own skills. If he is not willing to bet his own money on them, that's not a good sign.

11. Trust Your Instincts

As I've discussed earlier, I and my associates have an advantage in running a talent search: we can usually call up someone in the business who knows the people we're interested in. This is a field where just about everybody worked someplace else. We'll know a manager at Putnam or T. Rowe Price where this fellow used to work and he'll usually be frank in his evaluation. Managers who are good tend to have opinions about who else is good, who works hard, who really understands the market and values, who is plugged into the best research, and who is trouble and to be avoided. If I get bad reports, though they may at times be unfair, I'll probably stay clear of that person. You just can't take the chance of working with people who create victims.

You probably can't make such calls, but certainly make any cross-checks that you can, including, needless to say, calling some of the manager's clients. In addition to evaluating all the nitty gritty you have gathered about the firm from the brochure, the ADV II, and the responses to your questions, trust your subjective judgments about the people and the culture of the place. I've found that people are reluctant to rely on their own instincts. The investment business, they think, is some other kind of world. But if you've been alive for a while, you've developed good instincts about people and businesses. You are simply trying to align your intuitive sense of the integrity of the people with the integrity of the process. And that's no different than trying to decide whether your plumber is being honest with you or whether he or she sees an opportunity to milk you for a few hundred bucks.

I know some people are just hopeless in this regard. They couldn't tell an ax murderer with a bloody hatchet in his hand. But most of us, through normal interaction with others, have some intuitive barometer as to whether people have honesty, integrity, intelligence, and ability. So rely on your instincts, particularly if you sense something unsettling. If you feel something's out of whack, you don't have to define exactly what that something is. Just listen to that inner voice. If it whispers that there's something about this person or persons, there's something about their offices, there's something about their style of communication—if you have this visceral reaction that something's not quite right—then the best thing you can do is forget about that firm. There are plenty of other providers of the service. Or, at the least, go back again to test your premises as best you can. I react negatively to a firm, then hear something about it that makes me wonder if I've been hasty in my conclusions, and I revisit.

At the very least you certainly will have a sense of whether these are people with whom you are going to feel comfortable—or, more important, whether you're probably going to be uncomfortable with them. My advice, if you are uncomfortable, is that, again, you don't have to write an essay about how you feel and why you feel that way. You feel that way, and that's it. Check that firm off your list and keep looking for the one you feel is right for you. If you have money, you have choices.

If You Find You Can't Decide

Some people just can't do it. They find the whole process too confusing. They see ten managers and they cannot pick up on the differences. Instead, a blurring and blending takes place. They are overwhelmed by the similarities. They throw up their hands in frustration and say, "It's beyond my capacity to make an intelligent decision about something I have no knowledge of or interest in. I don't really care about investments. To tell you the truth, I have trouble paying attention to what these people are saying. It's boring and far too complicated."

If that proves the case, then you either choose mutual funds or pay a consultant like me to do the job for you. You can only mainstream people to the extent that they are willing to be mainstreamed. One of the nice things about being wealthy is that you get to create a world that accommodates you. You transfer an inconvenience to those who are compensated for dealing with it. We could probably all write our own wills, too, if we wanted to go to the law library and figure out how to do it. Most of us prefer to pay the lawyer's price.

If you *are* interested, if you are drawn into the process, it can be a fascinating intellectual game. Every time you speak to someone new, you are cross-checking. One manager's buying Merck at the same time another's selling. And when they start talking about the universe of stocks and their obsession with unearthing the next Merck, these managers—the good ones—bare their souls. You get to compare investment psyches.

Still, if it's not for you, it's just not for you. Several years ago I got a call from a gentleman in Florida who told me he had just sold his business and was in possession of a check for $50 million. "I'm quite anxious to get this done," he said.

So I gave him my usual response. "There's no hurry about this, because you are going to be in the investment business for a long time. We'll arrange to meet, talk things over, and I'll provide you with the names of several managers. . . . "

"No," he interrupted. "You don't understand. I want to get this done. Can you come to Florida in the next day or so?"

It was my turn to say "No." I had to go to New York the next day, Wednesday, and I had a really nasty travel schedule for the following two weeks.

"Look," he said, "I'm leaving for France at the end of the week—I have a house there—and I want this done before I leave."

Fifty million dollars by the end of the week! I thought a minute and told him, "I'm flying into Kennedy. Do you want to meet me there?"

"It would be easier for me to meet you in Chicago. Could you reroute through Chicago?"

I told him I'd see if there was space and get back to him. There was, and I arranged a three-hour layover in Chicago. We met at the American Airlines Admirals Club at O'Hare. He was a good-looking man, in his early 60s, quite nice. I told him again there was really no reason to hurry this, that it could be handled while he was in France, and that he could interview managers when he returned. But he just said, "As I told you, I just want to get this taken care of. I've checked on you. You've got a good reputation. You take care of it for me. Let's get it behind us."

So we went through the usual exercise, about how much income he wanted, how much risk he wanted to take. We decided to set aside something like $30 million and have his bank invest it in tax-exempts of a specific quality and maturity. Then we talked about stocks. "Just give me the names of four investment managers with different styles," he said. He never even talked to them. I arranged for the managers' contracts to be sent to him in Florida by Federal Express. The contracts were executed, his Florida bank was instructed, and he was live by the end of Friday, the day he left for France.

When hiring an investment manager

- Do your homework
- Trust your gut reactions
- Or hire a consultant to help you do the job

7

WATCHING OVER
YOUR MONEY

---

1. Your Investment Goals

When it comes to investments, the only history people are interested in is their own. They may have hired a money management firm on the strength of its prior record, but from then on they will judge it entirely on the basis of their own experience. The world begins anew the day they sign the contract.

On that day you should know what you will consider success and what you will deem a disappointment in your new relationship. And you should share your return expectations with your manager, for they are then his guidelines in running your account. Your aims are his job description. From the outset you both know when you will be satisfied and when you will be disappointed to the point where he can expect you'll be looking for a different association. If you buy into a mutual fund, you should write down just what outcome you expect from the decision to hire that fund's manager.

Success has to be defined, of course, in terms of achieving your goals during a period when it is possible to achieve them. There will be times when you will be frustrated because the market has been hostile and Bernard Baruch couldn't pull out a winner.

Over a three- to five-year period there are really three thresholds you need to cross to grasp the financial grail.

First, you want your investments to earn a return that compensates you for the risk you took for buying stocks instead of Treasury notes or leaving your money in a money market fund. That would mean annual average earnings in the 12 percent to 15 percent range (see Figure 7.1), the range that we have seen earlier is realistic and attainable.

Second, you want to earn returns that suggest that the person you've hired is better than the average money manager. *Better than average* means just that—you want your manager to be at least in the upper half—and preferably in the upper 30 percent or 40 percent—of the people managing money in the same style. You expect good relative returns as well as good absolute returns. You did not sign up for mediocrity. If you have gone through a couple of years when you've made 12 percent a year but everybody in the world has made 17 percent, clearly you have not been well served (see Table 7.1).

You are employing the test you would use to gauge the effectiveness of any employee, and your money manager is, in essence, on your payroll. Has he done what you have paid him to do? Has he performed better than other employees doing the same thing?

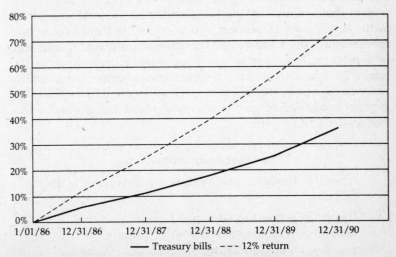

Figure 7.1 Treasury bills vs. 12 percent return from common stocks (five-year cumulative returns with dividends reinvested).

Table 7.1   Effect of Excellence

- $1000 invested for 10 years in the best-performing mutual fund produced $6833.* (Annualized return 21.19%.)

- $1000 invested for 10 years in the 50th best-performing mutual fund produced $4199.* (Annualized return 15.43%.)

---

*Value at 6/30/91.
Source: Morningstar.

Third, you should be able to earn a spread over the inflation rate on an after-tax basis. If I had to choose only one objective, it would be to earn an after-tax 3 percent return compounded over the inflation rate. Because that means you're winning. That is the bread-and-butter definition of coming out ahead in this game. Relative measures are fine and well, because we all want excellence, but they're less important than knowing you kept up with inflation, that you didn't lose capital in real terms, and, better yet, that you made money in those same terms. You can't buy a new car with relative performance. Common stocks provide that inflation-plus advantage (see Figure 7.2).

And that is where we get the absolute return goal we started with. If you earn 12 percent and you're 40 percent taxed, that leaves you with a little over 7 percent after taxes. If inflation is 4 percent, then you've got your 3 percent above that. It's hard, therefore, to set an absolute figure because the inflation rate varies, but in recent years a return in the 13 percent to 14 percent range would give you a comfortable margin above the rise in the cost of living.

Your investment objectives:

1. Absolute annual average return of 12 percent to 15 percent

2. Upper 30 percent to 40 percent of the universe of managers with a similar investment approach

3. Three percent above inflation rate, after taxes are paid

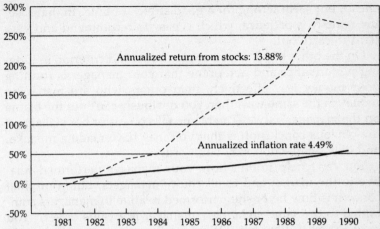

Figure 7.2 Inflation vs. S&P 500: 10 years' cumulative results.

2. When the Numbers Disappoint

Setting your goals is pretty uncomplicated. The complications arise when you go through periods when your manager or managers don't meet one or more of the above tests. Then you have to ask yourself what's causing the problem.

Usually, if you have chosen talented people, the disappointment is on the first scorecard. Stocks have been in a slump, and next to nobody's brought in even 10 percent returns. Or the disappointment stems from rotational patterns in the market; the manager has not earned 12 percent to 15 percent because his or her style has been out of phase. The manager was not stupid or inattentive. Anybody running money can be out of sync with the prevailing trend for a year or two. The manager can be right about cyclicals but the cycle takes longer than usual. He or she can be a growth stock manager when everyone wants value stocks, or a small company manager when the large capitalization stocks are in vogue. After all, you want a manager who thinks independently and who is likely to be early with his or her ideas. If your manager isn't something of a contrarian, you are just running with the pack. Well, contrarians can be right, and buying stocks when they are indeed cheap, but seem wrong for a good stretch of time. In that case, the remedy is patience, which is easy to recommend and very hard to carry out.

On the other hand, if you apply the second criterion in judging performance and determine that your manager is running your money less effectively than others who are managing money in the same way, then you obviously can't put the blame on the manager's style. The blame falls on his or her skills, and the obvious conclusion is that you may have made a mistake, and that a correction may be in order.

You can't help noting how your manager performed relative to the market and to all equity managers, but your chief concern is how he or she performed relative to managers committed to the same style. "My manager is a value buyer," you have to say to yourself. "Who are the other value investors, and how have they done?" If value buyers as a group haven't done well—which was true, for example, during much of the latter part of the 1980s—you can understand why your manager has fallen short of the market and of the universe of equity managers.

How do you get the names of other value managers, growth managers, small-capitalization managers, or whatever style your manager espouses? Some of them will come from *Barron's, Forbes,* and *The Wall Street Journal.* If, when you interviewed the manager you hired, you asked what other managers he or she admires, you probably have the names of some people important enough in the industry to have their records discussed in the press. You can check on mutual funds managed according to the same style. Magazines that publish mutual fund performance tables usually indicate the style of the managers. You can consult *Nelson's Directory of Investment Managers,* which breaks down managers and their performance by style. This annual costs $325, but it can be found in some libraries, particularly university libraries. You really don't have to be a CIA operative to develop this information.

If you find that value buyers have done badly and that your value buyer has done no worse—and maybe even better than his or her peers—then the best thing to do is to relax and wait it out. Better yet, you could increase your bet. Logic and mathematics suggest that response—styles out of favor in one cycle become very much in favor in the next—but most people won't double up. When emotion and logic clash, most people find reasons to ignore probabilities. Las Vegas has prospered on that simple phenomenon.

3. Time for a Probe

Suppose there have been two or three disappointing quarters, when the manager has not done well in absolute terms and relative to other managers following the same discipline. You are worried and you reach for the phone. You are polite, but you want a dialogue. You are looking for reassurance that your manager is on top of the situation. You want to get a sense of whether or not you will be rewarded if you stay put.

When I make such calls, they often go something like this:

"George, we haven't spoken in a while. What's going on?"

"This market's murder," is the answer. "Stocks are just too pricey. They were pricey six months ago. We're underinvested because we just can't find anything to buy that makes any sense."

"What would it take to encourage you to get invested again?"

"Either prices have to come down or we need some reason to believe corporate earnings are going to trend back up."

What I am listening for is information that will allow me to determine if George knows what he's doing and what would make him change course. I want to be sure that he hasn't become so steeped in dogma that he wants to be right more than he wants to be rich. I hired him as a value buyer, and if he tells me he can't find values, that's alright. But if he starts telling me that the banking system's coming unraveled and that the folding of 200 savings and loans is sure to send the market down 30 percent, I worry, because the fact that they're closing S&Ls doesn't mean the market has to blow up. There are other stimuli that can neutralize systemic blows like that. I want to hear analyses of particular companies and particular stocks, not macroeconomic forecasts. When I ask, "What would get you invested?", I want to hear, again, about stock prices and not about newspaper headlines.

What is reassuring is when you sense that your manager acknowledges that he has a problem, that he is concerned about it, and that he has thought through what would impel him to alter his strategy. At least you know somebody's minding the store, and if he has been off-track only two quarters and sounds like he knows what he's up to, you can give him more time.

I don't even mind hearing, "Hell, I don't know what to do in here. I don't understand it. The market's going up. I've got companies that are great growers. But nobody cares." If nothing else, I've had a statement of candor. I know the guy is upset. I know he's gone back and checked and rechecked his work. Most important, he isn't kidding himself. He is conscious of the problem and is trying to figure out what to do about it. He isn't telling me, "These are great companies, and I don't care what the market's doing." I don't like the arrogance of "the world's wrong and I'm right." That kind of rigidity kills you, or has the potential to kill you. You need some flexibility in this business.

The firm's history helps in making a judgment, and the more history, the better. You can go back and see if there were other periods when the numbers looked terrible for a time but the guy bounced back. If so, he's good, he knows how to pull himself together, and he should be able to do it again. What you can't do is look only at recent history. It can get very tough to make a decision when you've got someone who was going like gangbusters two years ago and then headed south, or who was a disaster five years ago, had a couple of good years, and then started to disintegrate again. You can't learn much from that kind of choppy record. But when you get a long-term picture, you can make a reasonable judgment about a manager's true abilities.

There is something else I want to hear: compassion for the client. And I want to hear fear. The fear should be that all the clients will go away and there won't be any money anymore.

When your manager's had two or three consecutive disappointing quarters

- Talk to the manager to judge if he or she is concerned and on top of the situation.
- Check manager's record for ability to pull out of similar stretches in the past.

4. When to Pull the Plug

In all likelihood, the manager's numbers will rally. If your selection process was at all responsible, you didn't hire a total
washout, and intellectual and judgmental skills are not per-
ishable. Most firings are premature and badly conceived. Of
course, if you have unrelieved poor results quarter after quarter, in relation both to the market and to other managers pursu-
ing a similar approach, you and your manager will split within
a year to a year and a half. But that would be rare. Normally,
even a manager who lost his or her touch will look good again
for at least several quarters. There will be up quarters and
down quarters, so you get mixed messages, and the only way
you can get a handle on how your account is faring is by link-
ing up those quarters. You have to look at the annual returns.

As you watch those returns, the time may come, however,
when you say to yourself, "This person is no longer credible."
There is a point at which the great market god tells you that,
in spite of how well reasoned everything he's told you may
be, you are on the wrong planet and that it is time to get
off. You've squandered an opportunity; you can't allow it to
continue and be trapped in a continuing decline. The longer
somebody underperforms—particularly if that failure is related
not to methodology but to execution—the more the manager's
credentials are stripped and the closer you are to abdication.
You have to say, "Yes, he's a nice guy. I know he's working
hard and trying hard. But he just doesn't have the right stuff."

How long do you wait before you make that decision? Three
or four years, unless you are convinced sooner that something is
very wrong, or you aren't getting the kind of answers that show
there is concern and effort, or the firm is so far under water that
even another good year or two won't bring it back to acceptable
territory. Otherwise, you give the manager the benefit of the
doubt—until three or four years show you it just won't work. "I
put in a million dollars three years ago, and it's worth $1,150,000.
I haven't lost money, but hell, I could have done better in the
bank. More important, the average mutual fund with the same
approach is not up 15 percent but up 30 percent." If you have to
say that, you know it's time to cash out.

It's not always an easy call. Three or four years of putting up with disappointing numbers may seem like forever, but it is a relatively short period in the scheme of things. If I were making all the rules, I'd give a manager five years, but that's too far out for most people. Three years seem to represent the outer limit of human endurance in bearing disappointment. So three to four years is a reasonable compromise. But in most instances it has to be at least that long. A shorter period than that, as I've said, will usually contain mixed messages. There will be a year when the manager had great numbers, far better than those who manage money in the same way. And there will be a year when the manager did substantially worse. But if you look back over the three-to-four-year history and ask, "Would I hire this person today?" and the answer is a conclusive "no"— that's the ultimate litmus test. The manager has to be replaced.

I know I haven't given you a precise recipe. I have long searched for some mechanical measure of judgment, something like, "After the passage of ten quarters if you're not at Point A, you get fired; if you're at Point B, you're on probation; and if you're at Point C, you get a gold star." But I've never been able to develop a set of measures as strict as I would like. You end up having to make subjective judgments. The short-term record is too confusing. You hire a manager. She underperforms the first quarter, then the second, and the reason is that she's at odds with the market. She's 50 percent in cash and the market's up 6 percent two quarters back to back. But the third quarter the market drops, and because she was still 50 percent in cash, she's had a great quarter. So for two quarters you've written "imbecile" on her forehead and the third quarter she looks like a visionary. Or was she? Was she, in fact, gifted and early? Or has she been second-rate all along? It gets muddled, and only the passage of more time will make things clear.

The first year you hire a manager doesn't matter so much in any case; the firm's getting the account invested, and one quarter can strongly impact the full year. The first quarter the market can be up 10 percent, but the manager is in the process of putting your money to work; you are only 30 percent invested. You may well be at the bottom of the performance rankings, but you can't terminate your manager at that point.

Even at the end of the year, your manager may have done well for the final three quarters but still look mediocre because of that first quarter, and again you have to be tolerant.

But if after six quarters into the process there is no sign of excellence, my anxiety spikes. And if after the seventh and eighth quarters there's a consistency that makes you suspect that you are going to have more bad quarters than good quarters, then you know you have a problem you have to deal with. If the first quarter of the third year is also disappointing, way below trend, then you've got to say, "I'll give him one more quarter, and unless something miraculous happens, he's gone." Is the evaluation process scientific? No. You just throw up your hands and say, "Enough is enough."

If there is a pattern of being chronically below the fiftieth percentile, you would worry early on. Now, if the guy's compounding money at 16 percent and the world's doing 18 percent, it isn't so bad. I would say to you, "If you could sign a five-year contract at these numbers, do it." But if somebody's doing 6 percent and other people are doing 12 percent, my tolerance is quite different. There are ranges of acceptability if you are to gratify long-term goals. If you can't find periods of demonstrated excellence, in relative terms, then you don't wait three years; you accelerate the process.

The same guidelines hold true whether you have an investment counselor or shares of a mutual fund. There certainly is no difference in the period of judgment, and the comparative numbers are easier to come by—in some ways, too easy to come by. You are exposed to too many rankings in the press. You want to compare your manager's three-to-five-year record against those of his or her peers, managers with similar mandates. You do not want to compare him or her to the top performer last year. If you keep switching to last year's top banana, you are acting exactly like the person who keeps buying the hot stock of the moment, so hot it is almost sure to cool off not long after you have bought it. The best-performing managers, the ones who will make you rich, are seldom at the top of the heap in any given year; they don't concentrate their portfolios that much, take on that kind of risk. Instead, they tend to be above-average performers year after year, which over the long pull *does* put them at the top of the universe.

When do you fire a manager?

- After three to four years of poor performance relative to the market

- More important, after three to four years of poor performance relative to other managers following the same style

- Sooner than that if the manager gets so far behind that he or she cannot catch up to the market or other managers within the time remaining until three to four years have passed, or whenever you have lost confidence in a manager because communication or administration has been unsatisfactory

---

5. Be Reasonable

Some investors will *never* be satisfied. They'll be up 18 percent a year for seven years and dump the manager because they hear about somebody who's done 22 percent. Or they leave because they have six great years in a row and the seventh year's flat—not a disaster, mind you, just flat. Such people tend to get greedier and greedier until they do themselves in and end up with terrible performance, a point I will come back to in the next chapter.

That is what worries me about the so-called wraparound accounts that we examined earlier. Brokers finding investment managers for clients assemble lists that are often based on the sexiest records of late. If you have a listed phone number, you are bound to get calls from stockbrokers who tell you, "We've done a screen of all the investment managers in the world and these are the best." So you say, "Send me something," and you see all these fancy numbers. Somebody's always bound to have done better than your manager, so you begin to wonder if you are adequately served. The pension funds are used to this sort of thing, and take the latest five-year wonders with a grain of salt. But individual investors aren't used to seeing a lot of comparative numbers, and they'll be seduced into joining up with the latest hot-shot. Wrap accounts will probably churn up the whole business, and encourage higher manager turnover rates for the worst reasons.

In a perfect world, you hire somebody and he or she loses your business when you die. The truth is, my firm hasn't had to go through many firings—about five managers in our 20 years in business. In those instances, we felt they had lost the skills that we had hired them for. Sometimes I think it is just age. At a certain time the manager's age becomes a problem, despite the durability of some old masters—Phil Fisher, Warren Buffett, John Templeton—who seem to go on forever.

One thing important to remember: most investment managers are reactive, not proactive, when it comes to clients. They'll talk to you when you call, but they aren't likely to call you. Sometimes people don't understand that. They complain to me: "George never calls me. He doesn't care about my account." I explain to them that it doesn't work that way. "That's the way the business operates. They don't have time to call and chit-chat."

Don't Call to Whine

Some people never understand the whole manager-client relationship. They think having hired an investment manager gives them the right to call any time with queries like, "George, why do we still own Amalgamated? Hell, it went down again yesterday." The first time your question will be answered, but the second time the manager will—politely, I hope—tell you that he simply can't explain his strategy daily to all his clients and still have time to run his portfolios competently. And the third time he will say, less politely, that there's obviously been some misunderstanding about the relationship, and perhaps your needs could be better served by someone else who has more time for communication. I don't mean that you can't call up now and then with a question, even a stupid question, and get an answer that is probably not too patronizing, but you have to be an adult about the relationship with your manager. If you ask such questions too often, you'll be reminded that what you are buying is professional judgment, not companionship. If it's entertainment you want, then it's back to a broker.

When my clients call me first, looking for permission to confront their manager, I try to make them understand that. "Yes, Amalgamated is down, but remember, it's not just your account, it's all the accounts. I mean, he probably owns 100,000 shares of the stock. When he looks at the price on the screen, it's not your face alone he sees, reproving him, but all his clients. Believe me, he knows he has a problem. If you ask him why he owns Amalgamated, what's he going to say? There really is only one thing he can say: 'I bought it because I thought it was going up. So far, it looks like I made a mistake. We're watching the stock very closely, and we see no reason, as yet anyway, to sell.'"

If you call just to complain, you've accomplished nothing, except to sour the relationship. You never get far putting people on the defensive. But if you call and—politely—tell your manager you've been genuinely concerned and ask what the story is with the stock, that's different. He'll explain, you'll understand better how he thinks, and that can strengthen the relationship. But as I said, you can't do that too often, and after you do understand how he operates and you have the reassurance of accumulating favorable returns, you won't need to.

What really drives people up the wall, and makes them want to scream into the phone, is when a manager sells a stock and then a week later there's a tender offer for the stock, ten points higher. The investor feels victimized, as though this perfidy has been committed against him and him alone. "How could that manager be so stupid as not to know?" Well, he didn't know. If he had, he wouldn't have sold.

Another frequent bone of contention arises over the tax consequence of some sales. Most portfolio managers aren't tax sensitive, partly because they are probably running tax-exempt pension money as well as taxable money, but mostly because they are far more keen on prices and registering gains than anything else. So a stock that's been a big winner starts to slide and the manager sells—in December. The investor then has to pay a capital gains tax in April, whereas if the manager had waited until January to sell, all the money would be available for investment for more than another year, until April of the following year. That can be an understandable criticism.

Still, I am of the school that believes that investment decisions should be made on investment, not tax, criteria. That stock could have taken a tumble from December to January, and if it fell far enough, the tax consequences would have been a moot point.

Try a Little Back-patting

I cannot see what good it does to grouse to managers. Instead, try calling your manager when there is reason to bestow praise. Pass on the opportunities to criticize and seize the opportunities to shower him or her with unqualified adoration. As I've said, managers love approval. This is their work product, and they relish having it appreciated. There may come a time when they can do a little favor for your account—maybe when apportioning a hot stock that's in short supply—and they'll remember who's been nice.

And if the day comes when you are so unhappy with your manager's performance that you want to call it quits, just phone and say, "I'm going to make other arrangements," and be done with it. No closing statements. I never saw the point. My advice is, give only praise until the day you terminate the manager, and then terminate without an accompanying bill of indictment.

It's not easy, I know, because I am a client of managers, too. I want to fire the manager with all the venom I'd feel like venting against an employee who'd screwed up and cost me a bundle. And I, unlike my clients, am supposed to know better. You feel almost betrayed when things don't go as expected. You hire a manager because her investment record says she's compounded at 18 percent for the last ten years, and two years later your account's up only 10 percent. There are reasons—probably the market hasn't done anything—but all you know is you got sold on an 18 percent script and you were delivered 5 percent a year. "This isn't what I signed up for. Yeah, she did her best, I suppose, but she didn't deliver." You are frustrated and angry and you feel like letting off steam.

In a way, the marketing practices of firms set people up for that kind of reaction. The brochure you are handed touts the 18 percent for a decade. True, a footnote states, "Past performance is not indicative of future results," and the manager, unless he or she is a real con artist, also tells you, "We've done 18 percent a year, but you should know that that's probably not sustainable." But at the same time, he or she is sure as heck showing you the 18 percent, not to mislead you, but that's just the way it is. You see the 18 percent and you read and hear that it is not likely to be that good in the future, but the one message is far more powerful than the other.

Manager-client etiquette

· Limit the number of calls to your manager; after the first year, four would be a maximum.

· Call for enlightenment, not to complain.

· Compliment your manager when thanks are due.

· If you have to fire your manager, forget the recriminations.

---

6. The Psychology of Losing

I get fired, too, with fair regularity. Eighty percent of my clients who leave walk out in the first 18 months. And so often it's a matter of the last-in, first-out syndrome. These people have been toying with the idea of the equity market for a long time, but resisted the notion. But the market keeps going up and up and they can't stand it any longer. So they come to me and say they want an equity manager. Well, the longer the market has been going up, the more probable it is that its next direction will be down. I tell them that, of course. "Listen, the market's been good for a long while. It's up a lot. There's a very good chance you might not make any money for a bit. You may, in fact, lose some. Ten years from now, you'll be fine, but two years from now you could still be just treading water. Your patience may be tested."

"Hey," they tell me, "I'm a big boy. I know that. Don't worry about me."

So they hire somebody. By the end of the first year the market has peeled off 12 percent. They're paying my fee. They're paying the manager 1 percent. In the old days, before they entered this crazy arena, they would have earned something like 8 percent in Treasuries. Instead, they're underwater to the tune of nearly 14 percent.

So we have a predictable little discussion. "Bear markets usually last 18 months or so," I say, "so much as I'd like to see you making big money, you are down and you may still be down a year from now."

Six months later I get a call. The market's come back 3 percent, or dropped another 3 percent, or it's flat—it doesn't matter. They can't take it any longer. "Hell, if I'd kept my money in the bank, I'd be up 15 percent. Well, I'm down 15 percent. I'm 30 percent in the hole. I've got a million dollars. This little exercise has cost me $300,000, plus what I paid that donkey you sent me to. This is not for me."

If that same guy is up 30 percent the first year, then gives back 15 percent the second, he could still argue that he's out $300,000, considering the opportunity cost of not switching into Treasuries at the end of the first year. But that doesn't happen. If somebody makes good money at first, then gives some of it back, that's all right. The psychology is different. The trick is to stay above the line. If an account is up 30 percent, I am almost assured it will be with me two years later—as long as the market doesn't punch him out and take the portfolio back to zero.

It's the same for most of us when we buy a stock. If you buy a stock and it goes up, then pulls back but you are still in the black, you feel pretty good. Because you've been right: the stock is worth more than you paid for it. But if it goes down after you bought it, you feel stupid, and the minute it gets back to your cost, you are out. Most people forget their original goal and think only of recovering their capital, even though nothing may have changed about the company or their reasons for buying it in the first place. Is that rational? No. Is that the way the world works? Absolutely.

It is very hard to talk logic to people when it comes to investments, but once in a while I succeed. I had a fellow whose father had been a client of mine since 1975, with great results—even better than 15 percent a year compounded. So his son, who was in his 40s, hired the same manager to run a profit-sharing plan for his company. After about 14 months, when the market and the account had done little, he called me and said, "I'm sorry, I know they've done well for my dad, but they haven't done a thing for me. I think I should get rid of them."

Fortunately, I knew the guy and could talk straight to him. "Fred, do yourself a favor and just go to sleep. Don't even think about this stuff for a while. It's going to work out fine. You've got a long history to look at. Based on your father's experience, these people know what they're doing. That's the way it is in the market. There are periods when you don't make money, periods when you lose money, and periods when you make big money."

He listened. He stuck it out. He had hired the firm late in 1987, after the crash, and it had done little in 1988. But in 1989 it was up 42 percent.

7. More Faith, Less Folly

The people who make money in stocks are those who recognize and accept the cyclical nature of the market. The hard part is to stay there when the heat gets turned on. History says if you hang in, the market gives you 10 percent on your money on average. Find people who can do better, and you come out very well indeed.

But it is not easy to stick it out. The market induces anxiety. Score is kept daily. And at the end of every tally, the radio and the newspaper give you some imbecilic explanation of why the score changed that day. We are all inundated with this stuff. "Analysts say the market's strength yesterday was attributable to the Department of Labor's announcing a 0.5 percent rise in unemployment." So you sit and think, "People out of work is good for stock prices?" Yes, you see, because it reduces inflationary pressures, which means the Fed can ease credit. But you say to yourself, "What inflationary pressures? There aren't any. This doesn't make any sense to me."

Whatever the convoluted reasoning, the market went up, and you just shrug off all the commentaries. But then it goes *down*, and, nervous about the drop and what's going to happen next, you start paying very close attention to all this information you are getting about why it went down. The reasons you are hearing are very disturbing, and you decide that you had better act. "I'm losing money. If I don't process this information, if I ignore it, I will lose more, maybe all of it. I've got to sell. I'll buy back later, when the news is better."

What people don't understand is that all of these explanations and the patterns of market behavior they suggest are sometimes meaningful and sometimes not. Interest rates, Fed action, corporate earnings, the Japanese market, budget problems, a fall in the Administration's popularity, trouble in some hot spot in the world—there is such a huge number of variables that it is impossible to know what they all add up to. But investors get scared and they vacate. They tend not to reenter until the news is better, and by that time the market has probably already had a decent run in anticipation of better times.

Those who make money in the market ignore all this noise. They say, "I'm going to have money in the market and I'm going to leave it with people who have historically done a good job. Unless they disappoint me for too long, I'm not going to change anything." They tend to their businesses or go and improve their backhand. Unless there is something in your past experience that suggests that you have the ability to time the market, to move in and out successfully, don't even try it. The Standard & Poor's 500 index returned 17.6 percent a year, on average, in the 1980s, but a study conducted by the brokerage and money management firm Sanford C. Bernstein & Co. showed that if you had been out of the market on the 10 best days in that decade—just 10 out of 2,528 trading days!—your return would have been only 12.6 percent. Bernstein called its study *Stock Market Timing May be Hazardous to Your Wealth*.

Even if the market goes up and you've called it right, you get edgy. Who knows what the psychology is? Profits generate anxiety. You fear that the great market god will take it away from you, I suppose. So you've made money, but you get out far too soon. If the market goes down, and you haven't ducked out, you beat yourself up. "I *knew* it was time to get out," you say at the end of the day the Dow is down 65 points. "Why didn't I follow my instincts?" The reality is that that morning you were torn between doubling your bet and leaving the game, but the way the human mind works, you forget about the fact that you had considered doubling up.

It is hard to find stocks that perform better than other stocks, but it is a hell of a lot easier than timing the market. Take a company like Wal-Mart. It's increased its earnings at 36.5 percent a year for the ten years through the end of 1990. There's a linear progression, uninterrupted, a line with a beautiful upward slope. But look at the lower half of Figure 7.3, which represents the price of Wal-Mart stock. It trends up, quarter by quarter but there were 30 percent to 40 percent price changes. That just illustrates the difference between picking a good stock and market timing. The company's doing fine all along, but investors are processing all sorts of information about interest rates, consumer confidence, or bank failures, and stock prices bounce around in response.

Prudence Dictates Caution

Timing the market—forecasting where it is heading—is different than reacting to prevailing market conditions. I *do* like managers who are responsive to the market, because they can smooth out some of those peaks and valleys. If the market is very high and they can't find stocks to buy, they don't buy anything. If their stocks are going down, they try to figure out why; if they can't, they will often reduce their positions, based on the notion that they might have missed something critical. They *respond* to change, but they don't try to *anticipate* it, or to figure out when it will occur and what its magnitude will be.

What I've said about responding to change suggests that you are not going to be fully invested all the time. Having 100 percent of my stock market money always on the table would generate considerable anxiety for me. The U.S. market has sold within certain valuation ranges, and when you are at the high end of that range—where everything looks dear—the

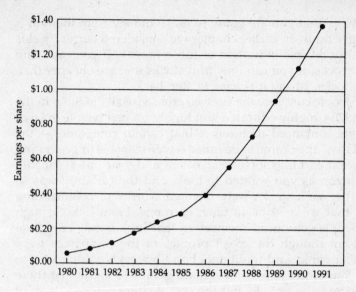

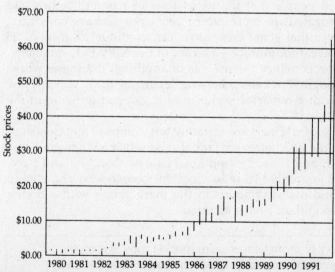

Figure 7.3 Wal-Mart earnings versus Wal-Mart Stock, 1980–1991.

probability that you are going to make money from then on is getting slim. In an earlier chapter we considered current yields as a fairly reliable indication of those ranges. If you can't find cheap stocks, if you can only find stocks that are cheaper than other stocks, I'd say it is wise to step back.

But people convince themselves otherwise all the time. In the early 1970s, highly educated and highly trained people in large numbers convinced themselves that certain companies—"the Nifty Fifty," they came to be called—were capable of generating 15 percent earnings increases year in and year out as far into the horizon as you wanted to look, and the certainty was so great that such stocks were deemed worthy of commanding prices that were 30 or 40 times earnings. From 1986 through 1988 people convinced themselves that junk bonds bore little risk, even though the credit profiles of the companies were such that banks and traditional bond buyers wouldn't lend to them. You didn't have to be a math genius to know that there was going to be trouble, but the combination of a repetition of the big lie and the fact that there had been no disaster as yet convinced people that the usual laws of risk and return had been abrogated. In more recent years people have convinced themselves that some companies can continue to grow at 25 percent a year for infinity—a replay of the Nifty-Fifty mentality. People can convince themselves of anything, if a thesis works long enough. But remember the lesson of IBM, which grew and grew at a remarkable clip until it stopped growing in the mid-1980s.

While professionals are certainly not immune from delusion, I believe the good ones are far better at sensing when craziness is abroad, and resisting emotional excess, than you and I are. At least I know that I'd rather look for people who understand under- and over-valuations in the marketplace with a higher level of skill than I have attained.

> To try to *predict* short-term market moves is coun-
> terproductive. To *react* when stocks have become
> very under- or overvalued is just common sense.

8

FINANCIALLY
SUICIDAL TENDENCIES

Anyone who unfailingly puts aside money over a lifetime of work and invests those savings sensibly so that compounding can do its magic will end up in the ranks of the affluent. And anyone who keeps enough of his or her accumulated money in Treasuries to produce the income needed to sustain a comfortable life is going to be free of financial angst.

Simple directions, but difficult to follow. Human proclivities get in the way. Considering what can go wrong, what often does go wrong, one can only conclude that some people have a death wish when it comes to financial security. They will detonate any financial plan set up for them. It is often said that some people can't stand success. It seems some can't stand financial security either. The various species of the genus are readily identifiable.

1. The Carpe Diem Spender

I sat next to a woman from Washington, D.C., on a plane recently who, when I told her what I do for a living and about the book I was working on, started musing aloud about her own ways with money. She said she and her husband both have good jobs, that their combined incomes are "a few hundred thousand a year." In their 40s, they have no children. "It's

terrible," she told me, "but we never save a nickel." She shook
her head in disbelief at her own indulgence.

"We have a charming brownstone. We have two nice cars.
We travel a lot. We think nothing of eating out, oh, three times
a week usually, and I don't mean the neighborhood bistro but
good restaurants. With a good bottle of wine the tab often runs
$150. We've talked about it and talked about it, but we never
seem to have set up any kind of savings routine. We don't
even have IRAs. We have the pension plans of our employers,
of course, but that's it."

She paused, shrugged, and added, "I know we need to do
something about putting money aside. But we just never seem
to get around to it."

She is an educated person, and so is her husband. In fact,
both have had business training, so it's not as though they
don't know how to set up a budget and impose a discipline.
The truth is, they just don't care enough to bother. When the
choices are laid out for them, the one they take habitually is
to consume.

I am not imposing moral or value judgments. People make
their choices. If you spend everything today, you will indeed
live well today. But you cannot look forward to living well
on the morrow, after work ceases. That is a financial law that
cannot be abrogated, unless you win the state lottery. Habitual,
compulsive spenders are either going to reform—and for the
truly addicted there is even a self-help group, called Debtors
Anonymous—or they are not going to join the empyrean of
the wealthy.

2. The Big-Picture Myopic

The first years of retirement, as we explored in an earlier chapter,
are rough on almost everyone. One is not used to leisure; there
is a persistent desire to *do* something, to accomplish, as one did
at one's office. And there is all that money you have assembled,
just sitting there. Maybe something can be done with *it*.

Those who sold their businesses are most vulnerable to this
urge. One, they were handed a check for a great deal of money,

probably several million dollars. Two, as business owners, entrepreneurs, they long ago became action junkies. They were so thoroughly involved in their enterprises that mere idleness is unthinkable for them.

Up early as they were wont, but now with time on their hands, they start reading the financial press for hours every morning. They become experts on interest rates and what "the Fed" is up to. Those whose entire experience with currency has been in converting pesos in Acapulco are now forecasting the future of the yen and deutsche mark.

For all the time these people ran their own show they thrived on being confronted with problems, studying them, and making decisions. Corporate people do, too, of course, but entrepreneurs are usually far more accustomed to making decisions autonomously. They have developed a simple dynamic: first there is input and then there is output.

Now that they are in possession of all this input from the financial press, a decision is obviously required. The only asset they have left to make a decision about is those millions. So they take what they have read and develop a macroeconomic point of view and then decide on a grand strategic investment scheme.

And they get very excited about their new prospects. When you are operating a business, 90 percent of the decisions you make deal with housekeeping matters. It is rare that you get to develop a global view and then change the course of an enterprise. Your average businesspeople are a lot more interested in their inventories, order books, the pricing of supplies, and what's going on in their own industries than they are in what's happening at the Treasury or the Japanese Ministry of Finance. Sure, they'll have a passing interest in the bigger picture. They read what the economists say because they're educated and aware of world issues. But they're not accustomed to making major policy changes in response to a global perspective.

Ah, but now is their chance. They'll postulate some view of the world, something thematic. Maybe it's hyperinflation, or disinflation, or the pending collapse of the banking system, or the resurrection of real estate. Whatever it is, once they have this view of the world, being action junkies, if they don't do something about it, it would be a sign that they've lost their courage. With men, there's a macho challenge; they are afraid they might go soft because they've reached retirement. It isn't the possibility of the money reward that drives them so much as the need to find an arena where they can continue to validate their judgmental skills.

I know just such a man who became obsessed ten years ago with the federal deficit. He had invested the money realized from the sale of his business in stocks, because he knew that from a financial perspective they would bring him the highest return. But he kept feeling uneasy, because any day now the government's profligacy was going to bring down the system. Several doomsday newsletters he subscribed to fueled his anxiety. His money, he just knew, should be in gold, 100 percent. Finally, as the deficit grew and grew, and Congress seemed unable or unwilling to really tackle the problem, he could stand it no longer. In 1986 he fired his equity manager and put all of his money in gold. I lost track of him after that, so I don't know if he ever reversed his decision. I do know that at the time he bought his gold, he paid $750 an ounce for it and that lately it's been $360 an ounce, and that the Dow Jones Average went from about 1800 to over 3000.

I have many clients afflicted with this post-retirement syndrome. They are not easy to live with. For one thing, today's headlines are different from yesterday's. The input keeps changing and so do their responses. One of them will call me, and as soon as I hear, "I've been reading a lot . . . ," I always want to say, "Oh, God, what next?" Then they will go into this very long and highly structured spiel about what is going to happen to the world soon and how they want to implement a strategy to take advantage of it. And they have conviction. I mean, they want to make a big, big bet. They either want to change the investment managers we have chosen or the allocation of their investments, or they want to call the managers whom they hired to provide a particular expertise and mandate that they change their approach to reflect these screamingly obvious impending changes in the world's economies. All of a sudden they expect a growth stock manager to start buying bankruptcy stocks.

If I can't dissuade my clients from committing dollars to back up their theories, I can at least inject some sense of proportion into their decisions. They'll usually calm down and make far smaller bets, or, if I am persuasive enough, hold off for a while to study the situation some more. But then, three months later, again I hear, "I've been reading a lot . . . " Again I listen, and this time I am told why they have abdicated their previous views of the world in favor of other, equally radical ones and they want, once more, to call the managers. And again I say, "Listen, I don't know if what you are telling me is right or wrong, but let's look at how it affects your life if you *are* wrong. A mistake could take you from a high level of comfort to marginal comfort, or maybe carry you below the line of comfort."

Most of the time, on some intuitive level, people know they really don't want to bet the store, take an outlandish risk that could threaten much of that money they've so recently obtained. Or they realize they were wrong in their first prognostications and gain a bit of humility and caution. If you study economics for a while and come up with some hypothesis, it is usually disproved in such a systematic and devastating way that you lose faith in your ability to forecast. So they quiet down, understand that their old skills as managers can't be so tidily applied to world news, and go back to concentrating on their golf swing or something else they can have some control over. Of course, there's always the possibility that I don't hear from them anymore because they don't like listening to my homilies.

3. The Compulsive Speculator

Incorrigible speculators are really no different from the compulsive gamblers who risk their money in casinos or at the track. But they have found it is far more respectable to gamble in securities. That is, if they lost the same amount of money at the crap tables, they'd have a divorce on their hands. But since markets are enveloped with the aura of "investment," it's far more acceptable to lose money there.

I can understand someone's speculating when he or she is trying to acquire a fortune fast, though I believe it's folly, because the odds are so heavily stacked against you, while slow-but-steady is certain to succeed. But what is the motivation if you are already rich? To make more money? You can't live any better, and your children are already assured of a decent inheritance. So you are probably trying to prove something, and I suspect the psychology in this case makes the odds of success even poorer.

Since these people are essentially gamblers, bent on financial destruction, maybe it takes a Doestoevsky to explain their psyches. But when I see people toss much of their money away in crapshoot investments, it doesn't take subtle analysis to conclude that many of them are filled with guilt about that money. They inherited it, and, therefore, feel they did nothing themselves to deserve it. Or they have made so much money as entrepreneurs or surgeons or litigation firm partners that they can't quite believe they are worth that kind of compensation. So they unconsciously want to give some of it back. Brokers who have clients like that have told me they have come to the same conclusion.

Whatever the reason, these people are driven to speculate—in frenetic stock trading, in start-up ventures and fragile young companies, in options and commodities futures, and even in bonds, in which case they make interest-rate calls and use the total allowable leverage. Their gambles certainly provide excitement for them. They can't wait to open the morning paper to check out their bets, and you get the phenomenon of the executive who leaves the meeting or the lawyer the courtroom to make a hasty call to his or her broker. They seem to need to get their anxiety level up to a point where they feel it's worth getting up in the morning. People who sell a business for $50 million and can't wait until they've acquired a new one have some of that same need for the thrills of financial risk.

It may take therapy to exorcise this need to speculate. When I have clients who are clearly infected with the disease, I advise them to take just 5 percent of their money and put it in futures programs, biotechnology stocks, venture capital, or whatever else turns them on. They can afford that, but it really is a game and not part of a financial plan. Another $20,000 from a successful fling isn't going to make much difference to their balance sheet, and none at all to their life-styles. Never mind that their 5 percent high-risk portfolio can only provide 100 percent of the anxiety for 5 percent of the benefits. That's fine. It satisfies their craving. They need that anxiety. It keeps life interesting for them. They can now read *Barron's* and watch "Wall Street Week" and feel they are part of the parade. In recommending the 5 percent, I am merely integrating economic and temperamental realities.

The risk is that the 5 percent bet doesn't pay off and another 5 percent purse is thrown on the table. The only sure way to know if you've gone over the edge is if you're lying awake at 3:00 in the morning, grinding your teeth, and wondering what could happen to you if your stake heads south. You then know for certain that you've gone beyond the amusement stage.

I also try to convince my clients whom I suspect suffer from these speculative itches to hold off for a bit. I urge them to start with just the Treasuries and a professionally managed stock portfolio. If after a year or so they find life is incomplete without the stimulation of more racy investments, they can always jump in then—with that 5 percent. But I'd just as soon they didn't tell me about it.

4. The Deal-Me-In Patsy

Earlier we discussed the entrepreneur who has sold his business for a lot of money and is offered participations in other business ventures out of respect for his knowledge, ability, and contacts. He is asked for little or no money of his own.

But if you have come into money, even though you are not knowledgeable about business, you, too, will be offered "deals." In your case, however, it is precisely your money, not your expertise, that is sought. These solicitations can suck you into some very costly situations and torpedo the comfortable life you have attained for yourself.

You are with friends, at lunch or on the golf course, and they will mention, say, a new business venture they are backing. They ask if you'd like to get in on it. It is so easy to say, "Sounds good. Count me in." That's the way these deals happen. You're at the fourteenth hole and Joe says he's in for fifty thousand and Bill says the same, and you just want to be one of the boys. If you say, "Seems like a good deal, but I'm just not a player anymore," it sounds like you've become nothing more than a spectator of the smart world around you, and that's hard to accept. Often the people soliciting the investment innately understand that; it's their leverage.

And once you've agreed to come in, it is very difficult to come back and say, "Listen, I've thought this over some more, and it really doesn't work for me." You are too embarrassed.

So don't rush into these deals mindlessly. Ask yourself some questions before you chime in with amicable consent. Is this an exercise in camaraderie or is it a financially sound investment? What happens if it doesn't prove sound? If you lose the money you invest, or if it gets tied up for years, would that create a problem for you or your estate? And even if a loss wouldn't hurt you financially, might it aggravate you to the point where it just isn't worth it? I think one of the blessings of money is the ability to avoid that kind of aggravation.

Fifty thousand might not be crippling, but what often makes the situation worse is that the original ante doesn't prove enough. The participants may say, "Yes, we have to sign a note, but we'll never have to put up another dime." And if the initial stage goes well, you won't. But so often that stage falters. You don't *have* to dig into your pocket contractually, but you feel pressure. You've got $50,000 vested in the deal that you don't want to walk away from, and the other parties are very convincing that another $50,000 from each will solve the problem. And if everyone else you know who's in on the deal is coughing up more, you wonder if you are behaving improperly, in a business protocol sense, if you stay out. Wouldn't that mean you are not a stand-up player? On the other hand, you realize that being a stand-up player could start to threaten this wonderful life-style you recently created for yourself.

So before you get involved in the first place, ask yourself, too, if you are willing to walk away from that money, even if it appears more money will carry the deal to success and even if you will feel you have acted badly toward friends.

Remember, too, that all the deals you are offered, and other involved investment schemes, can get you enmeshed in endless layers of complexity, for every investment generates an oversight role, legal burdens, accounting requirements, stacks of reports, and the need to file those reports.

Do you really want that hassle anymore? Do you want to involve yourself in an investment that could give you considerable anxiety and even threaten your security and comfort? My advice would be to pass on these deals. If you have money and are doing fine, don't take the risk of things going awry. Preserve what you have and let others handle the fireworks.

I know one man, in his late 60s, who is probably worth about $7 million. He doesn't have a lot of cash; probably $2 million of his money is in his house and $5 million in oil and gas properties, which are not readily marketable. One of the oil and gas fields he has an interest in is about to be developed. If he doesn't ante up with some big money—about $2 million—to participate in the development stage, his interest in the field will be greatly reduced.

He'd have to borrow the money. If he does, and the development works, it won't change his lifestyle. He lives extremely well now. It could make his children's lives substantially better financially—this project could make tens of millions of dollars—but not his own. But if it *doesn't* work, he's going to be 70 years old trying to pay off a $2 million obligation, which, with interest, is going to cost $3 million. In the worst case, he'd probably live the same way, but he'd have to liquidate some assets, so that his kids, instead of inheriting several million dollars, would inherit next to nothing.

I know this man pretty well, and I suspect he will hock himself to the hilt and go ahead. And I think I know why. His father was wealthy, too, and he's never outgrown the need to prove himself, to show that he can be even more successful than Dad.

5. The Impossible Client

Some people with a great deal of money seem to do all the right things to ensure its safety and growth. They make the proper allocations, and they research their manager options and hire a professional of proven ability. But somehow their long-term stock investment record is—not a disaster maybe—but mediocre at best. The reason is simple: they are impossible clients.

They call their manager constantly, usually to complain about a trade—the purchase of a stock that's dropped or the sale of a stock that continued to climb. Nothing seems to satisfy them. That account somehow turns into the manager's worst-performing, because she is hesitating to take the risks she should to avoid the phone call that will surely come in a week if her move isn't immediately successful.

Eventually, the manager probably drops the whiner, even though it is a good-sized account, because she can't stand dealing with this person any longer. If I have arranged the relationship, the manager usually calls me first. "This guy is unbelievable. I'm not going to put up with it any more. Not only is he impossible to please, he's rude to the secretaries, he's abusive to me, and he's extraordinarily demanding. I can't take it." I tell the manager to go ahead and dump the account. Client-manager relationships should be happy ones. Some people can be all sweetness and light before the hiring and are impossible from then on. There are some just plain nasty people in this world, and blessing them with money only makes them nastier. I wouldn't want them in my life and I wouldn't expect anyone else to want them in theirs.

Managers, too, can get nasty, by the way. If I think a manager has behaved inappropriately, I'll call and say, "Hey, this is not acceptable. I don't know what your problem is, but this client's paying your bills." And maybe he or she will say, "I know, and I am sorry. I was having a lousy day, trying to do six trades, and this guy's harping on me about a $12 dividend. I just lost it." "All right," I'll say, "it can happen. I just think you should apologize." The apology is made, and that's usually the end of it.

If the manager with the impossible client ignores the abuse in order to continue collecting his or her fee, it doesn't matter, because the client never stays long with any manager anyway. Such people are never satisfied. They'll be up 20 percent for three years running and drop the manager because they hear of somebody else who's up 25 percent. Or the manager has a rough quarter or two and is summarily terminated. "I don't know what it takes to make some people happy," managers tell me. "Forget my great record for three years. All they care about is what I've done for them yesterday." I remind them that such people probably came from some other shop and they are going to end up in still another shop a few years from now. That's the way with such people.

They probably think they are shrewd, aggressive caretakers of their money. The truth is, they don't get the best out of the manager they have, and they always end up dumping him or her in favor of some hot performer who, in the cyclical nature of styles and markets, is poised for a bad stretch ahead. So these people are almost assured of sub-par performance.

Such people, as I've said, can be dissemblers, but if I spot them, I won't have them as clients. When someone comes to see me and we start talking about his experience with the stock market and he tells me he's had 22 different stockbrokers and 7 different investment managers, the personality problem is transparent. "Why so many," I'll ask. "Because," I hear, "they've all screwed up." This poor soul has suffered abuse at the hands of anyone who ever rendered him financial advice. He is convinced that he has been perpetually victimized. He is greedy—he wants big, big returns—but he doesn't want to take any risk to get them. Such people shouldn't be in the investment business, but they'll never listen to advice, from me or anyone else. I'm not likely to change a life pattern of unsuccessful investing because I'm not a therapist, and these people need help. They are forever sending out fresh invitations to make trouble. I don't want clients like that. I don't want friends like that either.

9

WHERE THERE'S A WILL, THE WAY IS CLEAR

If the plan I have laid out in these pages has any elegance, it stems from its simplicity. When you are in the process of acquiring wealth, you merely compute what you need to set aside that will allow you smoothly to bridge the gap between a comfortable life while working to an equally comfortable life when you choose to stop working, whether that be at the age of 45 or 65. If you have reached the stage where you no longer have to work, you compute what you need to invest in bonds to provide sufficient income to maintain that comfortable life. If there is money left over, you invest it in stocks for growth and additional income.

The saving option for aspirants to wealth should begin as early in life as one can manage. You must not delude yourself that your capacity to earn will keep rising so that saving becomes "easy." You first have to make one large decision— that you will save for the goal you have in mind—followed by hundreds, if not thousands, of smaller decisions. Every time you contemplate a major expenditure, be aware of the relationship between what you consume now and what is available to fund your life-style in the future. When you are thinking of spending the weekend in New York, which will cost you $1500, consider the fact that the $1500 can be invested and turn into $25,000 twenty-five years later.

You have to train yourself to think in terms of such alternatives. It is a very painful exercise, much like sitting down to dinner and saying to yourself, "I am going to skip the potatoes." Too often, need I say, in the clinch most of us eat the potatoes—and the dessert. If you truly want to be well-off, you have to put yourself on a lifetime financial diet.

I hope this book has helped you recognize the consequences of the options and consider where you might be undisciplined, and that it has encouraged you to adopt some of the mechanical means of saving suggested—such as committing a few hundred dollars a month to buy zero-coupon bonds for your children's education or to pay off your mortgage on an accelerated schedule. If that $200 or $300 a month means driving a less glamorous car, so be it.

Simple ongoing decisions have enormous impact 20 to 30 years down the road. Look back at page 55 and reflect on the difference between investing $300 a month at 30 and not beginning until you are 40. It will give you a crystal-clear picture of what a modest sacrifice early on will represent on your fifty-fifth birthday, when retirement stops being an abstraction and starts to loom as an attractive, perhaps near-term possibility.

If that sounds like old-time religion, I suppose it is. Save and ye shall be saved. Maybe the most uncomfortable aspect of what's been advocated in these pages is having to admit that Mom and Dad were right. We've all had those lectures as kids, and many of us as adults, about the extravagance of our lives.

I have another suggestion to help you conserve consumption. Try a mantra—that is, a simple phrase that you can repeat to yourself over and over to concentrate your mind on your goals and to stiffen your will. Suppose it is "$800,000 at age 52." Every morning remind yourself what your goal is while you're doing your sit-ups. Or visualize becoming a six-handicap golfer because you're playing five days a week. Make your goal tangible. Visualize it, recite it, and sell yourself on the fact that it's going to happen. Hokey? I suppose so. But it works.

Forgoing some goods or experiences doesn't condemn you to a life of penury. If you start when you are young enough, it doesn't have to be that much that is put aside monthly. Also, as we said at the outset of this book, people's ideas of affluence differ except for the basic notion of living on the scale one is accustomed to without working. A $50,000-a-year household cannot, of course, save as much as a $500,000-a-year household, but whatever *is* saved can one day make it possible to live a $50,000-a-year life-style without working for it. Those with one-half-million-dollar incomes should be socking away enough to allow them to live just as grandly when they are ready to call it quits.

The 1990s may make it easier to save than the preceding decade. The 1980s were crazy days. You had recently impoverished students rising to six-figure, occasionally seven-figure, incomes before they were 30 who the next moment found themselves unemployed, and most of them completed that cycle between 1985 and 1989, a very fast round trip indeed. The whole yuppie phenomenon, whatever one's income, was one of instant gratification. It was always, "Let's go, and let's go first-cabin." Most Americans never saw the inside of a limo before 1980. Now the kids take them to their high school proms.

After all the excesses of the 1980s, the 1990s should see the clean-up crew come in to straighten things up a bit. Yet it's hard for me to believe that people have dismissed the notion that living well is attractive, desirable, and possible. It seems to me that in America it is just as acceptable to acquire money these days as it was in the Reagan years. But it is less acceptable to display it as openly. We are returning to a more traditional range of consumption. Not austerity—as has frequently been said, austerity is something we admire in our ancestors—but not extravagance either. That should make it easier to pass on the Porsche, buy the Pontiac, and put the savings in a mutual fund.

If you do that regularly, you will one day be able to say goodbye to your office—if you want to. With a little luck, that day will come sooner than you expected. Make your plans so that the only event that can derail them would be failing health—both because of its expense and the way it robs you of the enjoyment you were planning for. But then luck can help. When you invest, you need the wind at your back, and we have considered asset allocation with markets' recent returns in mind. But if you're fortunate enough to go through a period, as was true in the 1980s, when the winds were almost gale force, you have an opportunity to accelerate the day of retirement or substantially increase the life-style scale when that day comes.

I believe in planning on conservative assumptions—stock returns closer to 10 percent than 20 percent, tax rates that are on the high side of the probability scale, and incomes that don't increase as rapidly as hoped. If all that proves true, you'll retire when you're a little older, at 65 rather than 60, or 60 rather than 55. But if you are lucky, if there are favorable surprises, then you'll do better. If you start with all conservative assumptions, the chances of a happy surprise or two are very high.

Many people, of course, find that they have accumulated enough money to retire at 55, even earlier, but don't choose to do so. The truly blessed people are those for whom wealth has come as a byproduct of work they have enjoyed, be it in business or a profession. Acquiring wealth wasn't the dominant goal. They were happily engaged with the world and compensated in a way that allowed them, through continuous put-asides, to be able to walk away from that business or profession sooner than they'd planned. Some will indeed walk, and will start what they hope is a gratifying second chapter of their lives. But many like what they have been doing so much they can't think of anything else they would rather do more. So they stay at their desks. But it's nice to have the option.

Most people I've encountered would work a little bit until the day they die. Since they like what they do, the idea of not doing it at all is unattractive. It is a decision generally forced upon them by the system, rather than one they make voluntarily. When they pass 55, they find, because they have had a disciplined financial plan in place, that they have sufficient assets to sustain their life-style. The children are probably educated by then and the mortgage paid off, or nearly so. But they choose to continue until they reach their firm's mandatory retirement age. It is hard for those who have achieved in commerce to settle happily into raising orchids.

Unless they do it competitively. That helps. The same aggressive personality traits that conspired toward their economic success conspire against their success as retirees, so they transfer that competitiveness into a new channel that provides the same psychic, rather than economic, rewards. I think of an investment manager whose annual income the last ten years of his career probably wasn't below $3 million who is now consumed with breeding and training dogs for field trials with the same obsessive need to win.

The Sanctuary Years

As you work and save toward the day when your work days are over, whether voluntarily or prescribed, you'll be sustained by a vision of what it will be like. Wealth provides choices. When buying a new car, you do not have to choose between a Toyota Tercel and a Hyundai, and I consider that a blessing. Money enriches your life because it opens up the world to you and your children. It provides experiences that are simply impossible without it. You don't go on safari without money.

But there are some things money cannot do. It will not make you taller, able to run faster, or a better lover. It will not, as the sages say, buy you happiness. Happiness has to do with how you interact with your family and the rest of the world.

The people in your life who annoyed you will still annoy you. As a matter of fact, the annoyances may increase, because money does not allow you to insulate yourself quite as effectively as people would think. Money attracts people, and some who are newly rich mistake this attraction for adoration. They soon realize, however, that it is their money, not themselves, that is adored. If you use a beach house, Mercedes convertible, and other possessions for bait, you shouldn't be disappointed by the kind of people you attract. Or surprised.

Wealth will not even solve all your financial problems, and, as we've seen, it creates a few of its own. You won't be burdened with pedestrian anxieties about being able to pay the butcher and the auto mechanic in the same month. But you will quickly find that such concerns are replaced by others. Can you buy a Caribbean condo without threatening that wonderful new sense of security? Are you managing your money responsibly? And the proverbial question: how should you dispose of your assets to your children without impairing their development? Every generation wrestles with those same problems.

I hope the preceding pages have helped you deal with such questions. Since the most important benefit of money is a sense of security, the most valuable contribution I can make when advising the wealthy is the concept of sanctuary—the money that is not put at risk but that ensures an income that in turn ensures a continued, inviolable life-style of comfort.

Though with every passing year you will better understand the wisdom of that concept, it is not one that is immediately apparent. It took me several years, after I started counseling people, to realize that financial security is wealth's chief advantage, and that it therefore must take priority over other considerations. I tended to think in terms of *financial* solutions for people, of investing their money where returns have traditionally been highest. I assumed people wanted to make as much money as possible, period. I didn't grasp, at that time in my own life, how much more important the need for security and certainty becomes for people as they age. I soon began to see, however, that with very few exceptions, the hierarchy of needs changes as the calendar ticks away. When people are 55 or older, making money becomes secondary, maybe tertiary, in importance, and security becomes primary. They want to be able to hold their heads up as responsible investors, of course, but more money would have little meaning in the way they live their lives. They see little incremental benefit to incremental capital.

The other thing that influenced me was that I began to accrue money of my own, and I began to understand why people of wealth don't care much about amassing more material goods. When I was 30 years old, I fulfilled a lifelong ambition: I bought a Ferrari. Today I drive a Land Cruiser because I know the damn thing will start every day. The only way to understand how little acquisitions mean is to be able to act out some of your fantasies. Once you have stayed in suites, it doesn't seem so important anymore if you stay in a suite or a simple hotel room. Once you've tasted the grape, it's not mandatory to taste it at every meal.

Economics must be integrated with ever-changing human psychology. The word *sanctuary* came to me, because that is what people really want. Their goal is to feel invulnerable. That need became crystal clear to me, though it is not always so to my clients. It's like giving advice to the lovelorn. When you are uninvolved, it's easier to read the situation and suggest remedies.

There are two interrelated ways the affluent can threaten their sanctuary. The first way is that they can spend too much. And the second is that they can then move into riskier investments to make up their deficits. With the right deal, $200,000 could turn into $500,000 in a couple of years, and the prospect is so very alluring. But make a quick computation and you will see what will happen to your income if your investment goes sour and your capital is partially lost. Ask yourself, simultaneously, what your capacity is to replace that income. Most people soon get the message. As they move forward from 55, they see that there is simply not enough time they can count on to replace any serious dent in that sanctuary. If you are male and lose a large sum of money at 55, you face the expectation of 22 years—27 years if you are female—of living under the duress of a diminished life-style.

That is probably the chief benefit I bring to my clients. I make those who are already wealthy realize the hazards of spending too much and taking risks that are really no longer necessary. I cross people's lives at a point when they are rationalizing their finances and I, as an authority figure, can explain the consequences of jeopardizing their financial security and dissuade them from acts of folly. I show them in a crisp mathematical way, so that it has meaning, the unpleasant outcome of out-of-control spending and of imprudent and unnecessary investments.

I hope that I have done the same for you. If you are still striving toward wealth, I hope that you are going to make changes in your spending patterns so that savings can compound and bring you to the fulfillment of your goals. Once you say to yourself, "I have to do something about this spending," remedies begin to take shape.

If you are already wealthy, I hope that I have forced you to examine your consumption patterns and inventory your assets so that you can isolate enough of those assets to provide the income that will enable you to consume at a responsible level. If there is money left over and you still have the appetite, then you can consider risk investments. But the sanctuary stays inviolable. It is your security, and your reason for acquiring wealth in the first place.

INDEX